Explanation and Experiment
in Social Psychological Science

John D. Greenwood

Explanation and Experiment in Social Psychological Science

Realism and the Social Constitution of Action

Springer-Verlag New York Berlin Heidelberg
London Paris Tokyo

John D. Greenwood
Department of Philosophy
City College
City University of New York
New York, NY 10031

Library of Congress Cataloging-in-Publication Data
Greenwood, John D.
    Explanation and experiment in social psychological science :
realism and the social constitution of action / John D. Greenwood.
        p. cm.
    Bibliography: p.
    Includes index.
    ISBN 0-387-96799-0 (alk. paper)
    1. Social psychology—Methodology.   I. Title.
HM251.G7523   1989
302.01'8—dc19   88-37924

Printed on acid-free paper.

Typeset by ASCO Trade Typesetting Ltd., Hong Kong.
Printed and bound by R.R. Donnelley & Sons, Harrisonburg, Virginia.
Printed in the United States of America.

9 8 7 6 5 4 3 2 1

ISBN 0-387-96799-0 Springer-Verlag New York Berlin Heidelberg
ISBN 3-540-96799-0 Springer-Verlag Berlin Heidelberg New York

For my mother and father
In loving memory

Preface

This book is about explanation and experiment in a science of human action. It aims to provide a philosophy of social psychological science that both embodies sound principles of scientific reasoning and is sensitive to the social psychological dimensions of human action. The guiding principle of this book is the belief that the logical forms of causal explanation and experimental evaluation can be effectively employed in the scientific analysis of meaningful human action.

According to most accounts, social psychological science has been in a more or less constant state of crisis for the past decades, having been subject to a host of criticisms on moral, political, methodological, and philosophical grounds. Many of these critiques have been directed against the still dominant conception of social psychological enquiry as a causal and objective *scientific* discipline that is closely analogous to (if not to be identified as a branch of) the natural sciences. Thus, many of the most vigorous debates have concerned the nature of explanation and the utility of experimentation in a social psychological discipline.

Most psychologists maintain that their discipline is based upon principles of scientific reasoning. In fact, it has always been based upon a particular philosophical account of scientific reasoning that may be characterized as *scientific empiricism*. According to this account of science, causal explanation consists of the deduction of descriptions of events from "laws" that describe empirical regularities, which are confirmed by observed instances of such regularities. Theories serve to integrate and systematize such descriptions of observable regularity. Standard accounts of social psychological science based upon these philosophical principles may be characterized as *scientific psychology,* since this title seems to have been commandeered by those who profess that the goal of social psychological science is the explanation, prediction, and control of human behavior via the identification of antecedent causal determinants (usually via laboratory experiments).

Scientific empiricism has an obvious appeal to those concerned to provide a scientific account of human action, since it appears to promote objectivity by its restrictive emphasis upon the observable. The empiricist account of science has itself been the object of continuous criticism for the past half century. In particular, the traditional empiricist distinction between the observable and the theoretical has been dismissed as epistemologically naive. It has been argued that all observations are "theory-informed," and that the notion of a neutral empirical base for the evaluation of scientific theories is an intellectual fiction. Naturally enough, practicing psychologists have been disinclined to accept the implications of this *relativist* account of science, for this position is often interpreted (with some justification) as a denial of objectivity rather than an alternative conceptual framework for a science of human action.

Some contemporary criticisms of scientific psychology have been drawn from this relativist tradition in the philosophy of science. More fundamental criticisms question the very idea of a causal science of human action. This critical position may be characterized as *hermeneutical psychology,* since most commentators who object to a putatively scientific analysis stress the meaningful nature of human action. This emphasis on the meaning of human action has led some hermeneutical theorists to deny that explanations of human action are causal explanations, and others to deny the objectivity of action identification. In consequence, most hermeneutical psychologists deny the appropriateness of experimental studies in a social psychological discipline.

Over the years there has been no shortage of alternative meta-theories and "paradigms" that have promised to resolve the crisis, such as humanist psychology, hermeneutical-interpretative psychology, dialectics, sociorationalism, and social constructionism. Yet these have had little significant impact upon social psychological science. No doubt this is partly due to to ingrained commitments to scientific empiricism. However, it is no doubt also due to the justified belief among practitioners that to adopt the principles of such alternative paradigms would be to abandon a causal and experimental science. It would be to effectively abandon social psychological science. For most of the alternative paradigms are not alternative scientific psychologies. They promote altogether different forms of intellectual enquiry. In this respect the central crisis in social psychological science is a *philosophical* crisis concerning the identity of the discipline.

Most of these debates about the nature of social psychological science are vitiated by the uncritical adoption of the scientific empiricist account of science. The empiricist account is hopelessly inadequate as an account of causal explanation in science. Since it is (historically and conceptually) based upon the phenomenalist *idealism* of classical empiricism, it effectively denies the possibility of causal explanation. Consequently, the empiricist account cannot support the logic of scientific practice. The attempt to accommodate experimentation to this account distorts the logic of experimentation.

Most of the arguments of the scientific psychologist are vitiated because scientific psychology is not based upon the practice of causal and experimental sciences but upon an inadequate empiricist account. Most of the arguments of the hermeneutical psychologist based upon the meaningful nature of human action are vitiated for the same reason. The denials of the adequacy or appropriateness of causal explanations are not based upon contrasts with causal explanation in natural science but upon empiricist accounts of explanation. In consequence, the hermeneutical psychologist misconstrues the point and purpose of experimentation in a causal science.

The most radical form of hermeneutical psychology denies the objectivity of action identification, via the claim that human actions are *socially constructed*. This relativist account is based partly upon the doctrine of the theory informity of observations and partly upon a correct intuition about the especially intimate relation between representation and ontology in social psychological science. Nevertheless, this extreme position embodies a number of fundamental ontological and epistemological errors.

Relativism is no alternative to empiricism. In fact it is a species of *neo-empiricism* that returns scientific empiricism to its roots in philosophical idealism. Opposed to these forms of empiricism and idealism is philosophical *realism*. This book is a presentation of a realist philosophy for a causal and experimental science of action. Realism provides a coherent rationale for causal explanatory and experimental activity in science, and reveals that many contemporary characterizations and criticisms of social psychological science are misconceived. This does not mean, however, that a realist philosophy of natural science can be uncritically mapped upon the social psychological domain. This would be to repeat the original empiricist error. A causal and experimental science of action must respect and accommodate the unique ontological characteristics of human action. This requires an applied experimental commitment to the meaningful nature of human action and the possibility of human agency or self-determination.

Human action is meaningful because it is *socially constituted*. Human behaviors are constituted as meaningful actions by their social relations, and by participant agent and collective representations of them. Diverse human behaviors are constituted as the same form of action by their social location and intentional direction. The social constitution of action makes self-determination possible. Causal explanations of action in terms of human agency are not precluded by a realist science of human action, although neither is their accuracy conceptually guaranteed by realism or the social constitution of action.

The social constitution of action—and the possibility of human agency—does not preclude an experimental science of human action. However, it does demonstrate that much contemporary practice is misconceived. Traditional accounts of the problems of an experimental social psychological science are firmly committed to the standard empiricist account. Consequently, most experimentalists simply fail to recognize the most fundamental problems that arise by virtue of the social relational and representational dimensions of human action. These are not the traditional (and misconceived) problems about the generalizability of experimental results. Rather, they are serious doubts about the *identity* of experimentally produced behaviors. According to a realist philosophy of experimentation in social psychological science, the logic of experimental enquiry must be employed via techniques that ensure that the identity of human action is preserved in experiments.

A realist philosophy of social psychological science and a social constitutionist philosophy of action embody no theoretical, moral, or political commitments. This is how it should be if they are to provide a conceptual framework for a causal and experimental science of action. A realist philosophy of social psychological science does not entail a social constitutionist philosophy of action.

Yet they are uniquely consistent, since both preserve objectivity with respect to the identification and explanation of human action. This must also be the case if they are to serve as a conceptual framework for social psychological science, for a social psychological science that does not preserve objectivity is not really worth preserving.

Acknowledgments

My greatest intellectual debt is to Rom Harré. It is a huge debt that I cannot even begin to document. Suffice to say that I remain grateful for his inspired teaching, constructive criticism, and his advice and support over the years. Also for his personal example which transformed my own moral career. A very considerable debt is also owed to Roy Bhaskar, who originally got me interested in these questions, and awakened me from my own "dogmatic slumbers" about causality. The influence of both these mentors on the present volume will be obvious to all who have read their work.

I also owe a special thanks to Nicholas Capaldi and Paul Secord, who read earlier drafts of the book in manuscript form and provided me with much useful criticism. Also for their friendship and advice over the years.

A number of other persons who contributed to the development of the arguments of this volume deserve special mention. Thanks to Chong Kim Chong, Jerry Ginsburg, James and Diana Herbert, Jarrett Leplin, Cheryl Logan, Richard McDonough, Peter Manicas, Joe Margolis, Catherine Morris, Glyn Owen, Harry Purser, Joe Rychlach, Michael Tay, and Cecelia Wee.

Much of the material of this volume was rehearsed in courses on the philosophy of social and psychological science given at the National University of Singapore and the University of North Carolina at Greensboro. I thank the students who participated in these courses for their very often useful comments and criticisms. I am also grateful to Walter Salinger, Head of the Psychology Department at the University of North Carolina, Greensboro, for arranging for me to give a graduate psychology course entitled "Social Dimensions of Mind, Behavior, and Method" in the Spring of 1987. The present format of this volume is largely based on sections of that course.

I have drawn on material previously published in academic journals. I thank the editors of *Philosophy of Science, Philosophy of the Social Sciences, Journal for the Theory of Social Behaviour, Human Studies,* and *European Journal of Social Psychology* for their permission to reproduce some of this material.

Thanks to my wife Shelagh, son Robert, and daughter Holly for putting up with the periods of physical and mental distance during the writing of this volume.

Finally, my greatest debt is to my late mother and father, for their moral support. This volume is dedicated to their memory.

Contents

Reason, holding in one hand its principles . . . and in the other hand the experiment which it has devised in conformity with these principles, must approach nature in order to be taught by it. It must not, however, do so in the character of a pupil who listens to everything that the teacher chooses to say, but of an appointed judge who compels the witnesses to answer questions which he has himself formulated.

Kant, *Critique of Pure Reason*

To define the limits of freedom and dependence is very difficult, and the definition of those limits forms the sole and essential problem of psychology.

Tolstoy, *War and Peace*

1
Scientific Empiricism and Scientific Psychology

Philosophy and Psychology

It is a common opinion among psychologists that psychology[1] became a science when it developed as a discipline independent of philosophy and modeled itself upon the practice of the natural sciences. In fact it did nothing of the kind. While psychologists quite justifiably rejected philosophical speculations about human nature in favor of empirical research, from the earliest days psychology was modeled upon an *empiricist* philosophy of science, derived from the empiricist and *idealist* doctrines of the 18th-century philosophers John Locke (1632–1704), George Berkeley (1685–1753), and David Hume (1711–1776).

In the 19th century, the influential empiricist philosopher John Stuart Mill (1806–1873) complained that the "moral sciences" such as psychology and sociology were a "blot on the face of science." According to Mill the situation could only be redeemed by the application of the empiricist scientific methods of his "*A System of Logic*" (1843, p. 580) to the realm of human behavior: ". . . the backward state of the moral sciences can only be remedied by applying to them the methods of natural science, duly extended and generalized."

In the 20th century, those who wished to advance a scientific psychology quite explicitly embraced the *logical positivist* formalization of empiricist philosophy of science:

. . . in pursuit of these ends, psychology did not go directly to physics but turned instead for its directives to middlemen. These were, for the most part, philosophers of science (especially logical positivists) and a number of physical science methodologists who had been codifying a synoptic view of the nature of science and who, by the early thirties, were actively exporting that view from their specialities to the scholarly community at large. This view was based upon a "rational reconstruction" of a few selected formulations in theoretical physics and put forward a detailed model of the scientific enterprise which came to be known as the "hypothetico-deductive method." (Koch, 1964, p. 10)

When Wilhelm Wundt (1832–1920) made the symbolic move to the laboratory in 1893, he carried with him the intellectual baggage of 18th- and 19th-century empiricism. His attempt to identify and correlate mental "elements" by introspection was little more than an experimental investigation of the "laws" governing the association of mental "impressions" postulated by Locke, Berkeley, and Hume. When John Watson (1878–1958) rejected *introspective psychology* as unscientific and introduced *behaviorism* as the foundation of a psychological science, he simply replaced the private mental data of introspective psychology with publically observable stimuli and responses, but retained the essential empiricist characterization of causal explanatory laws as the description of de facto correlation between observables: "In effect they have given to us as the primary analytic concepts for the most ambitious science ever conceived a mildly camouflaged paradigm for Hume's analysis of causality" (Koch, 1964, p. 34). Later behaviorist theorists, such as E.C. Tolman (1856–1959) and C.L. Hull (1884–1952), found that the the empiricist prescriptions of logical positivism provided a convenient justification for their conception of an empiricial science of psychology:

This "new view" held forth an ideal of rigorous theory and seemed to define a route to its achievement. In barest outline, it asserts theory to be a hypothetico-deductive system. Laws or hypotheses believed fundamental are asserted as postulates, and the consequences of these (theorems) are deduced by strict logical and mathematical rules. The theorems are then to be tested by experiment. Positive results increase the probability of a hypothesis; negative results call it into question. Scientific theories differ from logical or mathematical systems only in that their basic terms are given empirical reference (made to describe the world) by operational definitions (Bridgeman) which state the observational conditions under which the terms may be applied. A science aims towards explicit and, if possible, quantitative hypothetico-deductive organization of events in its domain. (Koch, 1962, p. 12)

One of the ironies of this piece of intellectual history is that the empiricist conception of science was adopted by psychologists at almost precisely the time it began to be seriously questioned by philosophers. The confident empiricism of Rudolf Carnap (1928) and Ernest Nagel (1961) has long since given way to the neo-empiricist *relativism* of Thomas Kuhn (1970) and Paul Feyerabend (1974). Most contemporary philosophers of science would reject as hopelessly naive the traditional empiricist account of science advanced by scientific psychologists.

EMPIRICISM, IDEALISM, and PHENOMENALISM

To understand the problems of scientific empiricism and, thus, the problems of scientific psychology, it is necessary to return to the roots of these doctrines in the epistemological concerns of the 18th century British empiricists. One of the central problems of classical empiricism concerns our common claims to have knowledge of the existence and nature of objects in the external world: those physical objects that are commonly held to have real and continuous existence quite independently of our perception of them or thoughts about them.

Locke, Berkeley, and Hume were all empiricists insofar as they held that our knowledge of the external world is based upon our sensory experience of the world. More significantly, they were all *idealists* who held that strictly speaking we can have knowledge only of our mental states (our sense impressions or perceptions, and our ideas or concepts). All other putative forms of knowledge, and in particular our putative knowledge of physical objects, are subject to the possibility of human error. They employed the concept of knowledge in the rigid sense defined by the *rationalist* philosopher Rene Descartes (1596–1650), who distinguished certain knowledge (epistēmē) from fallible belief (doxa). Their justification of this claim was also based upon the Cartesian belief that we have a privileged form of introspective apprehension of our mental states that makes our knowledge of such states immune from error. Error only arises when we engage in speculation beyond the experiential content of our sense impressions, such as speculations about the material causes of our sense impressions (or about the nature and unity of the self or mind that has such mental impressions). Thus, they were all also *phenomenalists* about our knowledge of the external world: they held that we can only have knowledge of the contents of our sense experience, but not of the existence and properties of physical objects that we commonly believe produce our sense experiences.

They were, however, idealists in different senses. Locke, Berkeley, and Hume were all *epistemological idealists* who argued that we can have knowledge only of our sense impressions. Berkeley was also an *ontological idealist*, who denied the existence of a world of physical objects existing independently of our perceptions of or thoughts about them.

Locke, Berkeley, and Hume were also idealists for slightly different reasons. Locke thought that our putative knowledge about the existence, nature, and causal powers of physical objects in the external world is at best an uncertain *inference* from our sensory impressions of color, texture, solidity, and so forth. Although Locke talked about the postulation of an independently existing world of physical objects with causal powers as a "necessity of thought," he nevertheless insisted that we can only have knowledge of the *nominal* but not of the *real* essences of particular physical objects. That is, he held that we can have knowledge of such objects only as they appear to our senses, but not as they are in themselves. This suggests a sense in which the real essences of physical objects may be said to be forever hidden from us by the "veil of ideas," since we can only apprehend and comprehend such objects through our (sensory) ideas of them.

Despite these strong reservations, Locke, nevertheless, also seems to have held the view (possibly inconsistently) that at least some of our sensory ideas (derived from our sense impressions) resemble and thus accurately represent the real properties of physical objects existing in the external world independently of our perception of them. For this reason, Locke's special brand of empiricism is sometimes characterised as *representative realism*.

Berkeley and Hume denied that the postulation of an external world of physical objects existing independently of our perception of them is a "necessity of thought." Hume did claim that our belief in "bodies" is a *psychological* necessity of thought (like our belief in a "necessary connection" between cause and effect). Both he and Berkeley denied that such a belief is an intellectual necessity in the sense that our sensory experience obliges us to postulate the existence of physical objects. Berkeley did not even think that such a belief is a psychological necessity. He denied that such objects exist in any sense independently of our sense experience. He believed that most of our sensory ideas are directly caused by God. Despite common misconceptions about the role of philosophical scepticism in Hume's philosophy, he seems clearly to have remained an epistemological idealist only. There seems little doubt that Hume, like Locke and most of the rest of us, continued to believe in the real existence of physical objects.

It is not, however, obvious that Locke and Hume were entitled to remain ontological realists, given their strong version of epistemological idealism (i.e., that only the contents of sense experiences can be known since these are the only objects of our sense experience). In this respect, Berkeley is possibly the most consistent classical empiricist. His ontological idealism is not based upon any blind faith that God directly causes our sensory experiences. Rather, he held this view as a consequence of his claim that it is literally inconceivable that our sense impressions are caused by physical objects. This claim is itself a natural consequence of the epistemological idealism advanced by Locke, Berkeley, and Hume.

It is important to notice that the Lockean conception of a "veil of ideas" that denies us knowledge of the real essence of physical objects is not simply a powerful metaphor. Such a necessarily restrictive account of our knowledge of the physical world naturally follows from the classical empiricists' conception of the nature and origin of concepts, and the meaning of our linguistic expressions of them. In neither Locke, Berkeley, nor Hume is there any essential distinction between perception and cognition. Our concepts of physical objects are held to be derived from our sense experiences and are held to be "copies" or "reflections" of them in an almost literal sense. Ideas are more or less identified with transient images, which are themselves treated as simply weaker or fainter "copies" of sense impressions. Our concepts or ideas are held to be meaningful only if they are derived from sense experience.

Locke, Berkeley, and Hume were all committed to the principle of *meaning empiricism* (Bennett, 1971) in a very strong sense: our concepts (or ideas) are only meaningful if they describe the actual or possible contents of our sense experience. Whatever their ultimate beliefs about the ontology of the world, the consequences of epistemological idealism are the same for Locke, Berkeley, and Hume. Since our concepts are only meaningful if they are concepts *of* sense experience, they can only meaningfully refer to sense experience. Thus our concepts of "physical object" or "causal power" can only refer to certain formal properties of our sense experience. Specifically (in Berkeley and Hume), they can only refer to the "constancy," "coherence," and "constant conjunction" of certain complexes of sensory experience. Such concepts are held to play a useful and meaningful role only insofar as they provide an intellectual means of organizing sensory experience that can serve as a basis for anticipating future sensory experience (based upon the past conjunction of complexes of sense experience). These intellectual constructions are justified only insofar as they play such an *instrumental* role. It is an intellectual error to suppose that they do or can play a *referential* role with respect to any entities other than complexes of sense experience. This led both Berkeley and Hume (and ought to have led Locke) to endorse a phenomenalist *linguistic idealism*: meaningful propositions that putatively refer to physical objects existing independently of our perception of them can only and do only refer to certain complexes of sense impressions. Our thought and discourse about physical reality are essentially cognitive and linguistic constructions from sense experience that legitimately relate to sense experience only.

LOGICAL POSITIVISM AND SCIENTIFIC EMPIRICISM

This conception of physical object concepts as purely intellectual constructions from sense experience was formalized in the early days of logical positivism by treating putative descriptions of physical objects in the external world as "logical constructions" out of sense data (the quasi-technical term introduced to describe the contents of our sensory experience). Propositions putatively "about" ordinary physical objects (such as pointers and arm movements) were held to be "molecular" propositions that could (in principle at least) be translated without remainder into a "protocol" language of "atomic propositions" about basic sense data (Carnap, 1928; Neurath, 1932; Schlick, 1936). Theoretical propositions putatively "about" theoretical entities (such as electrons and emotion) were simply held to be higher order molecular propositions that could (in principle at least) be translated into lower order molecular propositions about ordinary physical objects, and ultimately into atomic propositions about sense data. Thus, Russell (1962, p. 109), for example, was led to claim that: "Physics cannot be regarded as validly based upon empirical data until [light] waves have been expressed as functions of the colours and other sense data."

The justification of this formalized version of phenomenalist linguistic idealism (and instrumentalism) was the same as it was for the classical empiricists. It was based upon on a phenomenalist epistemological idealism to the effect that only propositions about sense data (the contents of which are "given" in sense experience) are immune from error and, thus, provide genuine knowledge. All other propositions, especially molecular propositions about the causal powers of physical objects, that describe correlations of complexes of sense data were held to be essentially speculative and subject to error. At best, such general propositions were held to be rendered more or less probable by observations of correlated molecular complexes of sense data. The claim that propositions about ordinary physical objects and theoretical entities in science are either meaningless or ultimately refer to sense data was based upon a rigid *verificationist* theory of meaning (Schlick, 1936), which held that only propositions that (ultimately) refer to (actual or possible) sense experience are meaningful, since only such propositions can be verified (in principle at least) by sense data.

However, this certain basis for knowledge was achieved in logical positivism (as it was achieved in classical empiricism) at some considerable cost. The bedrock of scientific knowledge is located in the private mental experiences of individual human beings, which are not themselves possible objects of experience for other human beings. With respect to scientific knowledge, this is especially peculiar, since scientific knowledge is paradigmatically a form of knowledge for which intersubjective replication of observations is an essential form of critical evaluation. The earlier phenomenalist (or *sensationalist*) forms of logical positivism seemed to have a form of *solipsism* as their logical consequence. Any putative science based upon sense data would ultimately be a multitude of descriptions of private sense data incapable of intersubjective verification.

Largely for this reason, a crucial modification of the basic empiricist thesis took place during the later stages of logical positivism in the 1930s. The later positivists simply abandoned the doctrines that sense data are the only objects of genuine knowledge and that propositions about physical objects refer to complexes of sense data. The later logical positivists, who preferred to characterize themselves as *scientific empiricists* (or logical empiricists), treated observations of physical objects as the foundation of scientific knowledge, and held that physical object descriptions do in fact refer to physical objects that can be directly observed by any human agent with healthy sense organs in normal conditions. This doctrine came to be known as *physicalism*.

It was for precisely this reason (in the form of their rejection of "introspective psychology") that the early behaviorists adopted the physicalist rather than the phenomenalist version of logical positivism as the philosophical justification for their methodological principles. They also adopted the instrumentalist doctrine about theories retained in scientific empiricism. Since "theoretical entities," such as magnetic fields, genes, social hierarchies, thoughts, and emotions, are not observable (or not directly observable), meaningful theoretical propositions putatively "about" such entities can only be cognitive and linguistic constructions that ultimately refer to the behavior of physical objects (by organizing and systematizing our descriptions of them). Thus, despite their joint commitment to the physicalist thesis, both scientific empiricism and scientific psychology remain profoundly anthropocentric (in the fashion of earlier phenomenalist versions of empiricism). The "realities" of the theoretical physicist, biologist, and psychologist remain intellectual constructions that serve to facilitate the description and prediction of the observable behavior of physical objects.

It is worth stressing that the scientific empiricists simply abandoned the earlier phenomenalist version of logical positivism. For in doing so they also abandoned the epistemological arguments that supported it. It is thus far from obvious that traditional empiricist doctrines about causality, explanation, and theory based upon the phenomenalism of Berkeley and Hume can be readily transferred to contemporary versions of scientific empiricism based upon physicalism.

It is true that some of the more rigid prescriptions of scientific empiricist philosophy of science have been modified or qualified by contemporary philosophers of science. It is also true that the days of the hegemony of behaviorism are over, and that many practicing psychologists now adopt a more liberal attitude toward theoretical discourse about postulated mental states. Nevertheless, it remains true to say that most practicing psychologists remain strongly committed to four central philosophical dogmas about science, which may be characterized collectively as *scientific empiricism* (since they are derived from the later physicalist formulations of logical positivism). These comprise the Humean or *regularity account of causality*, the *instance-statistics account of confirmation*, the *deductive-nomological account of explanation*, and the *instrumentalist conception of theory*. Those psychologists committed to these doctrines may be characterized as *scientific psychologists*. While some practitioners do recognize the philosophical origin of these doctrines, many present them quite uncritically, as if they represented some kind of scientific common sense.

In the following sections, these doctrines and their internal inadequacies are discussed in some detail. It is important to recognize that the most fundamental inadequacy of these doctrines derives not simply from their empiricist nature, but from their origin in phenomenalist forms of philosophical idealism. This explains why so many of the problems of contemporary philosophy of natural and social psychological science simply cannot be resolved within the framework of scientific empiricism.

Causality

The bête noire in the intellectual history of philosophy of science and psychology is the empiricist philosopher David Hume. Most of the doctrines of scientific empiricism and their scientific psychological versions may be seen as modifications and more sophisticated developments of Hume's account of causality.

THE HUMEAN ACCOUNT OF CAUSALITY

Only two ontological objects are possible objects of knowledge in Hume's philosophy: *impressions* of sense (or passion) and *ideas* (which were held to be fainter "copies" of impressions). Hume was committed to the view that an idea or concept relating to the "external world" has a legitimate epistemic application only if it is derived from some sense impression (and thus can be reapplied to sense experience).

Hume's most basic empiricist claim about causality is that the concept of causal "power" is not derived from any impression of sense. In any causal sequence, such as his own classic example of the motion of one billiard ball causing motion in another by collision, he noted that the only common features observable in sense experience are contiguity in space, priority in time, and "constant conjunction" in past experience. The concept of causality in its legitimate employment ought, therefore, to be restricted to the description of contiguity, priority, and constant conjunction in sense experience (Hume, 1739, 1748).

Hume recognized that this "philosophical" analysis of causality did not account for our common belief in some kind of "necessary connection" between cause and effect. Hume denied that there could be any philosophical justification of this belief, but he did provide a psychological explanation of it. As there is no sense impression from which our belief in a "necessary connection" can be derived, for Hume there could only be one other option: it must be derived from some "internal impression" or passion. According to Hume, the "necessary connection" of causality is simply a "connection . . . which we feel in the mind." This is a product of the mental association of sensory events via "habit" and "custom," based on past experiences of event conjunctions. As a natural consequence of the observation of past conjunctions of billiard ball motions, for example, the mind is determined to mentally associate such events, and anticipate their future conjunction.

It is worth stressing that this psychological account of our belief in causality is an account of the *causal determination of our belief in causality*. Causal judgments based upon experienced constant conjunctions are held to be:

. . . the necessary result of placing the mind in such circumstances. It is an operation of the soul, when we are so situated, as unavoidable as to feel the passion of love, when we receive benefits; or hatred when we meet with injuries. (Hume, 1748, p. 46)

Hume also gives a psychological account of the strength of any causal belief. This is itself causally determined by the number of observed conjunctions of sensory events:

As the habit, which produces the association, arises from the frequent conjunction of objects, it must arrive at its perfection by degrees, and must acquire new force from each instance, that falls under the observation. The first instance has little or no force: The second makes some additon to it: The third becomes still more sensible, and 'tis by these slow steps, that our judgement arrives at a full assurance. (Hume, 1739, p. 130)

Causality as Constant Conjunction

Hume's major philosophical legacy was the conception of causality as the simple description of observational conjunction or regularity. Although Hume provided the philosophical arguments, he was not in fact responsible for the widespread acceptance of the constant conjunction view of causality (Hacking, 1983). Newton's hypercautious attitude to universal gravitation led to the conception of gravitational theory as a series of descriptions of observable physical regularities (a view clearly expounded by Berkeley in *De Motu* (1721), for example). It was a short step to the treatment of all causal laws as simple descriptions of observable physical regularities, with "gravity" as the paradigmatic illustrative example. This step was quickly taken and clearly articulated in the writings of later empiricists and positivists such as John Stuart Mill (1806–1873), Auguste Compte (1798–1857), and Ernst Mach (1838–1916). All references to putatively explanatory causal powers were dismissed as appeals to "occult forces" or "empty metaphysics." An example from Mill will suffice:

We have no knowledge of anything but phaenomena; and our knowledge of phaenomena is relative not absolute. We know not the essence, nor real mode of production, of any fact, but only its relations to other facts in the way of succession or similitude. Their relations are constant; that is, always the same in the same circumstances. The constant resemblances which link phaenomena together, and the constant sequences which unite then as antecedent and consequent, are termed their laws. The laws of phaenomena are all we know respecting them. Their essential nature, and their ultimate causes, either efficient or final, are unknown and inscrutable to us. (Mill, 1866, p. 6)

This conception was formalized in logical positivism and encapsulated in Moritz Schlick's maxim that causal laws are descriptive rather than prescriptive.

One of the legacies of this conception of causality is a now standard problem for empiricist philosophy of science (already present in Hume's original account and noted by him). Whatever the other shortcomings of the Humean account, constant conjunction does not seem to provide an adequate or sufficient criterion for what laypersons and scientists characterize as causal sequences. In particular, constant conjunction does not suffice as a criterion to discriminate recognized causal sequences, such as the heating of a gas generating expansion in the gas, from purely accidental correlations, such as the soundings of the factory hooter in Manchester being regularly followed by the workers leaving the factory in London

(Broad, 1925), or the motions of two spacially adjacent pendulums, where no generation is involved. This problem reappears in scientific empiricism in a variety of different guises, as are noted in the following sections. The failure to provide an adequate criterion for distinguishing genuinely causal sequences is a continual source of embarrassment for empiricist philosophy of science, especially since laypersons and scientists appear to experience little practical difficulty. Worse still for the Humean psychological account, their actual causal judgments appear to have precious little to do with the number of observed correlations. Few are convinced that the ticking of one clock generates the ticking of a spatially adjacent clock (Braithwaite, 1953), no matter how frequently these events are conjoined in experience. Fewer still will regularly place their hands in an open fire to convince themselves that "proximate fire" (Berkeley, 1710) generates pain.

THE REGULARITY ACCOUNT OF CAUSALITY

Scientific empiricists treat publically observable physical events as the observational foundation of scientific knowledge of the world. Their statement of the regularity account of causality is a slightly more sophisticated syntactical version of Hume's account: causal propositions or laws are held to refer to the constant conjunction of publically observable physical objects and events (Braithwaite, 1953). This doctrine is often expressed in conditional terms, such that one event is held to be the cause of another if the first event is, ceteris paribus, a sufficient condition for the other (Braithwaite, 1953; Hempel, 1965; Popper, 1972).

Thus, for example, to say that tiger mosquito bites are the cause of yellow fever is to say that instances of tiger mosquito bites are regularly conjoined with instances of yellow fever, or that tiger mosquito bites are sufficient conditions (in conjunction with other necessary conditions) for yellow fever. Putative causal laws are analyzed as universally quantified conditional propositions relating observation predicates. For example, the causal claim that "tiger mosquito bites cause yellow fever" is analyzed as equivalent to "for all men, if any man is bitten by a tiger mosquito, he will contract yellow fever." This is represented by the symbolic formulation (x) $(Fx \rightarrow Gx)$, where the variable x ranges over men, the logical predicates F and G are interpreted as "is bitten by a tiger mosquito" and "will contract yellow fever," respectively, and the material implication sign $\rightarrow$ is interpreted as analogous to the ordinary language "if. . . then" connective.

CAUSALITY AND ACCIDENT

The basic problem with this analysis is the basic problem of its Humean predecessor. It fails to provide an adequate criterion for discriminating causal sequences from purely accidental correlations, or causal laws of nature (universals of law) from accidental generalizations (universals of fact): ". . . a scientific law cannot be adequately defined as a true statement of universal form: this characterization expresses a necessary, but not a sufficient, condition for laws . . ." (Hempel, 1966, p. 55)

Various additional criteria have been proposed by empiricist philosophers of science to account for the "surplus" element in causal laws, but with little success. Nelson Goodman (1947) proposed that genuine causal laws can be distinguished from accidental generalizations by the fact that causal laws "support" or "license" "unfulfilled hypotheticals," whereas accidental generalizations do not. Thus, for example, the causal law "all heated gases expand" supports or licenses counterfactual and subjunctive conditionals such as "if this gas had been heated, it would have expanded" and "if this gas is heated, it will expand." However, an accidental generalization such as "all the coins in my pocket are silver" does not support or license the conditionals "if this coin had been in my pocket, it would have been silver" or "if this coin should be in my pocket, it would be silver." Such a criterion raises its own novel problems (Kneale, 1949), not least of which is an explication of the sense in which causal laws "support" or "license" such conditionals. This cannot be treated as logical deduction, since both causal laws and accidental generalizations are supposed to be identical with respect to their logical form (both are universally quantified conditionals). No doubt the ability to support or license such conditionals is a mark of a causal law, but this feature is as much in need of explanation as the original distinction between causal laws and accidental generalizations. The same criticism applies to the claim that causal laws are explanatory, whereas accidental correlations are not. This is certainly true, but the empiricist needs to give an account of why some conjunctions are explanatory and others are not.

Other criteria fare no better. Braithwaite (1953) suggested that a genuine scientific law could be deduced from universal propositions of a higher order of generality. Thus "all heated gases expand" can be characterized as a scientific law because it can be deduced from the kinetic theory of gases. This criterion produces its own paradoxical consequences. On this account, the gas laws did not become laws until the kinetic theory was developed, and the highest order theoretical propositions, which provide the deductive grounding for scientific laws, are not themselves scientific laws. Furthermore, it is intuitively implausible. Scientists can and do successfully establish causal relations often long before they are in a position to provide an adequate theoretical account of the mechanisms of generation. They were able to establish that tiger mosquito bites are the cause of yellow fever long before they established the theory of viral transmission (and the gas laws were adequately confirmed long before the kinetic theory). In any case, there seems no reason why accidental generalizations such as "all the coins in my pocket are silver" could not in principle be deduced from higher order accidental generalizations such as "all the coins in everyone's pockets are silver," yet we would still be disinclined to call them scientific laws.

Nagel (1961) suggested that genuine laws are unrestricted in space and time, whereas accidental generalizations are restricted to particular spaces and times. However, some scientific laws do seem to be restricted in space, such as Kepler's laws, and others in time, such as the Newtonian gravitational constant (which varies in time). For this reason, many scientific empiricists themselves reject this criterion, recognizing that only the most basic laws of physics are unrestricted in space and time (Carnap, 1966).

The patent failure of scientific empiricism to discriminate causal laws from accidental generalizations is hardly surprising, given the idealist and phenomenalist origins of the regularity account of causality. Berkeley and Hume, respectively, denied and doubted the existence of generative causal relations between physical entities. Since they held that causal laws can only be legimately interpreted as descriptions of correlation among sense impressions, there is no logical difference between causal laws and accidental generalizations, nor any ontological difference between causal and accidental sequences. The same point applies equally for the physicalist empiricist. If causal laws are descriptions of observational regularity, there can be no basis for the distinction between causal laws and accidental generalizations, since *both* are simply descriptions of observational regularity. The scientific empiricist wants to deny what he or she believes to be a spurious metaphysical conception of generative causality, but retains precisely this conception by maintaining a distinction between causal sequences and causal laws on the one hand, and accidental sequences and generalizations on the other. Without a reference to generative causality, this distinction simply cannot be maintained or justified.

Causality and Regularity in Psychology

The same is true of the scientific psychologist. The scientific psychologist will often want to claim, for example, that a reference to television violence gives a causal explanation of (some forms of) aggression in young children. Yet because of his commitment to a "scientific" approach, he will insist that this only means that a regular correlation has been observed between television violence and aggression in young children. He might claim that a certain amount of television violence would be a sufficient condition for aggression in young children (in conjunction with other conditions such as maternal deprivation, weak peer bonding, frustration, etc). Yet few would be so incautious. In social and psychological sciences, causal propositions are usually given a weaker interpretation. They are held to describe a (unspecified) degree of statistical regularity rather than constant conjunction.

Still, such a degree of regular correlation between observational phenomena is held to be a *necessary* feature of any causal sequence:

Observational research cannot itself determine whether a relationship is causal or not; its purpose is to determine whether a relationship exists at all and if so, how strong it is. If no association had been found between watching violent behavior on television and displaying aggressive behaviour in primary school, researchers might have abandoned the whole issue. (McCall, 1980, p. 6)

Scientific psychologists also stress that regular correlation is not to be equated with causality. Yet they have no more basis than any other empiricist for discriminating causality from accidental correlation, and in practice treat degree of correlation as some kind of measure of the probability of a causal connection: the probability of a causal relation between television violence and aggression in children may be held to be low if there is a low correlation. There is no warrant for this, since accidental correlations (such as the correlation between the ticking of two spacially adjacent clocks) may exhibit a high degree of correlation, and causal relations (such as the relation between smoking and lung cancer) may exhibit a (very) low degree of correlation, although it can perhaps be explained in terms of the scientific empiricist account of confirmation.

Confirmation

THE INSTANCE-STATISTICS ACCOUNT OF CONFIRMATION

Most scientific empiricists also accept the Humean psychological account of causal judgment to the effect that our degree of belief or confidence in a causal judgment is determined by, and proportional to, the number of observed correlations. Indeed the instance-statistics account of confirmation seems little more than a syntactical formulation of the Humean psychological doctrine. This account states that causal laws (which describe observational regularities) are confirmed by "positive instances" of the putative law (Hempel, 1965; Nagel, 1939; Nicod, 1934). Thus a putative law such as "all men bitten by tiger mosquitos contract yellow fever" is confirmed by positive instances of men bitten by tiger mosquitos who consequently contract yellow fever.

It is further stated that the degree of confirmation or probability of a putative causal law is, ceteris paribus, proportional to the number of observed positive instances (Carnap, 1966; Hempel, 1966; Nagel, 1939). Thus the degree of confirmation or probability of a putative law such as "all men bitten by tiger mosquitos contract yellow fever" is held to be proportional to the number of observed instances of men bitten by tiger mosquitos who subsequently contract yellow fever.

This account is usually also supplemented by the further claim that the degree of confirmation or probability of a putative causal law increases in accord with the representative nature of the observed sample of positive instances. Thus our confidence in the putative causal law "all heated gases expand" increases according to the number of different gases that are observed to expand when heated in a variety of different circumstances.

There are a number of technical paradoxes associated with this account of confirmation.[2] But perhaps the main problem is that this account treats the confirmation relation as incredibly weak. It was noted earlier that Hume's account of causal judgment fails to explain why the child recognizes that fire causes pain after a single burn. The instance-statistics account likewise cannot explain why natural scientists regularly demonstrate causal laws on the basis of very few positive instances (Toulmin, 1953). On the empiricist account a scientist who injects a chemical that destroys a cell nucleus would have to repeat this process dozens if not hundreds of times to gain any confidence in a causal relationship. A natural scientist would doubt the sanity as well as the logic of anyone who seriously suggested this.

CONFIRMATION IN PSYCHOLOGY

Scientific psychologists are, however, equally strongly committed to this account of confirmation. Few clearer statements could be found than the following account of confirmation in psychological science: "An explanatory statement is regarded as being more probably true as the number of verified descriptive statements and confirmed explanatory statements with which it is found to be consistent increases" (Anderson, 1971, p. 29). The scientific psychologist also places great emphasis on the representative nature of such positive instances. Thus it is held that one's confidence in a causal relation between television violence and aggression in children ought to be increased if a large number of instances of the correlation are observed with respect to different classes of children (of different ages, sex, race, home background, etc.) in a wide variety of different circumstances (at school, at home, in the psychological laboratory, etc.).

This account of confirmation is also frequently found in justifications of experimental confirmation employing inferential statistics, although this seriously distorts the general logic of the experiment and the special logic of the psychology experiment (Rozeboom, 1970). The scientific psychologist gives the empiricist account of confirmation a special twist by treating the number of subjects employed in an experiment as some kind of measure of the adequacy of causal inference. This no doubt explains a rather dubious practice to which many commentators have objected: the fact that one statistically significant result will displace a number of nonsignificant results, especially when the study that achieves significance employs a larger subject sample than previous studies (Westland, 1978). It is doubly distorting if critics such as Bakan (1966) are correct in claiming that standard tests of statistical significance in psychology experiments are more sensitive with smaller samples.

Explanation

THE DEDUCTIVE-NOMOLOGICAL ACCOUNT OF EXPLANATION

A quite natural scientific empiricist development of the Humean or regularity account of causality is the deductive-nomological account of causal explanation, proposed independently by Popper and Hempel in the early part of the century, which treats causal explanation as essentially the description of observational regularity. On this account, the causal explanation of singular events (a man contracting yellow fever, a gas expanding, aggressive behavior in a child) is held to consist of the subsumption of the event to be explained, called the *explanandum*, under one or more "covering laws." (For this reason it is often called the "covering-law" account of explanation.) Explanation is held to proceed by the deduction of a description of the explanandum from one or more such laws, in conjunction with a description of the initial conditions, which jointly constitute the *explanans* (Hempel & Oppenheim, 1948; Popper, 1959).

Thus, for example, an explanation of a particular instance of the expansion of a gas is given by deducing the description "the gas expanded" from the causal law "all heated gases expand" and the initial condition description "the gas was heated." It is further stipulated that the explanans statements must have empirical content and be true. This simply means that, in addition to the truth of the initial condition description(s), the covering law(s) must describe de facto observational regularity.

EXPLANATION AND PREDICTION

One of the most significant consequences of this account is the claim that explanation and prediction are symmetrical with respect to their logical form, since the prediction of singular events is also held to consist of the deduction of descriptions of these events from causal laws and descriptions of initial conditions (Hempel, 1965). The only difference between explanation and prediction appears to be a difference in the tense of the event and initial condition descriptions. Thus the prediction that "the gas will expand" could be deduced from the initial condition description "the gas is being (will be) heated" and the covering law.

This doctrine was quickly elevated into a criterion for the adequacy of a causal explanation: ". . . an explanation is not fully adequate, unless its explanans if taken account of in time, could have served as the basis for predicting the phenomena under investigation," (Hempel and Oppenheim, 1948, p. 155). The treatment of predictive success as the acid test for the adequacy of a causal explanation is hardly surprising, given the roots of this doctrine in the Humean account of causality. One of the apparent virtues of the regularity account is that descriptions of observational regularity seem to provide a basis for the prediction of phenomena, which is seen as a primary (if not the exclusive) goal of scientific enquiry.

EXPLANATION AND PREDICTION IN PSYCHOLOGY

Certainly the scientific psychologist sees this as a virtue. The equation of explanation and prediction finds expression in practically every introductory and advanced text in psychology: "Science is deterministic in its mode of reasoning since only deterministic assumptions give us the licence to make predictions, and this we have already taken to be a distinguishing feature of scientific explanation in general" (Beloff, 1973, p. 7). However, despite the obvious appeal of this account of explanation to the scientific psychologist, it is generally recognized that psychological explanations do not (at present at least) live up to this ideal. It was noted earlier that few psychologists would be so incautious as to treat their causal explanatory factors (television violence, presence of other bystanders, cognitive dissonance, etc.) as sufficient conditions for the phenomena explained. Yet such factors must be treated as sufficient conditions if they are to provide deductive explanations and predictions. The same point can be expressed by recalling that the scientific psychologist interprets causal explanations as descriptions of a (unspecified but usually fairly high) degree of statistical regularity, whereas the description of constant conjunction is required for deductive explanation and prediction: "As anyone who has studied psychology would have quickly noticed, most of the arguments which assert a relationship (e.g. a causal one) between psychological phenomena are based on probabilistic statements, not universal generalizations" (Bell & Staines, 1981, p. 46).

STATISTICAL-PROBABILISTIC EXPLANATION

This problem or perceived inadequacy is not restricted to psychological science. It is also held to apply for example to explanations in sociology, economics, and, especially, history. Few would deny that these disciplines provide generally adequate explanations in their respective domains. To accommodate explanation in these disciplines, Hempel (1966) introduced another type of "covering-law" explanation known as *statistical* or *probabilistic* explanation.

In this type of explanation the covering law expresses a high probability (high relative frequency), not a universal regularity. Given the probabilistic law and statement of initial conditions, the explanandum event is implied with high probability (Hempel calls it "near certainty"). It is implied but not entailed because the relation between explanans and explanandum is one of support rather than logical deduction. In Hempel's own example, the covering law "the probability for persons exposed to the measles to catch the disease is high," in conjunction with the initial condition statement "Jim was exposed to measles," implies and "makes highly probable" the fact that "Jim caught the measles." Thus presumably in a psychological example, a covering law something like "the probability for children exposed to violence to become aggressive is high," in conjunction with the initial condition statement "Tommy was exposed to violence," implies or "makes highly probable" and thus explains the fact that "Tommy was aggressive."

One of the attractions of this account for the scientific psychologist is that it allows him to link his explanations with prediction. These predictions may not be deductively certain, but they have a high degree of probability, which is enough for a young and developing science. It also holds out the hope and promise that scientific psychology will eventually produce deductive-nomological explanations that will enable the scientific psychologist to make deductively certain predictions. Probabilistic or statistical explanation is clearly seen as a weaker form of explanation but also as an approximation toward the deductive ideal (Hempel, 1962).

EXPLANATION AND DESCRIPTION

The deductive-nomological account of explanation is not without its critics. The most common complaint is that predictive success is not a sufficient condition for an adequate causal explanation (Dray, 1957; Scriven, 1962; Zaffron, 1971). A description of the correlation between abnormal animal behavior and earthquakes might be formalized into a rather successful predictive device, but no one would imagine for a moment that this provided a causal explanation of earthquakes.

As a matter of fact neither Popper or Hempel ever claimed this. Predictive success was held to be the acid test of a causal explanation (a necessary condition), but both explicitly denied that successful prediction was equivalent to causal explanation. This, however, can be of little comfort to the scientific empiricist. For now of the old problem of discriminating causal sequences from purely accidental correlations returns in an only slightly modified form: What criterion or surplus factor distinguishes causal explanatory laws or deductions from nonexplanatory descriptions of regularity that may function as useful predictive devices? Once again there can be no answer to this problem for the scientific empiricist. Indeed the situation is much worse than this. The deductive account cannot be justified as an account of explanation at all.

PHENOMENALISM AND INSTRUMENTALISM

To illustrate this claim, one needs to return to the phenomenalist origins of the deductive-nomological account in the empiricism of Berkeley and Hume. Berkeley dismissed Locke's inference to an external world of physical objects with causal powers. For Berkeley, the only proper employment of physical object concepts is to describe recurring "complexes" of sensory "ideas." He had an obvious problem explaining the continued existence of such "objects" when they are not being perceived, and the origin of the sensory ideas that constitute them (having dismissed Locke's notion that they are causally generated by independently existing physical objects). Berkeley introduced God to provide a general causal explanation of the origin of our sensory ideas, and the "constancy" and "coherence" of complexes of such ideas which enable us to form physical object concepts.

Thus for Berkeley the only generative or efficient cause in the world is God. In any putative causal sequence, such as Hume's billiard ball collision, we do not have one physical object generating a change in the other, but simply one complex of sensory ideas followed by another. God generates both complexes of sensory ideas and ensures the regular and orderly progression of such complexes. Berkeley thought it is as pointless to search for generative causal explanations in the natural world as it is to try to discover the Lockean "real nature" of independently existing physical objects. The reason in both cases was the same. According to Berkeley, there are no physical objects existing independently of perceivers; there is no generative causality in the world save for God, who is beyond our sensory experience. Generative causal explanation has no place in a science of nature: "Real efficient causes of the motion of bodies do not in any way belong to the field of mechanics or experimental science. Nor can they throw any light on these." (Berkeley, 1721, p. 41).

Berkeley was an *instrumentalist*. Concepts such as "physical object" and "causal power" in their legitimate employment serve as useful descriptions of the order and regularity in sensory experience that enable us to anticipate experience. Theoretical concepts such as "gravity" do not describe the mechanisms of generative causality, but serve as useful computational devices that facilitate the description and prediction of sensory experience. Berkeley calls our sense experience of the natural world "the language of God." A benevolent God ensures the maintainance of regularities in sense experience, and it is the business of the devout scientist to identify these predetermined correlations of "sign" and "signified." What we call "fire" is not the generative cause of "pain": it is a "sign" that enables us to anticipate and thus avoid pain. The whole point of this argument is that causal laws are descriptive and *nonexplanatory*. They are only descriptions of regularity that enable us to predict the course of nature. The explanatory causes of phenomena are unknown and unknowable, since they are all produced by God.

In rejecting God, Hume created the problem of induction by removing a benevolent deity to ensure that descriptions of past and present regularities (causal laws) would hold true in the future. Later empiricists worried about this but remained committed to the view that generative causality plays no role in science. Causal laws are simple descriptions of observational regularity and therefore *nonexplanatory*, since we can have no knowledge of generative causality: "We have no knowledge of anything but phenomena. . . . We know not the essence, nor real mode of production, of any fact . . . " (Mill, 1866, p. 6).

POSITIVE EXPLANATION

The regularity account of causality owes much of its appeal to the fact that it appears to satisfy all the basic requirements of a scientific analysis. The treatment of causal laws as descriptions of observational regularity enables us to employ laws in the prediction of observational sequences. Thus, one can anticipate the motion of the second billiard ball on observing the motion of the first. Putative references to "forces" or "natures" appear to add no information that can be usefully employed in the prediction of further observational sequences. A classic example of this form of complaint is the popular example from Moliere. The scholastic doctor "explains" that the ingestion of opium is followed by drowsiness because of the "soporific power" of opium. What does it mean to say that opium has this soporific power? It means that if one ingests opium, one becomes drowsy. The soporific power of opium is itself explained in terms of the "dormative virtue" of opium. What does it mean to say that opium has this dormative virtue? It means that if someone ingests opium, they will become drowsy. Such references are held to be empty and otiose. They provide no useful information over and above the description of the observed regular association of opium ingestion and drowsiness, which is itself sufficient to enable the scientist to predict instances of drowsiness. The "analysis" of such "powers" or "natures" is of no scientific value and diverts the scientist from his true business: the identification of true and useful descriptions of observational regularity.

Thus, Berkeley's "language of God" became Mach's "analysis of sensations": "The communication of scientific knowledge involves description: that is, the mimetic reproduction of facts in thought, the object of which is to replace and save the trouble of new experience. This is all that scientific laws are" (Mach, 1894, p. 192). The positivist philosopher Auguste Compte (1830) treated the simple description of observational regularity as the final stage of his evolutionary "law of three stages." The theological stage produces "explanations" of phenomena in terms of anthropomorphic wills (gods and their activities). The metaphysical stage produces explanations in terms of "powers" and "natures" (force of attraction, gravity, etc.). The positive stage simply produces descriptions of observational regularity that enable the scientist to anticipate natural phenomena. The classic statement of this thesis in logical positivism is to be found in Schlick (1948).

Scientific empiricists reintroduced physical objects as the observational basis for science, but were equally vigorous in their rejection of generative causality as a metaphysical superfluity that plays no role in a rigorous science. But the consequences of this commitment should be squarely faced. *The deductive-nomological account cannot be said to provide an account of causal explanation*. It is an intellectual perversion for any scientific empiricist to employ the deductive-nomological account as an account of causal explanation.

It cannot provide an account of causal explanation because it is based on the regularity account of causality, which effectively denies the significance of generative causality. Thus, the critics are in fact correct to equate deductive predictions with explanations in the deductive-nomological account. For all the covering laws appealed to are simply descriptions of observational regularity. The scientific psychologist who adopts this account often articulates the goal of social psychological science as the explanation and prediction of human behavior: all that can be consistently meant by this is description and prediction.

Theory

INSTRUMENTALISM

According to the deductive-nomological account of explanation, observational causal laws are themselves explained by deduction from more general or abstract or inclusive law statements, which are treated as theoretical principles, and which are in turn explained by deduction from even more general statements (Braithwaite, 1953; Hempel, 1965; Nagel, 1961). Thus, for example, Charles's law is explained by deduction from the kinetic theory; the wavelength for the emission spectrum of hydrogen is explained by deduction from Bohr's theory of the atom.

Theoretical principles such as the propositions of kinetic theory and the Bohr theory of the atom are treated as postulates in a theoretical deductive system. They are expressed as interrelated definitions of theoretical terms, such as "molecule," "elastic collision," and "kinetic energy" in the kinetic theory, and "electron orbit" and "electromagnetic energy" in the Bohr theory of the atom. The deduction of laws from these postulates is held to be closely analogous to the deduction of theorems from axioms in a mathematical system. There is, however, one important and significant difference. Laws or theorems in science must be given an empirical interpretation: they must employ predicates that are descriptive of publically observable physical events. Thus, the effective deduction of observational causal laws from theoretical principles requires the inclusion of "correspondence rules" or "bridge principles." These function as operational definitions that enable theoretical principles to be translated into observational laws. In the kinetic theory the correspondence rules relate "mean kinetic energy of molecules" with "temperature"; in the Bohr theory of the atom they relate changes in electron orbit with changes in spectral emissions.

This conception partly derives from the logical positivist account of meaning, expressed in Moritz Schlick's maxim that "the meaning of a proposition is the method of its verification" (1936, p. 148). Any proposition that cannot be (in principle) confirmed or verified by observation (of publically observable physical reality) is dismissed as nonsensical. It is well known that logical positivists dismissed the propositions of metaphysics, morality, and religion as "literally meaningless."

The positivists were, however, disinclined to treat theoretical propositions in science as metaphysical nonsense. These were interpreted as indirectly confirmed or verified by the successful observational predictions that could be deduced from them via correspondence rules. This view was also heavily influenced by the physicist Bridgeman's (1927, 1936) doctrine of *operationalism*, which was itself influenced by Einstein's analysis of simultaneity in relativity theory, and some interpretations (notably the Copenhagen) of quantum mechanics. Bridgeman argued that any legitimate theoretical concept must be linked to operational procedures that establish its observational values. Thus, theoretical concepts such as "electrical charge" must be specified in terms of procedures that would justify the attribution of the theoretical term: for example, observations of the divergence of leaves in an electroscope. This "logical constructionist" account of the language of science created a mutually exclusive distinction between theoretical and observation statements: scientific language forms a hierarchical deductive structure, with theoretical principles at the apex and observational laws at the base (linked by correspondence rules).

The scientific empiricist account provides an *instrumentalist* conception of theory, which again is hardly surprising given its origin in the empiricism of Berkeley and Hume. Theoretical propositions are not held to be descriptive of an independent theoretical reality: they are only indirect descriptions of observational reality. They function as purely logical devices to integrate and systematize the deduction of observational causal laws. Thus, like Berkeley, the scientific empiricist treats Newtonian gravitational theory as simply serving to integrate and systematize the deductive prediction of descriptions of terrestial and planetary observational regularity, such as Galileo's law of free fall and Kepler's laws of planetary motion. Analogously, the kinetic theory simply serves to integrate and systematize the gas laws. According to Hempel (1965), a theory serves to provide the "conceptual integration" of a set of observational laws.

The information content of the theory is essentially no more and no less than the sum of the observational laws that are its deductive consequences. This follows from the fact that the meaning of theoretical propositions is specified via the correspondence rules, without which theoretical propositions would be empty and vacuous. Theories do not provide a reference to the real mechanisms that explain generative causality. They are sentential instruments that facilitate the prediction of observational regularities.

THEORY EVALUATION

However, the empiricist account of theoretical explanation is itself plagued by a now familiar if not tedious problem. The ability to successfully predict observational laws is at best a necessary requirement for an adequate theory. A basic feature of the logic of scientific inference is that observational predictions can only support but not demonstrate a scientific theory. The same true conclusion can be deduced from true or false premises; the same observational laws can be deduced from two or more competing theories. The Aristotelian or Ptolemeic geocentric astronomical theory and the Copernican heliocentric theory were equally successful in predicting the observational data. The Newtonian corpuscularian and Huygen's wave theory of light were equally successful in predicting the rectilinear motion of light, and the laws of refraction and reflection (and in both cases both theories got things wrong). The new problem for the empiricist is the problem of determining between competing theoretical explanations.

Once again the empiricist tries to appeal to additional criteria to distinguish between competing theories. A common criterion is *simplicity* or *economy*. All other things being equal, the simpler theory is to be preferred. Thus, it may be argued that the Copernican theory replaced the Aristotelian/Ptolemeic theory because it employed fewer epicycles and the geometry was mathematically more harmonious. It is in fact doubtful if the Copernican theory is simpler than the Ptolemeic theory (Hesse [1976], for example, takes the opposite view). One of the reasons it is doubtful is because of the ambiguities of the concept of simplicity. It is not clear whether the "simplicity" appealed to refers to the number of theoretical postulates, the degree of complexity of the mathematics, or something rather more obscure, such as mathematical harmony or aesthetic appeal. Whatever the definition, the history of science seems to represent a history of increasing theoretical complexity. It is not at all clear, for example, in what sense Einstein's theory or quantum mechanics could be said to be simpler than Newton's theory or classical mechanics.

Another popular criterion is *fertility*. Newton's theory, for example, was successful because it turned apparent predictive failures into dramatic victories (as when the accommodation of the anomalous motion of Uranus led to the discovery of Neptune). Einstein's theory made novel predictions such as the gravitational deflection of light rays and the retardation of clocks at high relative velocities. The problem with this criterion is that it is retrospective. The theories of Newton and Einstein were successes, but the Lamarckian and Phlogiston theories turned out to be failures. Nor can we appeal to a weaker interpretation of fertility as "promise." Newton's theory did not originally appear promising to Europeans: it could not predict the orbit of the moon, and failed to account for the fact that the planets revolved around the sun in the same direction (although this was a natural consequence of Descartes' vortex theory). The Lamarckian and Phlogiston theories were promising and fertile but wrong.

This is not to deny that the ability of a theory to produce a series of successful *novel* predictions counts significantly in favor of that theory. Unfortunately, this is no help to the scientific empiricist, who can provide no justification of the epistemic significance of this special subclass of predictions,[3] since for the empiricist their historical significance has no bearing on their epistemic significance (Hempel, 1966).

How Do Theories Explain?

There are deeper problems for the instrumentalist account of theory. In the previous section it is argued at some length that the scientific empiricist cannot consistently claim that deductions from statements of observational regularity provide causal explanations. The same is true of the empiricist account of theoretical explanations. If theoretical principles really contain no more information than the observational laws deduced from them, if the meaning of theoretical principles really filters up from the observational level via "capiliary action" (Koertge, 1972), it is extremely hard to understand how such "theories" can provide any kind of explanation of observational laws, since they can provide us with no new information about the phenomena related in such laws.

Indeed, the situation is worse than this, for these considerations seem to suggest that theory is in fact unnecessary and in principle dispensible. This problem was articulated by Hempel (1965, p. 186) as the "theoretician's dilemma":

If the terms and principles of a theory serve their purpose, that is, they establish definite connections among observable phenomena, then they can be dispensed with, since any chain of laws and interpretative statements establishing such a connection should then be replaceable by a law that directly links observational antecedents to observational consequences.

Now one of the ways in which this dilemma is supposed to be resolved is by allowing that some of the theoretical terms or principles are undefined or only partially defined (in terms of observables). Further interpretations of the "partially interpreted calculus," or new correspondence rules, are introduced as the theory develops. Of course in a fully comprehensive theory, theoretical principles are held to be dispensible,[4] but a critical function of theory for the empiricist is not merely to integrate already established observational laws, but to predict new ones (the fertility requirement noted above).

It is important to recognize that the meaning of theoretical propositions must be partially indeterminate, since this is necessary to allow for theory development. But it is equally important to recognize that the empiricist's account of this features does nothing to resolve the problem about explanation. A partially interpreted calculus includes no more additional information than one fully specified in terms of observational consequences (it simply contains the possibility of the development of new correspondence rules). Furthermore, it creates a new and more fundamental problem that threatens to undermine the whole point of the instrumental conception of theory, which is the claim that theories serve as sentential instruments for the prediction of observational laws. Since the empiricist does not interpret theory as an explanatory reference to mechanisms of generative causality, he can provide no account of why the theoretical scientist chooses to introduce one new interpretation (or correspondence rule) rather than any other. The fact that he does so successfully can only be fortuitous. In short, the instrumentalist can provide no rational account of theory development. She can provide no rational account of the way scientists develop theory to generate novel and successful predictions (Hesse, 1976).

BEHAVIORISM: THE HUMEAN ACCOUNT OF HUMAN ACTION

Perhaps the most rigorous illustration of the instrumentalist account of theory in any science is to be found in behaviorism. J.B. Watson (1913, 1924) denied that references to cognitive states play any useful role in a psychological science, partly because of the perceived inadequacy of introspective psychology, which was held to be unverifiable intersubjectively, but primarily on instrumental grounds. Watson did not relate the logical positivist or scientific empiricist analysis of theory to psychology, for the simple reason that these accounts had not been developed in detail at the time he produced his major theoretical works. However, his justification of behaviorism was the product of methodological reasoning that is an almost exact logical parallel of Hume's philosophical analysis of the concept of causality. Watson's behaviorism derived primarily from the methodological decision of workers in the field of animal psychology to restrict their studies to the observable behavior of animals. It was held to be idle to speculate about the cognitive states of animals.

The methodological reasoning behind this was roughly as follows. It was claimed that a putative causal explanation such as "the rat fled because it was afraid of the flashing light" essentially comprises of two components. The first component embodies the claim that "the rat was afraid." The second component embodies the general claim that "whenever a rat is confronted with a flashing light (observable stimulus), it will flee (observable response)." It was argued that the first component plays no useful role in the causal explanation of the rat's behavior. It is not directly and intersubjectively verifiable by observation. As it cannot be verified independently of the rat's behavior, from which it is indirectly inferred, it was held to be more profitable to investigate the observable antecedents of the rat's behavior. A reference to the rat's fear was also held to be redundant, since it has no predictive advantage over the second component. The second component provides sufficient grounds for the prediction of behavior. At best, a proposition about cognitive states was held to be a convenient redescription of correlations between observable stimuli and responses: to assert that the rat was afraid of the flashing light is to assert no more than a series of correlations between flashing lights and the rat's flight behavior, heart rate, epinephrine and urine secretion, and so forth. At worst, a proposition about cognitive states was held to be a metaphysical superfluity: a putative reference to cognitive states plays no more useful role than a putative reference to the "dormative virtue" or "soporific power" of opium. In either case, the conclusion is the same: any S-O-R proposition—where S and R refer to observable stimuli and responses, and O is a theoretical proposition about cognitive states of the organism—can be replaced by a S-R proposition simpliciter. For this reason, behaviorism gave birth to a stimulus-response psychology.

Watson and other behaviorists simply extended this justification to the study of human behavior: "The behaviourist asks: Why don't we make what we can observe the real field of psychology? Let us limit ourselves to things that can be observed, and formulate laws concerning only these things" (Watson, 1924, p. 6).

Although his grounds for rejecting propositions about cognitive states were essentially methodological, Watson was one of the few to draw an ontological conclusion: he in fact denied that cognitive states exist. Later behaviorists, such as Hull and Tolman, were convinced by Watson's methodological arguments but were also strongly influenced by logical positivist and scientific empiricist accounts of theoretical explanation as the deduction of observational regularities from theoretical postulates. Hull, for example, originally thought that propositions about cognitive states did have a possible role as "theoretical postulates." He simply argued that as a matter of fact their inclusion in a deductive structure did not facilitate the deduction of any observational behavioral regularity (Hull, 1937).

Tolman, on the other hand, did think that cognitive theoretical postulates, such as "mental maps" (Tolman, 1948), served a useful role in the description and prediction of behavioral regularity, and Hull eventually came to accept the utility of postulated "intervening variables" such as "habit strength" (Hull, 1943).

Radical Behaviorism

The contemporary behaviorist B.F. Skinner (1938, 1974) presents a radical denial of theory, claiming that it has no useful role in a psychological science. He is highly critical of Tolman's cognitive postulates and, indeed, Hull's references to "drive" states and Pavlov's physiological speculations. Skinner (in contrast to Watson) does not deny the reality of cognitive states, or their possible causal efficacy. Rather, he denies that they play any useful role in the explanation and prediction of behavior.

Skinner is perhaps the most consistent proponent of scientific empiricism in a scientific psychology, and is probably the only pure specimen of empiricist scientist. He thinks that propositions about cognitive states are entirely superfluous, and do nothing to advance scientific psychological knowledge. According to Skinner, propositions about cognitive states such as anxiety, fear, purpose, motive, and so forth are simply redescriptions of observable antecedents and behavior. They are "explanatory fictions."

In this important respect, the behaviorism of Skinner (and Watson) is avowedly antitheoretical and atheoretical. Yet as a metatheoretical perspective it presents a substantive theory in a methodological guise. This may be demonstrated by noting a typical Skinnerian justification of the disutility of theoretical propositions about cognitive states:

The objection to inner states is not that they do not exist, but that they are not relevant in a functional analysis. We cannot account for the behavior of any system while staying wholly inside it; eventually we must turn to forces operating from the organism from without. (Skinner, 1953, p. 35)

The logical fallacy in this justification should be noted. It is no doubt true that we cannot account for the behavior of the human system without reference to factors external and extrinsic to that system. Some human powers and liabilities need to be explained in developmental terms, and many explanations of individual human action require some reference to environmental events, either as stimulus conditions or opportunities for action. It simply does not follow that human behavior can be wholly explained by reference to such extrinsic and external factors. (This seems to hold true for any natural, biological, social, or psychological system.)

However, this is precisely what Skinner claims (and Watson also claimed). Skinner (like Watson) is committed to the remarkable and substantive thesis of a linear causal relation between observable stimuli and behavior. This is quite clearly stated in Skinner's answer to Hull's articulation of the "theoretician's dilemma" (Hempel, 1958). Hull (1943, p. 284) raises the question: "If you have a secure equational linkage extending from the antecedent observable conditions through to the consequent observable conditions, why . . . use several equations where one would do?" Skinner (1953, p. 35) answers it in the following way:

Unless there is a weak link in our causal chain so that the second link is not lawfully determined by the first, or the third by the second, then the first and third links must be lawfully related. If we must always go back beyond the second link for prediction and control, we may avoid many tiresome and exhausting digressions by examining the third link as a function of the first.

According to Skinner, references to mental states are "exhausting digressions."

But this thesis begs an important *empirical* question about the explanation of human action, both insofar as it simply denies that cognitive factors or human agency can override environmental influences, and insofar as it claims that a wholly adequate explanation of the generation of human behavior can always be given in terms of environmental factors. (This is like claiming that any disease can be best explained in terms of environmental factors just because a causal chain can ultimately be traced to them, or that the process of expellation can be totally explained in terms of the ingestion of food just because these factors can be related in a functional equation.)

The methodological prescriptions of behaviorism in fact produce a theory of human action to the effect that human action is wholly determined by and thus explained by environmental stimulus variables and reinforcement history. Since a reference to such factors always provides a sufficient causal account, there is no need for any reference to cognitive factors. More significantly and seriously, there is no logical room for an alternative account in terms of cognitive factors. For behaviorism does not simply promote a special theory of human behavior, but its special version of the philosophy of scientific psychology rules out the possibility of an alternative theoretical causal account (e.g., in terms of cognitive states or autonomous action). The real irony of this situation is that given the behaviorist's rigid interpretation of a scientific psychology, behaviorist theory is in consequence unfalsifiable and therefore untestable in principle, since for the behaviorist no evidence can conceivably count against the theory. The researcher can only be mistaken in identifying particular controlling stimulus variables and reinforcement, not in his general judgment that behavior is in fact controlled by stimulus variables and reinforcement.

THE COGNITIVE REVOLUTION

Behaviorists such as Hull and Tolman were equally committed to the substantive thesis about the invariant linear causal relation between human behavior and its observable environmental antecedents. However, their claims about the utility of theory seem to have won the day. Tolman especially stressed that the utility of cognitive theoretical postulates lies in their fertility: their ability to generate novel predictions of observational stimulus-response regularities. Like any scientific empiricist they were committed to the view that cognitive theoretical postulates are always in principle eliminable in favor of purely observational descriptions, but they stressed the useful role of these postulates in the acquisition and development of scientific knowledge.

This attitude toward theory eventually enabled liberalized forms of behaviorism to develop into cognitive psychology. For many psychologists have essentially adopted Hempel's own solution to the "theoretician's dilemma" by treating psychological theories as "partially interpreted systems" that can be further interpreted to generate novel predictions on the observational level. This account provides the basis for MacCorquodale and Meehl's (1948) classic distinction between "intervening variables" and "theoretical constructs." According to MacCorquodale and Meehl (1948, p. 107), with respect to intervening variables, "the statement of such a concept does not contain any words which are not reducible to the empirical laws." Theoretical constructs, on the other hand, involve "words which are not reducible to the empirical laws." While it is generally agreed that intervening variables are essentially redundant and eliminable, it is argued that theoretical constructs are essential in a developing science.

It is precisely this instrumentalist conception of theory that finds expression in contemporary accounts of theory in scientific psychology. Since the "cognitive revolution" of the 1950s and the more recent development of "cognitive behaviorism," theoretical propositions concerning cognitive states are held to play a legitimate role in a scientific psychology. However, it is insisted that the sole justification of such theoretical constructs lies in their integrative and predictive utility on the level of observational regularity:

> The relationship between the observables mediated by the mental process must be operationally defined, this relationship must be tested by critical experiments, and the mental concept thus defined must increase our ability to predict and control behavior, or else its use is not justified. (Ledwidge, 1978, p. 360)

There is no point in raising questions about the psychological reality of the cognitive states and processes putatively represented by cognitive theories, since the same behavioral data are held to be consistent with a variety of competing cognitive theories, and since we cannot discriminate the correct theory by the observation of cognitive states and processes (Anderson, 1978, 1981).

Yet this conception of the predictive utility of "cognitive constructs" will not bear critical investigation. Although B.F. Skinner's grounds for claiming that such constructs are redundant are unsound, nevertheless his conclusion is correct. It was noted earlier that the scientific empiricist can provide no rational account of how theories are developed to generate novel empirical predictions. But in fact the situation is much worse than this. For one needs to ask how the potential "surplus meaning" of "partially interpreted" theoretical systems is supposed to be developed from their present determinate meaning to generate novel predictions of empirical correlation.

In order to generate such novel predictions, the empiricist account requires the creation of *new* correspondence rules relating "partially interpreted" theoretical constructs with the description of novel empirical laws. But the only ground for the development of such rules is the present determinate meaning of the theoretical constructs, *which is specified by correspondence rules relating such constructs to previously established empirical laws*. On this account then, the only guide to the discovery and prediction of novel empirical correlations is our knowledge of already established empirical correlations. But if this is the case, then the logical apparatus of theoretical constructs and correspondence rules does no useful work. Previously established empirical laws simpliciter will serve as good or as bad a guide to novel empirical laws as any system of theoretical postulates and correspondence rules. Skinner is thus correct to dismiss theoretical constructs as redundant with respect to scientific development, *given this empiricist account of the meaning of psychological theories*.

2
Relativism

Neo-empiricism

The problems discussed so far have been largely internal to traditional scientific empiricism. The criticisms of the relativist undermine standard scientific empiricist assumptions about the objectivity of scientific knowledge by questioning the central claim that observation provides an objective basis for the evaluation of scientific theories.

The scientific empiricist claims that scientific theories are instrumental intellectual constructions that facilitate the prediction of observables, but also maintains that competing constructions can be evaluated on the basis of observational predictions (and other criteria such as the simplicity of theoretical principles, etc.). In Chapter 1 it is argued that the scientific empiricist has little warrant to maintain this thesis about theory evaluation. The whole empiricist enterprise seems to be completely undermined if observations themselves are constructed intellectually, which is the central relativist thesis.

According to Kuhn (1970) and Feyerabend (1975), scientific theories provide an intellectual structure analogous to a gestalt that (inter alia) serves to organize observations according to the theory. Since different theories organize or construct observations in different ways, scientists committed to different theories make different observations when assessing the evidence for and against competing theories. All observations are held to be theory dependent or theory informed. In consequence, there can be no theory independent observations that can serve as an objective basis for the evaluation of competing theories.

This account simply assumes epistemological and linguistic idealism with regard to theories. It advances further and different reasons for epistemological idealism by arguing that observations themselves involve theoretical construction and thus cannot serve as an objective basis for the evaluation of scientific theories. In this important respect, the relativist treatment of physical object observations as embodying theoretical construction returns scientific empiricism to its intellectual roots in the epistemological idealism of Berkeley, Hume, and the earlier logical positivists, who likewise held that our ordinary physical object observations embody forms of intellectual construction. The critical difference between the two positions is that whereas the earlier versions of empiricism introduced a form of relativism based upon the privacy of sense impressions, neo-empiricist accounts based upon the theory informity of observations introduce a form of relativism based upon the theoretical commitments of the observer.

In scientific empiricism (and indeed in the earlier forms of empiricism), intersubjective agreement is treated as the mark of objectivity. In neo-empiricism, any intersubjective agreement about observations is treated as simply the social product of shared theoretical commitments. The scientific empiricist account presupposes intersubjective agreement at the observational level. In the relativist account, there is no such presumption: observers committed to different theories will make different observations and consequently disagree about whether a piece of evidence counts for or against a theory. If this is the case, there would seem to be no objective way of deciding between two (or more) competing theories, since no observations could ever be made to settle the matter.

Relativist philosophy of science is essentially a form of neo-empiricism that compounds the original problems of scientific empiricism. Many of the relativist arguments are, however, only indirectly targeted toward the standard scientific empiricist account. They are usually directed toward the special form of scientific empiricism advanced by Sir Karl Popper.

Popper: Falsification

According to Popper (1959, 1963) the mark of a scientific theory is its *falsifiability* or *testability*. A scientific theory generates "risky predictions" that, if falsified, would lead to the refutation of the theory. The mark of a scientific theory is its ability to survive rigorous attempts to falsify it. Thus, for example, Einstein's theory of relativity is characterized as scientific because its risky prediction about the bending of light rays was supported by Eddington's photographs taken during the solar eclipse of 1919.

Popper uses this criterion to distinguish between genuine sciences and pseudo-sciences. He dismisses intellectual disciplines such as astrology and depth psychology because of their failure to generate risky predictions (the predictions of astrology are too vague and those of depth psychology are consistent with any form of human behavior). He is especially critical of theories (such as Marx's theory of history) that employ the "conventionalist stratagem" of accommodating failed predictions by ad hoc modifications of the theory. According to Popper, this reduces the scientific status of a theory. A falsified theory ought to be rejected and replaced by a superior theory that survives critical tests of its risky predictions.

THE QUINE-DUHEM THESIS

One of the apparent virtues of Popper's account is that it suggests the possibility of decisive refutations of theories. It also suggests the possibility of an "experimentum crucis" (crucial experiment) to determine between two or more competing theories (what Francis Bacon [1620] called an "Instance of the Fingerpost"). If competing theories successfully explain a common range of empirical phenomona, and are thus evidentially equivalent, then one ought to focus on an area in which such theories make different predictions. The experimental data would then provide additional support for one theory and decisively falsify its rival (or rivals).

However, the real situation is nothing like as simple as these remarks suggest. To suppose that theories are tested individually in this manner is an artificial abstraction. Theories are always tested in conjunction with a number of auxiliary hypotheses. When an observational prediction is falsified, this only shows that something is wrong with the conjunction of theory and auxiliary hypotheses. This point was clearly stated by the French physicist Pierre Duhem (1906, p. 87):

> . . . the physicist can never subject an isolated hypothesis to experimental test, but only a whole group of hypotheses; when the experiment is in disagreement with his predictions, what he learns is that at least one of the hypotheses constituting this group is unacceptable and ought to be modified; but the experiment does not designate which should be changed.

It is further claimed by the American logician W.V.O. Quine that the scientist is never obliged to reject his theory in the face of recalcitrant observational evidence. The theory can always be preserved by the modification of one or more auxiliary hypotheses (Quine, 1953, p. 43): "Any statement can be held true come what may, if we make drastic enough changes elsewhere in the system."

Collectively these arguments constitute a doctrine often characterized as the *Quine-Duhem thesis*: a theory that makes a falsified prediction can always accommodate the recalcitrant evidence by the addition or replacement or modification of auxiliary hypotheses. Furthermore, there are many cases in the history of science when scientists have successfully modified auxiliary hypotheses in order to accommodate failed predictions. Newton's theory was able to accommodate its original failure to predict the orbit of Uranus by modifing an auxiliary hypothesis about the number of the planets, by postulating that irregularities in the orbit of Uranus might be attributable to the gravitational effects of another planet beyond Uranus. This modification led to the discovery of Neptune.

The Quine-Duhem thesis appears to undermine the concept of decisive falsification and the possibility of a crucial experiment. For it appears that any theory can always accommodate a falsified prediction and preserve evidential equivalence with a competing theory by the modification or replacement of auxiliary hypotheses.

Lakatos: Research Programs

Lakatos (1970) maintains the objectivity of theory evaluation by distinguishing between different forms of theoretical accommodation of failed predictions. Scientific research programs comprise a "hard core" of theory made "irrefutable by methodological fiat," and a "protective belt" of auxiliary hypothesis that may be modified in the face of falsified predictions. Lakatos claims that the falsification of a theory by a failed prediction should not lead to automatic rejection, since theories need time to develop to accommodate initial problems. Rather, theories should be evaluated in terms of their development, by distinguishing between "progressive" and "degenerating" research programs.

A *progressive* research program is one in which auxiliary hypothesis modification in the face of failed predictions generates novel and sucessful predictions. In the case of Newton's theory and Uranus, the modification of the auxiliary hypothesis about the number of the planets not only accommodated the orbit of Uranus but led to the discovery of Neptune. A *degenerating* research program is one in which auxiliary hypothesis modification accommodates the failed preditions but does not generate any new and successful predictions. Thus the Ptolemeic and phlogiston theories (and Marx's theory of history) were degenerating research programs because the modification of auxiliary hypotheses accommodated failed predictions only, or generated additional predictions that were in turn falsified.

The main problem with this account of theory evaluation is that it is retrospective (Feyerabend, 1970), and restrospective over a long historical period given the changing fortunes of some scientific theories. Prout's hypothesis about integral atomic weights was progressive in the early part of the 19th century since many purified samples of elements approximated integral values, became degenerating in the mid-century over the recalcitrant fractional weights of some elements such as chlorine, and became progressive again later in the century with the postulation of isotopes. Since Lakatos recognizes that the decision to stick with a degenerating research program is methodologically sound (because it may make a comeback), his account cannot be said to identify decisive grounds for preferring one theoretical account over its rivals *at any historical moment*.

Kuhn: Paradigms

THE THEORY INFORMITY OF OBSERVATIONS

Many recent critics of the standard empiricist account have raised a more serious threat to the concept of decisive falsification and the possibility of a crucial experiment, by arguing that observations themselves are theory dependent or theory informed. It is claimed that what an individual observes is dependent upon his prior theories and expectations (Chalmers, 1976). Thus, a child or untrained observer in a physics laboratory sees only spools, mirrors, and iron bars; the trained physicist sees fluctuations in electrical resistance (Duhem, 1906). The untrained medical student sees mere marks on an X-ray plate; the trained medical practitioner sees scars on the lung and chronic infections (Polanyi, 1958). What one sees is held to depend upon what one *sees it as* (Hanson, 1958). What one sees it as is held to depend upon one's prior theories (Brown, 1977).

It is held to follow from this that scientists committed to different theories will make different observations. Thus, for example, it is claimed that whether a microbiologist sees and reports a "cell organ, a Golgi body," or sees and reports a "cluster of foreign matter, a coagulum resulting from faulty staining techniques," depends upon what he sees it as. If his theory commits him to the existence of Golgi bodies, he will see a Golgi body; if it does not, he will not. Analogously, it is argued that Brahe and Kepler (defenders of the geocentric and heliocentric theories, respectively) facing east at dawn see different things. Brahe sees the sun rising against a fixed horizon; Kepler sees the horizon rolling beneath a stationary sun (Hanson, 1958). Or again, it is argued that defenders of Prout's hypothesis tended to dismiss deviant weight measurements as failures of the separation and purification of elements; the critics treated such measurements as falsifications of the atomic theory (Harré, 1972).

The situation is held to be closely analogous to the ambiguous figures of gestalt psychology, such as the duck-rabbit example popularized in the philosophical literature by Wittgenstein (1953). The line drawing can be seen as a rabbit or as a duck: we see it in different ways as our total gestalt construction switches. According to the relativist, scientific theories provide a structure analogous to a gestalt that serves to organize the material of observations according to the gestalt. Different theories organize observations in different ways. A scientist who transfers his allegiances from one theory to another is like a man undergoing a gestalt-switch: after he changes his theoretical commitments he sees the world in a different way. In fact he is held to inhabit a different world (Kuhn, 1970).

INCOMMENSURABILITY OF THEORIES

According to Kuhn (1962, 1970) amd Feyerabend (1975), competing theories are "incompatible but incommensurable." Competing theories cannot be objectively evaluated by reference to observations because observations are themselves theory informed. Kuhn characterizes the development of science in terms of the historical acceptance and rejection of "paradigms," which are "theoretical or methodological schemata" shared by the majority of members of "scientific communities," and which guide and support "puzzle-solving" traditions.

But since theoretical paradigms are observationally incommensurable because of the theory informity of observations, no account of the evaluation of theoretical paradigms in terms of observations can in principle be provided. There can be no crucial experiments because experimental results can always be accommodated by interpretation according to competing theories. The acceptance and rejection of theoretical paradigms can only be explained in terms of social psychological and other extra-scientific factors that may influence the theoretical commitments of individual scientists and scientific communities (Barnes, 1977; Bloor, 1976). Thus, for example, Feyerabend (1975) argues that the Copernican theory superseded the Ptolemeic theory not because it was superior in terms of successful observational predictions, or because it was simpler or more fertile, but because of Galileo's highly effective publicity and propaganda, or, in less flattering terms, his "trickery and deception."

Kuhn denies that his own position is a form of relativism by providing a rather weak instrumentalist account of progress in science. He claims (1970, p. 206) that successive paradigm-shifts do represent some kind of increment in puzzle-solving ability:

Later scientific theories are better than earlier ones for solving puzzles in the often quite different environments to which they are applied. That is not a relativist's position, and it displays the sense in which I am a convinced believer in scientific progress.

Yet it hard to see how Kuhn can justify this claim if he also holds that different theories or paradigms embody different theoretical concepts, observations, problems, and solutions.

Paradigms and Research Programs in Psychology

Scientific psychologists are naturally wary when talking of paradigms, and generally prefer to ignore the unpalatable consequences of the relativist's arguments about the theory informity of observations and the incommensurability of theories. Much of the discussion about paradigms in psychology tends to revolve around the question of whether psychology is still at a preparadigmatic state where no dominating paradigm has yet emerged (Palermo, 1971), or the question of what is, or should be, the dominant paradigm (Peterson, 1981). It all depends on what you mean by "paradigm." According to Mary Masterson (1970), in the 1962 version of *Structure of Scientific Revolutions*, Kuhn meant about 21 different things. Most of the time, Kuhn is talking about theories, but scientific psychologists tend to avoid that sense of paradigm because of Kuhn's relativist account of theory conflict and evaluation.

When talking about theories, scientific psychologists prefer to explain theoretical conflicts in terms of Lakatos's research programs (Gholson

& Barker, 1985). Thus, for example, the conflict between "cognitive dissonance" (Festinger, 1957; Festinger & Carlsmith, 1959) and "self-perception" (Bem, 1967, 1972) theories of attitude change is explained in these terms. Both successfully predict a common range of phenomena; both can accommodate putative crucial experiments by auxiliary hypothesis modification. The self-perception theory has superseded the cognitive dissonance theory because the former is a progressive research program, while the latter is degenerating. Self-perception theory has proved fertile by predicting novel phenomena such as actor-observer congruances, whereas the cognitive dissonance theory has simply accommodated new conflicting evidence.

Of course, few dissonance theorists would agree. They argue that self-perception theory only accommodates a very limited range of attitude-change phenomena (Wicklund & Frey, 1981). The question threatens to degenerate to social psychological explanations in terms of current fashions and interests.

PHILOSOPHY AND METHODOLOGY: THE NEW PARADIGMS

Most of the current psychological discussion of paradigms is in terms of philosophical and methodological commitments (Weimer, 1974). This is often represented in terms of a philosophical and methodological conflict between behaviorist and cognitive psychological forms of the scientific empiricist paradigm (Palermo, 1971), or between these forms of the scientific psychological paradigm based on causal explanation and alternative paradigms such as hermeneutical psychology based on the explication of meaning (Chapman & Jones, 1980).

Kuhn does employ this sense of paradigm, but understandably with extreme caution. For it is in fact doubtful if the history of the natural and biological sciences exhibits major paradigm-shifts in this sense. Many historical accounts focus on the Copernican revolution as an obvious example: the Copernican revolution not only introduced the novel heliocentric theory, but ushered in a whole new philosophy of science and methodology to replace the sterile and rigid Aristotelian dogmas.

Such an account is largely fictitious. The leading exponents of the "new science" were Galileo and Francis Bacon. Yet much of Galileo's new science was based on the eclectic Aristotelian teachings of the Jesuit College Romano (Wallace, 1984), including the emphasis on the role of mathematics. Many of the descriptions of scientific practice in Francis Bacon's *Novum Organum* (1620) are also to be found in the writings of the Medieval Aristotelian scholars Roger Bacon (c. 1214–1292), Duns Scotus (1265–1308), and Robert Grosseteste (c. 1168–1253), and in Aristotle's own writings.

No doubt there have been considerable differences in philosophical emphasis. Yet the so-called "methods" of agreement and difference described by Mill (and Hume), Francis Bacon, and Roger Bacon are all descriptions of the basic logic of the experimental investigation of generative causality. Apart from the few scientific empiricist or positivist moments (Osiander's instrumentalist interpretation of Copernicus's theory, the atomic debates, and the "Copenhagen" interpretation of quantum mechanics), the work of natural scientists throughout the history of science has been guided by a search for the explanatory mechanisms of generative causality.

Kuhn is rightly cautious about the philosophical and methodological interpretation of paradigms. This is because a belief in the progress of science (even Kuhn's insipid version) is difficult to sustain if past proponents of different paradigms were doing it wrong (at least according to the current paradigm). Argyle (1978) astutely notes that if many of the proponents of the "new paradigm" (or "new paradigms") in social psychological science are correct in their methodological prescriptions, then most of the work done according to the "old paradigm" of scientific psychology is worthless.

This is possibly true, although perhaps not for the reasons avowed by the hermeneutical psychologist. The fundamental hermeneutical objection to scientific psychology is that it has illegitimately tried to model itself upon the natural sciences. The central debate about paradigms in psychology is a philosophical and methodological issue. It is essentially the question of whether social psychological science should be based upon natural scientific practice, or upon some other form of intellectual inquiry such as literary criticism (Hekman, 1986) or history (Gergen, 1973). The scientific psychologist is committed to the former alternative. The hermeneutical psychologist is committed to the latter.

REALISM AND IDEALISM

In the following chapters it is argued that a scientific investigation of generative causality in the social psychological domain is entirely legitimate: a causal explanatory and experimental science is possible. This introduces a realist philosophical and methodological paradigm that is new for psychology (Manicas & Secord, 1983), but not for the natural sciences. Much of the experimental work done according to the "old paradigm" in psychology is inadequate, not because it is modeled upon natural science (which it must be if it is to constitute a causal explanatory and experimental enquiry), but because it is based upon a totally inadequate scientific empiricist account of science. It is also inadequate because it fails to take seriously (because of its commitment to scientific empiricism) the meaningful nature of human action and the potential for agency, which are stressed by the hermeneutical psychologist.

This is not to say that hermeneutical psychology is a causal explanatory alternative to scientific psychology. It is a different animal altogether. In the end, however, there seems to be a rather surprising identity. The hermeneutical psychologist, unlike the scientific psychologist, is not reticent about talking of paradigms as theories, and often actively embraces the theses of the theory informity of observations and the incommensurability of competing theories. Thus, for example, the conflict between cognitive dissonance and self-perception theories is presented as simply a conflict between theoretical constructions that organize our observations of attitude change. For this reason, there can be no crucial experiments or accumulations of observational evidence to resolve the issue, since practically any experimental result can be interpreted in terms of either theory (Forsyth, 1976; Greenwald, 1975). There could be few more explicit statements of the relativist thesis (based upon the Quine-Duhem thesis and the theory informity of observations) than the following claim by Gergen (1982, p. 72): "Virtually any experiment used as support for a given theory may be used to support virtually any alternative theory."

It has already been noted that relativist criticisms of scientific empiricism return scientific empiricism to its roots in epistemological idealism about "observables." Much the same is true of hermeneutical psychology in its critical reaction to scientific psychology. This is partly based upon the relativist arguments drawn from philosophy of science, but is also based upon a more radical claim about the theory informity of observations in social psychological science. The hermeneutical psychologist notes that ordinary folk as well as professional social psychologists have theories about the social psychological world, and claims that these theories are themselves social constructions of social psychological reality, which does not exist independently of these constructions. These theoretical constructions may be in conflict, but those of the professional psychologist have no special priority or observational warrant. This strong version of epistemological, linguistic and ontological *idealism* is again clearly articulated by Gergen (1985, p. 266): "Social constructionism views discourse about the world not as a reflection or map of the world but as an artifact of communal interchange."

3
Realism

Realism as a general philosophical doctrine is the thesis that the nature of physical, biological, social, and psychological reality is quite independent of human representations of physical, biological, social, and psychological reality. The realism advocated in this volume includes the seperate theses of ontological, epistemological, and linguistic realism that are directly opposed to the forms of ontological, epistemological, and linguistic idealism advanced by scientific empiricists and relativists.

Varieties of Realism

Ontological realism, with respect to physical objects, is the thesis that there are physical objects that exist independently of our perception of them and thoughts about them. It is opposed to ontological idealism, which denies the real existence of physical objects. Few of the classical empiricists (except Berkeley) and certainly few contemporary scientific empiricists, relativists, or scientific psychologists seem committed to ontological idealism with respect to physical objects; most seem to be firmly committed to ontological realism. Ontological realism, with respect to theoretical entities, is the thesis that at least some of the entities described by scientific theories have real existence in precisely the same sense as physical objects; ontological idealism denies this. Again, few scientific empiricists (with the exception of Watson) or relativists would dispute this view in general: they would, however, remain sceptical about the real existence of any particular set of theoretical entities in science, because of their commitment to epistemological idealism. Many practicing scientists become ontological realists with respect to particular theoretical entities in the sense that they come to believe in the real existence and properties of some entities such as genes, electromagnetic fields, and asymmetrical social structures of power and status. Most empiricist and relativist philosophers remain agnostic about theoretical entities because their epistemological idealism precludes the possiblity of knowledge of such entities.

Epistemological realism about theoretical entities is the thesis that one can have knowledge of the existence and nature of entities, structures, and mechanisms that provide explanations of generative causality. This form of knowledge is, of course, different from the ideal of knowledge advanced by empiricists in the sense that it is not infallible. Epistemological realism is the thesis that one can have good grounds for believing that the entities represented by scientific theories exist and have the properties that they are represented as having, and good grounds for preferring one set of theoretical representations over another (or others) when these are in conflict. Epistemological idealism denies this, either in the empiricist fashion of claiming that one cannot have knowledge of unobservables, or in the relativist fashion of denying that there are any theoretically neutral observations that can serve as an objective basis for theoretical inferences or comparisons.

Linguistic realism is the thesis that theoretical terms in scientific language are referential in nature: they aim to provide and sometimes do provide accurate representations of reality that furnish explanations of generative causality. Linguistic idealism or instrumentalism denies this by claiming that theoretical terms are useful constructs that are accepted or rejected according to their efficiency as predictive devices (in scientific empiricism) or other criteria that make no reference to the nature of the reality putatively represented by the theory.

Ontological realism about generative causality is the thesis that particulars in the physical, biological, and social psychological world have causal powers that cannot be equated with constancies or regularities of empirical succession. *Epistemological realism* about generative causality is the thesis that causal sequences can be discriminated from accidental constancies or regularities of empirical succession. *Linguistic realism* about causality is the thesis that causal power ascriptions are descriptive of the causal powers of particulars, and not descriptive of constancies or regularities of empirical succession.

REALISM AND CAUSAL LAWS

This does not mean that causal laws are descriptive of causal powers or any other "surplus element" that may be held to distinguish causal from accidental descriptions of empirical invariance. It is true (as noted above) that an ontological and epistemological realist about causality is committed to a linguistic realism about causal power ascriptions: causal power ascriptions are held to be descriptive of the causal powers of particulars. But a linguistic realism about causal power ascriptions does not entail a linguistic realism about causal laws. Although natural causal laws are true (when true) by virtue of causal powers, they are not descriptive of causal powers or any other additional (observable or unobservable) entities. Yet because they are true (when true) by virtue of causal powers, they have a different logic from simple descriptions of constant conjunction or regular succession.

The empiricist mistakenly assumes that because causality is only revealed by the observation of empirical sequences, causal propositions are therefore descriptive of constant conjunction or regular succession. E.H. Madden (1971) has noted that the basic disagreement between realists and empiricists boils down to a dispute about justifiable ontological commitments in scientific and everyday thought. For the empiricist, the objective world is a historical sequence of events within which invariant or regular sequences can be discriminated. For the realist, the objective world consists of enduring particulars in causal interaction.

Now, a science descriptive of autonomous and independent events is only possible given an ontology of sense impressions. It may be true that if the only legitimate objects of scientific knowledge are sense impressions, then the Humean account of causality in terms of the constant or regular succession of sensory events is the only possible account (although even this is doubtful). Yet scientific empiricists since the 1930s have abandoned phenomenalism in favor of physicalism. But given the commitment to physicalism, events cannot be conceived as autonomous and independent: they are alterations and transformations of particulars (e.g., the heating of a gas, the stricking of a match, the flicking of a switch).

Nevertheless, despite his rejection of phenomenalism, the scientific empiricist wishes to retain the Humean analysis of causal law: causal laws are held to be descriptive of the constant conjunction or regular succession of physical events and processes. What the scientific empiricist fails to realize is that *one cannot accept an ontology of enduring physical particulars and retain the constant conjunction analysis of causal laws.*

This is because the causal powers of physical objects are constrained not only by their enabling and stimulus conditions, but by the conditions of other physical objects. Any causal power of any particular can in principle be constrained by the causal powers of other particulars to prevent its exercise. The frequency with which any particular manifests a causal power is partly a function of the frequency with which it is correlated with other particulars that have the power to interfere and prevent its exercise. We simply cannot tell a priori the frequency with which any causal power will be manifested: it may vary from never to always, and will be different for different causal powers and different particulars. This is an empirical question that is quite independent of an empirical question about the *existence* of a causal power.

Newton may have followed Berkeley and Hume in part in his doubts about the ontological significance of some causal powers, such as the gravitational force of attraction. Yet Newton's laws do not describe constant conjunctions. Newton's first law, for example, states that "every body continues in a state of rest, or uniform motion in a right line, unless it is compelled to change that state by forces impressed upon it." This law does not itself describe any frequency with which bodies continue in a state of rest or uniform motion in a straight line. It is a contingent fact that, strictly speaking, none do, and that some (an unknown number) do relative to particular frames of reference and others do not. Newton's first law is not descriptive of any force of attraction, but neither is it descriptive of any degree of empirical correlation.

TRANSCENDENTAL REALISM

The present account is also committed to *transcendental realism* (Bhaskhar, 1975). This is the claim that scientists do and ought to employ transcendental arguments in the justification of causal and theoretical claims. The logic of experimentation is designed to demonstrate that if a certain effect is manifested in an *isolated* system, this is possible *only if* the system (or some part thereof) is causally responsible for the effect. However difficult this may be to achieve in practice, the isolation of systems is the only means of discriminating causal powers.

The same form of argument lies behind theory evaluation in science. Theoretical scientists aim to develop arguments of the form: certain observations or experimental results would be possible *only if* reality has the properties or structures represented by a theory. No matter how difficult it is to achieve in practice, the creation of a crucial experiment is the only way of discriminating between competing theories.

These claims are developed in the following chapters and defended against standard empiricist and relativist objections to these forms of argument. At the present juncture, it is important to note that such forms of argument certainly would be illegitimate were it not for a critical element ignored in practically every empiricist and relativist account of scientific reasoning and practice.

Realism and Agency

Popper has characterized inductive (as opposed to hypothetico-deductive) accounts of science as articulations of the "bucket theory of the mind." More sophisticated empiricist and relativist accounts emphasize the active role of the human mind in theory construction. Yet in neither of these accounts is there any place for the *agency* of scientists in the generation of scientific knowledge. Scientific knowledge is essentially held to be an intellectual construction of sensory experience of physical objects. They are exemplars of the sorts of accounts that Dewey rightly dismissed as articulations of "the spectator theory of knowledge."

For the realist, the agency of scientists is a critical factor in the production of scientific knowledge. One of the crucial implications of the realist position is that the scientist (and lay epistemologist) must also be recognized as and must also function as a *powerful particular*. Scientific knowledge is generally the product of goal-directed and active intervention in the course of nature to create conditions of observation that would not arise naturally (Anscombe, 1971; Bhaskar, 1975; Hacking, 1983; von Wright, 1971). Nor is this a mere convenience. Without intervention, there would be a host of cases in which causal relations could not be discriminated from accidental correlations. Without intervention, many alternative and competing theoretical explanations would remain forever underdetermined by observational data.

With the exception of the occasionally revealing contingencies of the natural and social psychological world, the discrimination of generative causality from accidental correlations and the determination of the accuracy of theoretical representations depends upon the scientist's ability to *create* situations in which epistemically critical observations can be made (in laboratory and field experiments in which the relevant structures and variables can be reproduced and controlled), or to *position* herself to make epistemologically critical comparisons of naturally occurring and varying systems (when the relevant structures and variables cannot be controlled).

It is precisely because successful science is based as much upon intervention as it is upon hypothesis and theory that the dividend of scientific knowledge is often more effective intervention rather than more accurate prediction. The characteristic outcome of medical knowledge is not simply the more accurate prediction of correlations between environmental or physiological events and disease, and sometimes *no* gains are made on this score. More often than not, it is the elimination or attenuation of diseases via the exploitation of knowledge of the composition and structure of disease-producing organisms.

The realist is committed to the following theses about scientific knowledge. Causal laws are true (when true) by virtue of generative causality, which can be effectively discriminated from accidental correlation. Theories provide explanations by aiming to produce reasonably accurate representations of reality, and can be effectively tested and evaluated in comparison with alternative and competing theoretical accounts. These epistemic achievements are the product of scientific work through human agency. These claims are developed and defended in the following chapters on causal explanation and theory.

The following chapters offer no sustained general philosophical justification of realism. Rather, realism is advanced as a coherent, and perhaps the *only* coherent, rationale for scientific explanation and experimentation (which some may not unreasonably hold to be a sufficient justification of realism). Since realism is the dominant philosophy of most scientists most of the time, the following account of realism in science is no more than an articulation of the *logic of scientific activity*, which in a very real sense provides an informal social psychological analysis of the rule-governed practices that constitute scientific activity.

4
Causal Explanation

Causality

CAUSALITY AND CORRELATION

The empiricist account of causality is based upon a myth. The scientific empiricist and scientific psychologist recognize that regular correlation is not sufficient for causality, but it is always presented as a necessary condition. However, in the real world any causal power can be interfered with (Bhaskar, 1975; Geach, 1975). Although water, tiger mosquito bites, and increased voltage can generate rusting in iron, yellow fever in men, and increased current in an electric circuit, respectively, the mechanisms responsible for the generation of such effects can be interfered with. Paint and oil can prevent rusting in iron, a variety of drugs can prevent yellow fever, and increase in temperature can prevent increase in current. There are entities that rarely (if ever) manifest their causal powers because they are regularly interfered with (e.g., Plutonium 238 rarely manifests its power to generate tissue damage in humans because of protective lead screening). Some "regularities" only manifest themselves as a result of experimental intervention (e.g., all bodies only fall with constant and uniform acceleration in specially constructed vacuum experiments). As Geach (1975, p. 93) notes:

Prevention and interference are notions extraordinarily neglected in accounts of efficient causality. If we take them seriously we may be . . . preserved from the Humean error of thinking that causality is a matter of invariable succession. Because of interference and prevention, true causal laws do not state what *de facto* always happens, but only what happens *if* nothing interferes—and that is a quite different matter.

Thus, to claim that "tiger mosquito bites are a cause of yellow fever" is not to claim that "all men bitten by tiger mosquitos will contract yellow fever," but that "all men bitten by tiger mosquitos will contract yellow fever *unless* something interferes." Analogously, it is not to claim that tiger mosquito bites are sufficient conditions for yellow fever, but sufficient conditions *unless* something interferes. The most appropriate symbolic representation of a causal law is not (x) $(Fx \rightarrow Gx)$ but (x) $(Fx \rightarrow (Gx \Lambda I))$, where Λ is interpreted as the exclusive "or" (either . . or . . but not both), and I as an interference. A classic example is Newton's first law: "every body continues in its state of rest, or of uniform motion in a right line, *unless* it is compelled to change that state by forces impressed upon it." The constant or regular manifestation of a causal power is simply not a necessary condition of a causal power.

The realist conception of causality is based upon an ontology of enduring "powerful particulars" (including human agents) in causal interaction (Harré & Madden, 1975). A realist account locates the generative powers of physical particulars in their intrinsic natures (their composition and structure) and extrinsic enabling and stimulus conditions.[1] Thus, the superconductive power of tin is explained in terms of long-range electron coupling, given a very low temperature and creation of a potential difference.

To ascribe a causal power to a particular X is to say that given certain conditions, it will (or can[2]) generate a certain effect e by virtue of its intrinsic nature, unless something interferes. Thus, to ascribe the power of superconductivity to tin is to say that tin will (or can) act as a superconductor given various enabling and stimulus conditions, in the absence of interference (such as a local magnetic field). A theoretical explanation of causal powers makes reference to the mechanism of generative causality: thus, a reference to the molecular structure of chlorpromazine explains its power to relieve schizophrenia by blocking dopamine receptor sites in the nervous system.

Causality cannot be equated with the constant or regular correlation of events, since interferences may always prevent the manifestation of an effect in open (i.e., nonisolated) systems. Only a realist account of causality can provide a systematic account of the behavior of physical particulars in open systems (Bhaskar, 1975).

EXPLANATION AND DESCRIPTION

This means that the scientific empiricist "problem" about the distinction between causal sequences and laws on the one hand, and accidental correlations and generalizations on the other, is a pseudo-problem. This is because the "problem" is based upon the false assumptions that a causal sequence is simply a constant or regular conjunction, and that a causal law is simply a description of such a constant or regular conjunction. Causal laws cannot be mistaken for accidental generalizations because causal laws are not descriptions of constant or regular correlations. A clear distinction must be drawn between what may be termed *causal explanatory* and *descriptive correlative* propositions.

A *causal explanatory* proposition, or causal explanatory law, is of the (abbreviated) symbolic form: (x) $(Fx \rightarrow (Gx \Lambda I)$. Such a proposition is not descriptive of any degree of correlation. It is a conditional statement about what would happen (or would have happened or will happen) given certain conditions and the absence of interference. It is true (when true) quite independently of whether the causal power in question is rarely or regularly manifested. Mercifully, stockpiled chemical weapons rarely manifest their power to generate fatal biological diseases. Regrettably, a rabies virus infection, at present, (after a certain period of incubation), almost invariably manifests its power to generate nervous system disease and death. A causal explanatory law is true by virtue of generative causality; it is true by virtue of a *natural necessity* in the world. For this reason, the modal operator "must" can be employed in conjunction with such propositions. Thus, one can say that if a man has been bitten by a tiger mosquito, then he *must* contract yellow fever, unless something interferes. In this class there will also be included *functional* explanatory laws relating an increase or decrease in a variable generated by an increase or decrease in another variable, unless something interferes, such as "all heated gases expand, unless the pressure is increased."

A *descriptive correlative* proposition is essentially a statistical generalization of the form "a certain percentage of Fs are or are followed by G"; "all" (100%) is just a special case and in practice often means "most." Such propositions can be represented symbolically as (where $n\%x$ is interpreted as a certain determinate percentage of a specified class of things): $(n\%x) Fx$ (thus, "50% of parakeets are blue" would be represented as $(50\%x) Fx$, where the variable x ranges over the class of parakeets, and F is interpreted as "is blue."). Some examples of descriptive correlative propositions are: "all adders are venomous"; "most persons infected by the rabies virus die of the disease"; "92% of right-handed persons have speech centers located in the left cerebral hemisphere"; "49% of zinc atoms have atomic weight 64"; "0.0011% of cigarette smokers contract lung cancer"; "0.00028% of persons exposed to the polio virus contract polio." This class of propositions also includes descriptions of correlations in which one variable increases in direct or inverse proportion to the other, such as "electric current increases as temperature decreases" or "levels of child aggression increase with levels of television violence."

Such propositions are true (when true) by virtue of contingent correlations in the world, which are themselves maintained by contingent but relatively stable distributions of generative and interference conditions. For this reason, the modal operator "must" cannot be employed in conjunction with such propositions, even if the described degree of correlation is 100%. Even if "all men infected by the rabies virus die of the disease" is true (of a particular time and place), it cannot be concluded that "if this man has been infected by the rabies virus, he *must* die of the disease." At any point the contingent and relatively stable distribution of generative and interference conditions may break down.

The term *descriptive correlative proposition* is preferred to the misleading term *accidental generalization*, since few correlations are truly accidental in the sense that the causal mechanisms responsible for the generation of the associated phenomena are quite independent of each other. A classic statistical example of an accidental correlation is the proportional relation between the mule and Ph.D. populations in the state of California. A descriptive correlative proposition describing such a correlation is true (if true) because the causal generative processes that produce increases and decreases in the respective populations are independent but run in synchronous cyclical (and homeostatic) sequences. This *may* also be the case with respect to the correlation between television violence and aggression in young children.

However, this is not the case with many descriptive correlative propositions. The correlation described is often the joint effect of a single mechanism. This is perhaps more likely to be the case with the correlation between television violence and childhood aggression. Both may be joint effects of a single causal mechanism (e.g., a breakdown in social order) responsible for the general increase in violence and aggression in the media and on the streets. In other propositions, the correlation described may in fact be a linear generative causal sequence. This is the case in the rabies, lung cancer, and polio examples; it may be the case with respect to the correlation between television violence and childhood aggression. In all these examples, however, the descriptive correlative proposition is true (if true) by virtue of contingent degrees of correlation that are maintained by contingent but relatively stable distributions of generative and interference conditions.

Any descriptive correlative proposition is extremely sensitive to changes in such distributions. A descriptive correlative proposition about television violence and childhood aggression may be true at one time but false at another, given increased or decreased parental control. It may also be true of one culture and social group but not another.

It must be stressed that descriptive correlative propositions are in no sense approximations to causal explanatory laws, in the way that Hempel's (1966) statistical or probabilistic "laws" are approximations to deductive-nomological "laws." One might suppose that a descriptive correlative proposition making reference to 100% correlation, would, like a causal explanatory law, qualify as a universal generalization. However, this would be to misunderstand the most fundamental difference between causal explanatory and descriptive correlative propositions. Since causal explanatory propositions are true because of a generative causal relation, they are essentially concerned with *possibilities*: they are statements about what would happen or what would have happened (or will happen) given certain conditions and the absence of interference. Since descriptive correlative propositions are true by virtue of contingent correlations that are maintained by contingent but relatively stable distributions of generative and interference conditions, they are essentially concerned with *actualities*:

they are statements about what does happen, what has happened, and what will happen. Thus, although one might legitimately use the term *universal generalization* of both causal explanatory and descriptive correlative propositions, only causal explanatory propositions are properly expressed as *universal conditionals*, since only propositions based upon generative causality (or propositions true by definition) can be related to hypothetical cases that may never be actualized.

A causal explanatory law licenses or supports counterfactual and subjective conditionals in the sense of logical deduction. Since a causal explanatory law is about possibilities, it enables us to deduce what would happen (now or in the future) or would have happened in any possible situation, if nothing interferes or interfered. Since it is true by virtue of generative causality, we know what would happen or would have happened in any hypothetical situation if nothing interferes or interfered. A descriptive correlative proposition cannot license or support a counterfactual or subjunctive conditional in the sense of logical deduction. Since such propositions are about actual correlation, nothing can be deduced about what would or would have happened in possible situations. Since contingent degrees of actual correlation are maintained by contingent but relatively stable distributions of generative and interference conditions, we do not know what would happen in any hypothetical situation, since the actual distribution might not be maintained. The prediction and retrodiction (deduction of descriptions relating to the past) of actual correlations is a hazardous enterprise for this very reason.

The difference between the two types of propositions may be expressed in the following fashion. *Assuming the same ontological particulars in the world* (acids, mosquitos, rabies and polio viruses, etc.), the causal explanatory law "all men bitten by tiger mosquitos contract yellow fever unless something interferes" would be true given any possible history of the world. It would be true given any possible distribution of generative and interference conditions. Descriptive correlative propositions such as "most people infected by the rabies virus die of the disease" and "0.00028% of people exposed to the polio virus contract polio" would not be true given any possible history of the world: they would not be true given many possible distributions of generative and interference conditions. The former proposition would not be true in a possible (and possibly future and hopefully eventually actual) world in which a treatment for rabies is developed and distributed. The latter proposition would not be true in a possible world in which persons are not innoculated against polio (and it was not true of the actual world about 50 years ago).

CAUSALITY AND CORRELATION IN PSYCHOLOGY

The implication of these points for social psychological science is a necessary shift of emphasis from a form of enquiry concerned with the description of observed regularities, to a form of enquiry concerned with the explanation of human powers and liabilities.[3] As in the case of physical causality, to attribute a causal power or liability to a person or persons is not to describe any degree of correlation. A causal explanatory proposition based on the power of violent stimuli to generate aggression, or the power of agents to spontaneously intervene in an emergency is not descriptive of any constant or regular conjunction of these phenomena. The power of violent stimuli to generate aggression in some persons can be interfered with by social inhibition (Berkowitz & Donnerstein, 1982). The power to spontaneously intervene in an emergency may be interfered with by the presence of other bystanders (Latané & Darley, 1970) or anxiety about public performance. Statements about such powers and liabilities are true (or false) quite independently of the degree of correlation in the world. A descriptive correlative proposition will describe the actual degree of correlation in any particular time and place.

Psychologists committed to the scientific empiricist account of causality regularly confuse generative causality and correlation, and consequently fail to distinguish between causal explanatory and descriptive correlative propositions, and the different roles played by each. In consequence, the scientific psychologist is committed to standard scientific empiricist misunderstandings about explanation and prediction, and the role of experimentation in a causal science.

These matters are discussed in the following sections. At this point it is important to note that these misunderstandings are shared by hermeneutical critics of a causal and experimental science of action, who regularly equate generative causality and correlation, and make no distinction between causal explanatory and descriptive correlative propositions. It is often argued that there are no causal laws in social psychological science, either because they are never more than statistical regularities, or because even statistical regularities cannot be assumed to be invariant across different cultures or social groups, or across historical time. Thus it is claimed (Gergen, 1982), for example, that Asch's (1951) conclusions about group influences on conformity based upon his classic experiments are no longer valid today, since the high levels of conformity manifested in the original experiments are not manifested in contemporary repetitions, such as those of Perrin and Spencer (1980), who found an almost negligable degree of conformity among students from a variety of disciplines.

Now it may be true that a descriptive correlative proposition attributing a high degree of correlation between group pressure and conformity that held in the 1950s is no longer true today. Perhaps it ought to be replaced by a descriptive correlative proposition describing a very low degree of correlation. However, it is far from obvious that a causal explanatory proposition about the influence of group pressure on conformity no longer holds. It provides a plausible causal explanation for the conformity manifested by those who still do conform in contemporary repetitions of the original Asch experiment. If the descriptive correlative proposition attributing a high degree of correlation between group pressure and conformity no longer holds, this may simply indicate that many contemporary students have managed to overcome this common human liability. But the group pressure may still be there.

It is not claimed ex cathedra that this is necessarily the case. What is claimed is that historical or cultural variations in degree of correlation are quite independent of and (thus) irrelevant to the question of whether it is or not. Social pressure may be present in any form of life given any degree of social conformity. Nor is it denied that some human powers and liabilities may not be present in some culturally or historically specific forms of human life. In fact, this is a consequence of the present analysis given the additional (and reasonable) assumption that social psychological enabling and stimulus conditions for some human powers and liabilities may not be reidentifiable cross-culturally and transhistorically. This issue is discussed in Chapter 8. The present point to stress is that this question is also quite independent of questions about degree of correlation.

Confirmation

A recognition of the difference between causality and correlation, and between causal explanatory and descriptive correlative enquiries, is clear in the practice of natural science. The "instance statistics" account of the confirmation of causal laws is inadequate, because it fails to square with the fact that such laws are regularly established on the basis of relatively few instances:

> . . . physicists seem to be satisfied with far fewer observations than logicians would expect them to make: one finds in practice none of the relentless accummulation of confirming instances which one would expect from reading books in logic. (Toulmin, 1953, p. 99)

In fact, "positive instances" simpliciter are quite irrelevant to the confirmation of a causal explanatory law, since such propositions are not descriptive of any degree of correlation.

EXPERIMENTAL PRODUCTION: CLOSED AND OPEN SYSTEMS

A causal explanatory law is true by virtue of a generative causal relation. It describes what would happen given certain (enabling and stimulus) conditions if nothing interferes with the mechanism responsible for the causal relation. To test such a proposition, the scientist must establish that this is in fact the case, and this is normally achieved by the experimental production of a certain effect. In the investigation of a putative causal law, the natural scientist will act to isolate the system under investigation from possible interference conditions and alternative hypothetical generative causes. The system under investigation will be a certain particular and hypothetical enabling and stimulus conditions. If such a *closed system* manifests a certain effect, *e*, the scientist has demonstrated that *S* has the power to generate *e*. Thus it can be established on the basis of *closed experiments* that iron is liable to rust when exposed to air and water, that tiger mosquito bites cause yellow fever, that acids have the power to corrode, and that increasing the temperature generates expansion in a gas.

The scientist does not, however, conclude that *S* will be constantly or regularly correlated with *e*. After a few careful experiments, he may cautiously conclude that *S* will invariably be followed by *e* in any other closed system. He will certainly not conclude that *S* will be invariably followed by *e* in an *open system*: that is, a system not isolated from potential mechanisms of interference. The establishment of a generative causal relation between *S* and *e* tells the scientist *nothing* about the degree of correlation of such phenomena in real-world open systems outside the artificial confines of the closed experiment. Indeed, the degree of correlation of such phenomena in open systems is of no special interest to the investigative scientist who is concerned with gaining causal explanatory knowledge. Such a scientist will create further closed experiments to identify alternative generative causes and interference conditions (by adding and eliminating extrinsic conditions), and the mechanism(s) responsible for the generative causal relation. It is worth noting that a significant number of generative causal processes investigated by the natural scientist simply do not occur outside of experimental laboratories, or only occur within specially constructed closed systems outside the experimental laboratory. One could search for generations without finding naturally occurring instances of the Compton or Zeeman effects, or naturally occurring systems that obey Ohm's law. Sometimes the investigated systems themselves only occur in closed laboratory conditions, as in the transmution of transuranic elements.

It must be stressed that the production of experimental closures is often a necesssity and not a mere convenience in the development of causal explanatory knowledge. The scientific psychologist and scientific empiricist often treat experiments as mere conveniences, since the regularity account of causality creates a conception of confirmation as the active identification of observed correlations passively received. However, the scientist often needs to intervene and interfere with the course of nature in order to discriminate generative causality. The actual patterning of events in the world is not a reliable guide to generative causality; the determination of degrees of correlation is of no value.

A fairly simple example should suffice to illustrate this point. Around the turn of the century there were essentially three competing generative causal explanations of yellow fever. It was claimed that yellow fever was contracted by contagion from fellow sufferers, by exposure to "noxious vapors" from marshes, and from the bite of the tiger mosquito (*Aëdes aegypti*). All and any of these causal explanations might have been true. All of these conditions were established by careful observation to be antecedent to the contraction of yellow fever. However, simple observation alone could not establish which of these hypothetical causes was an actual cause of yellow fever, since all three conditions were found to be antecedent to any particular instance of yellow fever (for fairly obvious reasons: tiger mosquitos breed in marsh areas, and people who have been bitten by tiger mosquitos naturally come into contact with people suffering from the disease).

To discriminate the real cause (or causes) of yellow fever, scientists had to intervene and interfere with the course of nature to create closed systems that enabled them to make unambiguous identifications. In 1900, W.Reed and J.Carroll isolated nonimmune volunteers in specially constructed huts at Camp Lazear in Havana. Subjects were exposed for an extended period of time to the soiled clothing of fellow sufferers only, to noxious vapors only, and to tiger mosquitos only. Only those in the last condition contracted yellow fever. On the basis of experimentally produced instances of the disease in only a very small sample of volunteers, Reed and Carroll clearly demonstrated that the bite of the tiger mosquito is a generative cause of yellow fever, and that contagion and exposure to noxious vapors are not.

THE REPETITION OF EXPERIMENTS

It is almost axiomatic that experiments in any science should be repeatable and in fact repeated. However, the scientific empiricist and scientific psychologist misconstrue the reason for this. Experiments are not repeated to simply generate further positive instance statistics, but to determine that the experimental system was successfully closed. That is, repetition of the experiment is a test of the experiment itself: ". . . for the main point of the experimental method is that under the same experimental conditions the same results can be obtained over and over, to confirm the original experiment" (Przibram, 1926, p. 401). The failure to repeat positive or negative instances neither falsifies nor protects the investigated causal generative hypothesis. It simply indicates that some of the experimental systems were not successfully closed: "All experimenters occasionally obtain results which they are unable to reproduce later. And in such cases, they deem the experiment a faulty one rather than condemn a theory which happens to conflict with it" (Musgrave, 1973, p. 394).

Failed experiments do not produce results that are significant in the determination of generative causality. The scientist knows that there was some difference in generative and interference conditions that made a difference in the experimental results, but the experiments themselves do not usually display that difference. If a certain effect is manifested in one version of the same experiment but not in another, it might be because an additional generative condition was present in the former but not in the latter (the investigated system was not in fact a generative cause), or it might be because an interference condition was present in the latter but not in the former (the investigated system was in fact a generative cause). The scientist will persevere with further closed experiments until she finds the difference that made the difference. Once this has been done, however, the scientist will not laboriously reproduce the experiment to gather a multitude of positive instances. The basic point may be expressed by saying that in the investigation of generative causality, the scientist is concerned about the *quality* of the experimental closure, and not at all concerned about the *quantity* of instance correlations.

The scientific empiricist will often also claim that the degree of confirmation of a causal explanatory law is a function of the variety of positive instances. It is true that a scientist will vary the experimental conditions in modifications of an original set of experiments which establish a generative causal relation. Yet to suppose that such experiments provide further confirmation of the causal law by providing a greater variety of positive instances is also to misconstrue the point of this practice. Conditions are varied in further experiments not to produce further confirmation of the law, but to identify interference conditions, and possible alternative stimulus and enabling conditions for the exercise of the previously demonstrated causal power.

CORRELATION IN OPEN SYSTEMS

Successfully closed experiments constitute the preferred means of confirming and falsifying putative causal laws in science. Correlations in open systems do not in general count as confirmation instances because alternative possible generative conditions may be co-present. By the same token, causal explanatory propositions are not falsified by negative instances in open systems, because of interference conditions. Indeed, correlation in open systems bears only the most tenuous relation to generative causality. For the number of times a particular will manifest its power to generate effect *e* in an open system depends upon the contingent distribution of enabling, stimulus, and interference conditions. Thus, this number will vary from never to always, and will be different for different generative causal sequences. For this reason, degree of correlation in open systems cannot be taken as any measure of the probability or degree of confirmation of a putative causal explanatory law. Invariant correlation in closed systems is sufficient for the confirmation of a causal explanatory law. Invariant or regular correlation in open systems is neither necessary nor sufficient.

It is true that descriptive correlative propositions are confirmed by positive instances in open systems. The instance statistics account of confirmation does provide an adequate account of the basic logic of confirmation for such propositions. The degree of confirmation or probability of such propositions is proportional to the size and representative nature of the observed sample. Our confidence in the descriptive correlative propositions, "92% of right-handed persons have speech centers located on the left hemisphere" and "0.0011% of cigarette smokers contract lung cancer," is proportional to the number of right-handed persons and cigarette smokers studied, and the absence of systematic bias in their selection. Invariant correlations in closed experiments are neither necessary nor sufficient for the confirmation of a descriptive correlative proposition. In fact, they are quite irrelevant, since an experimentally closed system is *never* representative of an open system.

Two Empiricist Objections

A scientific empiricist might deny the difference between generative causality and regular correlation, or between causal explanatory and descriptive correlative propositions, by appealing to the ceteris paribus clause ("all other things being equal") in a putative causal law that describes an empirical regularity. He might appeal to the fact that in cases of interference, all other things are not equal.

This only shifts the empiricist's problem, but does nothing to resolve it. For the critical question arises: all other things being equal to what? If it is admitted that causal laws are confirmed in closed systems, then the empiricist must either accept that causal laws do not describe regular correlation, since the degree of correlation may be very low in open systems, or that causal laws do not hold in open systems, since the only actual correlations may be those artificially produced in experimental closed systems. Bhaskar (1975) articulates the dilemma in the following fashion: the empiricist who equates causality and correlation must either sacrifice the descriptive thesis that causal laws describe regular correlation, or the universal thesis that causal laws hold in any kind of system.

To deny that causal laws are confirmed by closed systems is of no help either. Again the critical question arises: all other things being equal to what? Whatever observational situation is taken as definitive, a specification of the conditions that must be equal will restrict the applicability of the causal law in order to preserve the invariance claim. For given some different conditions, a system capable of generating effect e will not generate e, if those conditions include an interference condition. But in many other different conditions S will generate e, if these conditions do not include an interference condition. Thus, many instances of generative causality would not be "covered" by the causal law. Nor can the applicability of the causal law be extended by dispensing with the ceteris paribus clause, for if the regularity thesis is maintained, then many causal explanatory propositions would be simply false.

The empiricist would no doubt protest that a ceteris paribus clause makes reference to "causally relevant conditions." However, it is hard to see how such a reference could be justified, if causal laws are held to be descriptions of observational regularity. The only causally relevant conditions for the empiricist are those observable antecedent to the observed effect, and these will include conditions that are not relevant in a generative causal sense (thus restricting the applicability of the law). The empiricist might with more prima facie justification complain that, prior to the identification of actual interference conditions, the open-ended nature of the clause, "unless some interfering condition is present," is no improvement on the ambiguity and vagueness of the clause "all other things being equal." However, the only way to preserve the "all other things being equal" clause is to abandon the regularity claim. The logical schema "unless some interfering condition is present" can be made quite specific by further experimental work.

An attempt has been made (Mackie, 1974) to preserve the regularity thesis by treating what the realist calls "interference conditions" as conditions whose negation form part of the set of antecedent conditions that are jointly sufficient for an effect. Any causal explanatory law of the (abbreviated) form (x) $(Fx \rightarrow (Gx \wedge I))$ can be rewritten as (x) $((Fx\ \&\ -I) \rightarrow Gx)$. The two propositions are logically equivalent. Yet this is a strange defense of the regularity thesis, since it already sacrifices the link between causality and regularity. Such a proposition will often be true even if there are very few instances of de facto correlation.

Furthermore, there is some point in including the interference clause in the consequent of the law. The clause, "unless some interference condition is present," is an empty logical schema until it is filled in with further causal knowledge gleaned from further experimental work. It should be noted, however, that even after particular interferences have been identified, the logical schema will remain in the form of "or any other interference condition." A lot of work may be needed to identify interference conditions, and we can never be certain that we have identified them all. The interference clause is always provisional and promissory.

In both the empiricist and realist accounts it a reference to the phenomena described in the antecedent of the law that is supposed to furnish the causal explanation. If negated interference conditions are included in the antecedent, such an explanation will always be provisional and incomplete (and the range of phenomena "covered" by the causal explanation indeterminate). It is true that any causal explanatory law is provisional and incomplete in the sense that the putative explanatory law might in fact turn out to be false (there might have been an experimental error), and in the sense that a causal explanation needs to be filled out by a theoretical reference to the mechanism involved. However, a causal explanation confirmed by a closed experiment is *not* provisional and incomplete in the sense that the explanation is inadequate unless we have identified the interference conditions. A causal explanation is fully adequate as a causal explanation if it has been confirmed by closed experiments. It is frequently the case that we can provide fully adequate causal explanations (based on closed experiments) long before one can identify interference conditions. The causes of yellow fever and tuberculosis were known long before effective means of treatment were identified.

CLOSURE BY ONTOLOGICAL AND CONTROL ISOLATION

The main point of the present section is that causal explanatory laws are confirmed by the observation of relatively few invariant correlations in a closed system. The discussion so far has been concerned essentially with *ontological closure*: the system is isolated from possible interference conditions and alternative hypothetical generative conditions. There are, however, limits to such *ontological isolation*. Experimental techniques to produce ontological closures are supplemented by techniques designed to produce *control closures*. Generative conditions may be isolated by *control isolation*, in which a control system reproduces all the features of the experimental system except the investigated conditions (or varies the levels of a variable in the investigation of a functional law). Both techniques are frequently employed, and frequently employed in conjunction, in closed experiments in causal sciences, since experimentally produced instances of correlation in closed systems constitute the preferred confirmation instances of causal explanatory laws.

NATURAL CLOSURES

This is not to say that such closed systems are always the artificial product of the experimental work of scientists, or that legitimate confirmation instances of generative causality only occur within the confines of experimental laboratories. There are many *natural closures*: systems that are naturally isolated from interference, or closely similar systems that may be compared to identify generative conditions. By virtue of such natural closures, one usually recognizes immediately (on the basis of a single instance) that proximate fire is the cause of pain, sliced onions the cause of tearing eyes, and morally abhorrent actions the cause of rejection by our peers (interference conditions are absent, and closely similar situations have been observed in the past without the novel causal factor and the effect). The scientist may through careful investigation or good fortune come across instances of ontological closure: in evolutionary biology one might observe bird populations on a remote and isolated island affected by a natural disaster; in physics one might observe the dip of a needle suspended in water in the absence of any significant local magnetic field. Or control closures may be discriminated by the careful comparison of similarities and differences in systems that vary naturally: in astronomy one observes the different distances, velocities, and positions of planets over a period of time; in meteorology one observes the different combinations of atmospheric conditions at different times and in different places.

The trouble with natural closures is that they often remain ambiguous (we can rarely be sure that all hypothetical generative and interference conditions have been included and eliminated), and nature simply cannot be relied upon to always oblige us with such epistemically privileged observational situations. For this reason, the scientist regularly intervenes, and alters the course of nature to create experimental closures. He need not, however, create these systems in a laboratory, although he usually prefers this since a laboratory (at least in natural science) is a place where effective instruments for controlling variables can be assembled. A field experiment is a closed system created by ontological or control isolation outside of any designated experimental laboratory.

Experimental and Observational Sciences

Any causal science bases its causal explanations on the observation of closed systems, but not all causal sciences are experimental. Some causal sciences have to rely on the observation of natural closures, since active interference in the course of nature is impractical, disruptive, or impossible. Thus, sciences such as astronomy, economics, and ethology are characterized by their emphasis on large amounts of observational data (not large numbers of "positive instances") and long periods of waiting for the right observation situation to arise. It is by virtue of the increased control over generative and interference conditions that the causal scientist prefers to create experimental closures whenever this is possible. It is the ability to intervene in the course of nature to control conditions of generation and interference that distinguishes the few controlled observations of the experimental physicist and the single-case designs of experimental studies of animal behavior, from the many and patient observations of the astronomer and ethologist.

It is true that an experimental scientist can never be *certain* that she has created an adequate ontological or control closure. The experimental scientist can never be certain that all the generative and interference conditions have been considered, and previous causal judgments are always open to revision in the light of later and more rigorously controlled experiments. In this respect, any closed experiment is always *epistemically open*, even though the scientist may have in fact effectively created an ontological or control closure. Nevertheless, the scientist has greater confidence in causal judgments as greater control is gained over the investigated system, and ineffective closed experiments are only superseded by more effective closures.

Experiments in Social Psychological Science

A common complaint advanced by both defenders and critics of a causal and experimental science of action is that experiments in social psychological science are "artificial" or "restricted" (Borgatta & Bohrnstedt, 1974; Campbell & Stanley, 1966; Harré & Secord, 1972; Kelman, 1972; McClintock, 1972; McGuire, 1967; Tajfel, 1972). It is complained that the regularities of the laboratory are not manifested in real life or natural settings:

> We must pay strict attention to the meaning of laboratory experiments and their relation to ordinary behaviour. We must discover a strategy for making empirical studies and for designing experiments that permit the person to behave as he would outside the laboratory under similar conditions. For many areas of social behaviour we may even need to abandon the laboratory for the actual world.
>
> (Harré & Secord, 1972, pp. 49–50)[4]

There are some fundamental problems about experimentation in a science of action, and these are discussed in Chapters 11 and 12. However, this is not one of them. The experimental method in social psychological science is not invalidated just because powers and liabilities manifested in closed experimental systems do not manifest themselves regularly in real-world open systems, since interference conditions eliminated from closed experimental systems may be present in real-world open systems. A successfully closed experiment can establish a power or liability, but nothing can be concluded about degrees of correlation in real-world open systems. Some powers and liabilities will regularly manifest themselves (when interference conditions are rarely present), others will rarely do so (when interference conditions are regularly present). The artificiality of ontological and control isolation is essential to the logic of experimentation in any science. Unless a closure obtains, instances of correlation do not count as confirmation instances of a causal explanation.

If examples of "violent stimuli" or "powerful and credible sources" can be isolated from interference conditions and alternative hypothetical causes, and correlated with manifestations of "aggression" and "persuasive communication" in laboratory experiments, then it can be established that violent stimuli are a generative cause of aggression (Berkowitz & LePage, 1967), and that powerful and credible sources are a generative cause of persuasive communication (Secord & Backman, 1974). Violent stimuli have the power to generate aggression in some persons; some persons are liable to become aggressive when presented with violent stimuli. Some persons have the power to persuade others; some persons are liable to be persuaded. Such experiments tell us nothing about the degree to which these powers and liabilities are manifested in open systems. Aggressive behavior in the presence of violent stimuli can be prevented by social inhibition; communications from powerful and credible sources can be resisted by contrary norms derived from local reference groups. To establish the actual degree of correlation in real-world open systems, a descriptive correlative enquiry would be required. Closed experiments are irrelevant in this form of enquiry, since such experiments are simply not representative.

Conversely, many representative instances in real-world open systems may confirm descriptive correlative propositions documenting a high degree of correlation between violent stimuli and aggression and a low degree of correlation between powerful and credible sources and persuasive communication. In neither case do such representative samples tell us anything about generative conditions (unless such instances happen to include identified natural closures). The descriptive correlative propositions may be true simply because violent stimuli just happen to be present in places where aggression occurs for other reasons (e.g., police stations, football matches, street gangs, etc.), and powerful and credible sources may simply tend to voice minority opinions. Such propositions are true or false by virtue of contingent correlations maintained by contingent but relatively stable distributions (at certain times and places) of generative and interference conditions. Assuming a generative causal relation, the high degree of correlation between violent stimuli and aggression may be a product of the breakdown of parental and social inhibitions. The low degree of correlation between powerful and credible sources and persuasive communication may be the outcome of more powerful group loyalties. A large and representative sample of instances in open systems is required to provide a reliable estimate of the degree of correlation in open systems, since it must be representative of such distributions.

RANDOM SELECTION: A SOURCE OF CONFUSION

Causal explanatory and descriptive correlative enquiries and their respective modes of confirmation are regularly confused in the social psychological literature. One potential source of confusion is the fact that subjects must be randomly selected for both types of enquiry. In a descriptive correlative enquiry, an inference is made from an observed degree of correlation between conditions and action (or nonaction) in a sample of persons to the population of persons in such conditions in real-world open systems. Subjects in an observational sample must be randomly selected to constitute a representative sample of the distribution of generative and interference conditions that are responsible for the actual degree of correlation between the investigated conditions and actions. If one was trying to estimate the percentage of students who gave up their studies (or reduced their efforts) as a result of test failures (or number of test failures), a sample of students whose parents always withdrew financial and moral support would not be representative. For the same reason, a sample of students in a closed experiment designed to investigate the effects of peer encouragement on renewed effort after failure would not be representative either (since steps have been taken to exclude more negative pressures). Of course, randomizing subjects in such studies does not ensure the absence of systematic bias and distortion, but it is the only means of guarding against it.

In a causal explanatory enquiry, an inference is made to a causal power or liability on the basis of its manifestation in a closed experiment. However, in a social psychological experiment it cannot be assumed that each subject will manifest a postulated human power or liability. Unlike experimentally produced instances of sulfur, acids, and tubercle bacilli, it cannot be assumed that the class of human persons forms a unitary natural kind with a common nature. Perhaps there are some uniformities of nature on the biological, social, and psychological levels among all persons and across all cultures and eras, but this simply cannot be presumed in general or in particular in social psychological experiments. And any real differences in personal natures will certainly make a difference in experiments designed to identify human powers and liabilities.

This does not mean that effective experimentation is impossible in a science of action. If a power or liability is manifested (or manifested to a greater degree) among subjects in an experimental group exposed to an enabling or stimulus condition, but not manifested (or manifested to a lesser degree) in a control group not exposed to the condition, then such a condition can be established as a stimulus or enabling condition. But since human powers and liabilities may be variably distributed in the general population of persons, the random selection of subjects is needed to ensure that no systematic bias will obscure the experimental effect.

If Milgram's (1974) subjects had all been liberal college professors or Catholic priests, then the power of authoritative commands to generate destructive obedience (or the liability of some people to follow such commands) might well have been obscured. The power of emotive content to generate errors in logical reasoning (or the liability of some persons to make errors when faced with emotionally loaded arguments) would be obscured if all the subjects in an experimental group were professional logicians. In consequence, such experimental studies do provide a basis for an inference about the relative frequency of such powers and liabilities in the general population, although it does not provide a basis for an inference about degrees of correlation between conditions and action. A randomly selected experimental sample provides an estimate of their distribution but not their manifestation in open systems.

This is only true of experiments that are designed to determine the existence of human powers and liabilities, and such experiments only provide preliminary guides to stimulus and enabling conditions. Experiments designed to determine more rigorously the stimulus, enabling, and interference conditions for a human liability, and those designed to determine whether there are in fact any stimulus conditions for the exercise of a human power, will employ subjects who demonstrably have or lack the relevant power or liability (on the basis of previous experimental tests).

There is no reason in principle why experimentation (laboratory and field) should not make a major contribution to a causal science of human action, although there is much in present practice to prevent it. These questions are discussed in more detail in Chapters 11 to 13.

Explanation

EXPLANATION AND PREDICTION

A causal explanatory proposition of the form (x) $(Fx \rightarrow (Gx \wedge I))$, confirmed by invariant correlation in a natural or experimental closure, can be used to provide a generative causal explanation of instances of G in open systems. The establishment of a causal relation in a closed experiment enables one to make a causal explanatory inference to instances of an effect in open systems. If S has been established as a generative cause of e by closed experiment, then instances of e in open systems can be explained by antecedent instances of S (when these occur). Thus instances of corrosion can be explained by reference to the corrosive power of acids, instances of yellow fever can be explained in terms of mosquito bites, and instances of gas expansion can be explained in terms of an increase in temperature.

However, a causal explanatory law of the form (x) $(Fx \rightarrow (Gx \wedge I))$ will not license categorical predictions about actual effects or degrees of correlation between conditions and effects in open systems. A causal explanatory law relating tiger mosquito bites and yellow fever can only license predictions about what will happen *if* nothing interferes. It can only produce predictions about hypothetical possibilities. Contrary to the deductive-nomological account, given the initial conditions and the causal explanatory law, it cannot be concluded *with certainty* that a man will contract yellow fever or that tin will act as a superconductor, since the generative power may be interfered with in open systems. A causal explanatory law cannot license predictions about degree of correlation in open systems for the same reason.

It is true that one can use knowledge of generative causality to facilitate the prediction of actual effects and degree of correlation in open systems. However, this requires much more than knowledge of generative conditions. For the prediction of particular effects, one needs to have knowledge of all the generative and interference conditions, and be able to anticipate their presence and absence in any particular situation. Such a Laplacean ideal is beyond the capability of most sciences, including experimental physics. Physicists are rightly modest about their ability to predict the trajectory of a leaf falling from a tree on a gusty day. Of course, the physicist could *make* the leaf fall with a specific trajectory in a specially created closed system, but that is a quite different matter.

To predict the degree of correlation between conditions and effects in open systems requires knowledge of the distribution of generative and interference conditions. This requires a descriptive correlative enquiry, which could itself determine degree of correlation, quite independently of the presence or absence of a generative causal relation between conditions and effects. The point of causal explanatory laws is not to provide predictions of effects or degree of correlation in open systems. The point of causal explanatory laws is to provide explanations of effects in open systems. The criterion of adequacy for causal explanatory propositions is not their ability to make predictions in open systems. The criterion of adequacy is the demonstration of a correlation between conditions and effects in a closed (usually experimental) system.

DESCRIPTIVE CORRELATIVE PREDICTIONS

A descriptive correlative proposition serves an entirely different purpose. It provides a description of the degree of correlation of phenomena in open systems. Such propositions enable the scientist to make probabilistic predictions about individual events given antecedent conditions. If conditions and consequent events are correlated to a high degree, then it can be concluded that it is highly probable that a particular event will follow, given such conditions. If "noxious vapors" from swamps and television violence are correlated to a high degree with yellow fever in men and aggression in children, respectively, then it can be concluded that these phenomena are highly probable, given such antecedent conditions. If conditions and events are correlated to a low degree, then it can be concluded that it is highly improbable that a particular event will follow, given such conditions. If exposure to the polio virus and powerful and credible sources are correlated to a low degree with polio and persuasive communications, then it can be concluded that such events are highly improbable, given such conditions. This is true quite independently of whether there is a causal relation between conditions and events.

If there is a high degree of correlation between conditions and events, this will enable the scientist to anticipate instances of the event in open systems, given the antecedent conditions. A high correlation between noxious vapors from marshes and yellow fever will enable him to anticipate instances of yellow fever, given this condition. If there is a low degree of correlation between conditions and events, the scientist cannot employ descriptive correlative knowledge to anticipate such events on the basis of antecedent conditions. A low correlation between exposure to the polio virus and polio will not enable him to anticipate instances of polio, given this condition. Again, this is true quite independently of whether there is a generative causal relation between conditions and events. Indeed, it is often the case that a description of a high degree of correlation between conditions and events that are not causally related will provide a far better instrument for anticipating instances of an event than a description of a low degree of correlation between conditions and events that are. Thus, for example, the predictive diagnosis of certain diseases, such as syphilis and tuberculosis, is best facilitated by reference to early symptoms, which are correlated to a high degree with instances of the disease, rather than by reference to exposure to microorganisms, which is not (because of individual resistance and prophylactics).

But a descriptive correlative proposition does not provide a generative causal explanation, since the relation between conditions and events may not be causal. One cannot presume that it is, since descriptive correlative propositions cannot be confirmed by reference to closed systems, which are unrepresentative of the degree of correlation manifested in open systems. A reference to early symptoms does not provide a causal explanation of diseases, no matter how high the degree of correlation in open systems. A reference to exposure to a bacterium or virus (based upon a closed experiment) does provide an explanation of diseases, no matter how low the degree of correlation in open systems.

It is, thus, quite wrong for scientific empiricists such as Hempel (1966) to suggest that a descriptive correlative proposition (statistical or probabilistic law) approximates a causal explanatory law (deductive-nomological law) as the documented degree of correlation between conditions and events increases. It has already been noted that the observed degree of correlation between conditions and events in open systems is no measure of the probability of a causal relation between conditions and events. Indeed, it may be said that degrees of correlation between conditions and events in open systems documented by descriptive correlative propositions, in conjunction with particular events themselves, constitute part of the subject matter of a causal explanatory scientific enquiry. Such contingent degrees of correlation are themselves causally explained by reference to generative and interference conditions identified by reference to closed systems, and estimates of the relative distribution of such conditions in open systems derived from descriptive correlative enquiries based on representative samples from open systems.

Thus, one can explain the high degree of correlation between infection by the rabies virus and the disease in terms of a generative causal relation, and the low relative frequency of interference conditions (such as resistance and treatment) when persons are exposed to the virus. Analogously, one could explain the low degree of correlation between exposure to the polio virus and the disease itself, in terms of a causal relation and high relative frequency of interference conditions. Or one could explain the high degree of correlation between abnormal animal behavior and earthquakes, in terms of a joint cause and the low relative frequency with which interference conditions are co-present.

Explanation and Intervention

It ought to be stressed, however, that although a reference to generative and interference conditions can be used to provide such an explanation of degrees of correlation in open systems, this is not usually the primary goal of experimental enquiries designed to identify causal explanatory conditions and interference conditions. Often the primary goal of such research is to create or eliminate a class of effects in the real world. Rather than attempting to describe or explain a regularity, the scientist aims to create or eliminate a regularity. Once the scientist has discovered a generative causal power and interference conditions in closed experiments, he will employ this knowledge to create new effects by creating specially designed closures outside of the experimental laboratory. He will create electrical systems that obey Ohm's law; he will create railway systems that operate on superconductive power; he will create a new form of power by the bombardment of a radioactive nucleus with neutrons. Or she will employ such knowledge to eliminate a class of effects, either by eliminating generative conditions or introducing or creating interferences. Medical researchers create experimental closures (or make careful observations of natural closures) in order to identify the generative and interference conditions of a disease. The researcher may then use this knowledge to eliminate instances of the disease by elimination of the generative condition. This is possible in the case of typhoid via the elimination of rickettsiae by the disinfection of sewage and drinking water, and in the case of malaria via the elimination of the plasmodium-transmitting female anopheles mosquito by swamp drainage or the application of DDT. It is not possible in the case of syphilis or influenza. If the elimination of a generative condition is not possible or not practical, the medical researcher will introduce or artificially create an interference condition, either in the form of a prophylactic or form of treatment. This will prevent the occurrence of the disease, even if the generative condition is present. The antibiotic penicillin (which inhibits bacterial growth) is effective against syphilis even when the generative organism *Treponema pallidum* is present. The antibiotic streptomycin was specially created to eliminate instances of tuberculosis despite exposure to the tubercle bacillus.

When the generative cause has been identified and means of prevention and treatment identified and distributed, there may be very few, if any, instances of the generative condition followed by the disease. Yet we surely would not claim, for example, that plasmodium was no longer the cause of malaria, or *Treponema pallidum* no longer the cause of syphilis. Those rare cases who were not treated with the prophylactic or antibiotic (or where the prophylactic or antibiotic was ineffective) would still contract the disease, and this would be explained in terms of the generative causal condition (established by closure). Medical researchers and scientists in general do not usually alter the powers or natures of particulars or change the laws of nature. Rather, they employ causal explanatory knowledge of generative and interference conditions, and of real natures and mechanisms, in order to change the course of nature (for good or ill). The causal knowledge derived from experimental interventions in the course of nature in the form of closed experiments enables the scientist to intervene more effectively in the general course of nature.

EXPLANATION AND EXPERIMENT IN SOCIAL PSYCHOLOGICAL SCIENCE

The effective isolation of generative causal conditions in closed experiments in a social psychological science does not enable the human scientist to predict particular effects in real-world open systems. Even if violent stimuli have been established as a generative cause of aggression in a laboratory experiment, it only follows that anyone subject to this liability and exposed to violent stimuli will become aggressive *if nothing interferes*. It does not follow that the person will become aggressive in any actual real-world situation. However, if this has been established as a generative cause of aggression, then instances of aggression in open systems can be explained by reference to antecedent instances of violent stimuli.[5]

Analogously, let it be assumed that Milgram, in his famous experiments on "destructive obedience" (1974), was successful in isolating what may be termed a "wisdom-authoritarian" command structure, in which individuals defer to another because of the other's superior knowledge, as in a doctor-patient or scientist-technician relationship; as distinct from a "sanction-authoritarian" command structure, in which individuals defer to another because of the possible or actual application of sanctions, as in an officer-soldier or warder-prisoner relationship. Then, it might be cautiously concluded that Milgram's experiments demonstrated the power of such structures to generate destructive obedience in some persons. Some persons are liable to obey commands to harm others from persons represented as competent in their field. If this is the case, then such experiments support causal explanatory inferences to instances of destructive obedience in real-world open systems.

A reference to antecedent commands by authorities perceived as competent can be used to explain the behavior of nurses in the Hofling et al. (1966) study, who obeyed orders from doctors to administer quantities of a drug that exceeded the maximum dosage levels; or the humiliating behavior of the patients of unscrupulous and unqualified mental health practitioners; and perhaps the behavior of some Nazi administrators according to Arendt's (1964) "banality of evil" thesis (the behavior of others is perhaps best explained in terms of "sanction-authoritarian" command structures).

However, consider the conclusion Milgram (1974, p. 188) himself drew from the experiments: "Something far more dangerous is revealed; the capacity for man to abandon his humanity, indeed the inevitability that he does so, as he merges his unique personality into larger institutional structures." There is nothing inevitable about this at all. Indeed, Milgram's own experiments illustrate a variety of interference conditions: for example, many subjects refused to continue, given moral support from peers. Thus, such experiments cannot be used to predict what a particular person will do in an open system when commanded to harm another. Furthermore, there is the additional problem already noted. Some persons (e.g., liberal college professors or Catholic priests) may simply not be liable to follow such orders, even in the absence of interference conditions.

Causal explanatory knowledge of generative and interference conditions gleaned from closures can be employed to provide explanations of the degree of correlation in open systems between conditions and actions described in descriptive correlative propositions, in conjuction with descriptive correlative knowledge of the relative frequency with which generative and interference conditions are correlated (and the relative frequency of liabilities themselves). A reference to such generative and interference conditions can explain the prevalence or absence or degree of destructive obedience in different societies and different historical eras. Descriptive correlative propositions simply describe degree of correlation between conditions and actions. They enable the scientist to make predictions about the high or low probability of actions, given certain conditions, on the basis of high or low correlations between conditions and actions. Such propositions are nonexplanatory and true or false quite independently of whether the condition is a generative condition of the associated event.

It is important to stress again that even descriptive correlative propositions documenting a high degree of correlation that license the prediction of events with high probability, and thus enable the scientist to effectively anticipate events on the basis of antecedent conditions, are neither causal explanatory *nor the least approximation to it*. One must be especially careful to distinguish the probabilistic predictive utility of a condition in open systems from the logic of control isolation in experimentation.

EXPLANATION AND STATISTICAL RELEVANCE

A common complaint about the deductive-nomological and probabilistic covering-law accounts of scientific explanation is that too little attention is paid to the requirement that initial conditions must be causally relevant to the explanandum event. Since the scientific empiricist effectively denies there is such a thing as generative causality, this is hardly surprising. An alternative account of causal explanation has been provided by Salmon (1971) in terms of the "statistical relevance" of a condition to an event, and this has proved popular with some psychologists (Bell & Staines, 1981). An example given by Salmon that has an obvious appeal to psychologists is the evaluation of psychotherapy. Salmon argues on familiar grounds that if the rates of spontaneous recovery from neurotic disorders for those who receive no treatment are as high as the recovery rates for those who receive a form of therapy such as psychoanalysis, then it cannot be concluded that a reference to psychoanalytic treatment provides an adequate causal explanation of recovery. Conversely, if the recovery rates for those who receive a form of therapy, such as behavior therapy, are higher than those who receive no therapy at all, it can be concluded that behavior therapy provides an adequate causal explanation of recovery. Eysenck, for example clearly thinks this is the case with respect to psychoanalytic treatments (1952) and behavior therapy (1960).

According to Salmon, a reference to a condition such as psychotherapy can only provide an adequate causal explanation if it increases the probability of an event such as recovery: if the presence of psychotherapy makes recovery more probable than if it was absent. This account has the advantage that it does not equate causality with a high degree of correlation or probability. Even if only a very few recover from schizophrenia or cancer, a reference to a treatment will give a causal explanation of recovery if the probability of recovery is greater with treatment than without (if more people recover with treatment than without).

However, the statistical relevance of conditions to events in open systems is no measure at all of the adequacy (or probability) of a causal explanation. The presence of early disease symptoms certainly does not provide an adequate causal explanation of a disease just because it increases the probability of the occurrence of the disease. A reference to early symptoms does not provide a better explanation of a disease than a reference to a bacterium just because the probability of contracting the disease is greater given early symptoms than it is given exposure to a bacterium.

In open systems, useful "signs" (Berkeley, 1710), such as abnormal animal behavior, early disease symptoms, and violence on television, which can be utilized to more effectively anticipate the course of nature, may not be the generative conditions of anticipated events such as earthquakes, diseases, and aggression in children. Exposure to noxious vapors from swamps, fellow sufferers, and tiger mosquito bites all increase the probability that a man will get yellow fever, and can thus be used to anticipate where hospital resources can be most usefully applied. But only a reference to the latter condition provides a causal explanation.

No doubt the admission of patients to hospitals increases their chances of dying. Only in very rare cases is it a cause of death. It is certainly not beyond the realms of possibility that certain forms of psychoanalytic treatment are effective in generating recovery, even though this condition actually decreases the probability of recovery in relation to no treatment. Conversely, it is entirely possible that some forms of behavior therapy actually increase the probability of recovery in relation to no treatment, but are themselves quite ineffective in generating recovery. The former might well be the case if only the more serious and resilient cases are referred to or seek professional treatments. The latter might be the case if client perceptions of credibility of treatment and expectancy of recovery are in fact the generative conditions for recovery.[6]

It has been noted already that statistical relevance can be used as a basis for the identification of generative and enabling conditions in closed experiments in a social psychological science (and alternatively in natural closures if these occur). Statistical relevance in open systems has no bearing at all on the adequacy of causal explanations, since this will depend upon contingent distributions of generative and interference conditions. Consequently, the statistical relevance of a condition in the social psychological world will vary across cultures and historical eras. Causal powers and liabilities do not wax and wane according to changes in such distributions. They only change if the nature of the particulars change.

PREDICTION IN SOCIAL PSYCHOLOGICAL SCIENCE

If the failure to distinguish causal explanation and probabilistic prediction leads to common scientific psychological misconceptions of explanation and experiment in a causal science of action, it also underlies many hermeneutical and other standard criticisms of such an enterprise. A common complaint is that theories and laws in psychology are poor predictive devices: "We have set ourselves to bring human behaviour under predictive control and our success—in our own terms—has been less than marked" (Hudson, 1970, pp. 289–290). Many writers go to great lengths to argue that putative causal explanations in a putative science of action are inadequate since it is extremely difficult to anticipate individual actions in open systems. (Gergen [1982] provides a detailed list of arguments and authors). This objection in large part accounts for the poor public reputation of the psychological and social sciences.

Whatever the weaknesses of contemporary social psychological science, this is just a mistake. It is about as appropriate to blame the psychologist for failures to anticipate individual instances of aggression or breakdown as it is to blame your doctor for not warning you that you were going to contract influenza, or the experimental physicist for not predicting the trajectory of the proverbial leaf falling from the tree. The success or failure of open system predictions has *nothing* to do with the adequacy of causal explanations. If generative conditions have been identified on the basis of closed experiments or natural closures, then perfectly adequate causal explanations can be provided for instances of aggression, breakdown, influenza, and individual leaf trajectories.

Descriptive correlative propositions do enable us to anticipate the course of the social psychological world *so long as they remain true* (and describe a high degree of regularity), although they may be more regularly subject to revision than the scientific psychologist finds comfortable. But this is not the purpose of causal explanations. Furthermore, the primary utility of causal knowledge in social psychological science is not that it enables us to explain or predict correlations, but that it enables us to promote some actions and eliminate others. Instances of violence may be reduced by legislation against the sale and carrying of arms, whether this is by virtue of the elimination of the "weapons effect" (Berkowitz & LePage, 1967) as stimulus condition, or simply the elimination of an enabling condition. Other liabilities are more resilient and require changes in biochemical, psychological, and social structures. Persons liable to self-destructive psychotic behavior may require transformational drug treatments or neurosurgery if instances of such behaviors are to be reduced. The reduction of instances of serious neurosis may involve a major change in psychological structures. The reduction of juvenile delinquency may involve a major transformation of social aspirations and opportunities within many youth cultures.

5
Theory

Theory and Observation

REALISM AND INSTRUMENTALISM

The realist holds that scientific theories are potentially accurate representations of reality. The instrumentalist holds that scientific theories are merely sentential instruments for the deductive integration and prediction of observational regularity. The instrumentalists Osiander and Ursus protected Copernicus's theory from church antogonism (since the Catholic church was committed to the Ptolemeic theory as church dogma) by arguing that the Copernican theory was nothing more than a useful device for calculating the observed orbits of the planets. The question of its accuracy as a representation of reality did not arise since it was not intended as a representation of reality. Galileo, as is well known, was forced to deny the Copernican theory before the Inquisition because he clearly advanced the view that the theory was an accurate representation of reality. He claimed that the planetary system really is heliocentric and not geocentric as Ptolemy and Aristotle claimed. The Jesuit theologian Clavius also provided a realist interpretation. He argued that the Copernican theory was not in fact an accurate representation of reality, and his arguments may have influenced the Inquisition to move against Galileo.

This is a popular illustration of the difference between realist and instrumentalist interpretations of theory. It also illustrates that there have been historical occasions when certain scientists have been inclined to argue the case for an instrumental interpretation of theory, although these have been relatively rare. It also illustrates the instrumentalists' preference for examples drawn from physics and astronomy.

It is no accident that fundamental dynamical theories (such as quantum mechanics and the theory of relativity) or fundamental aspects of physical theories (such as the space-time metric in relativity theory) have been the preferred illustrative examples for instrumentalists and antirealists from Berkeley to van Fraassen (1980). For it is precisely these kinds of theories that provide the strongest support for the instrumentalist account.

This is true for a number of reasons. In the first place, many of these theories (or aspects of them) are truly fundamental in the sense that (for long periods at least) there is no deeper level of theoretical or technical penetration that can be achieved (quantum mechanics presently comprehends all subatomic phenomena and the weak nuclear, strong nuclear, and electromagnetic forces; the theory of relativity comprehends all macroscopic phenomena and gravitation). And it may be the case that these fundamental theories, or fundamental aspects of them, may require an instrumentalist interpretation (Cartwright, 1983). Second, many of these theories, or aspects of them, may be said to be *systemic* in nature (Ellis, 1985). They were never designed to provide *explanations* by reference to causal processes, but were introduced as (often mathematical) constructs designed to systematize and integrate a whole range of established causal and functional and theoretical laws. It seems fairly clear, for example, that Newtonian point masses were never intended to play a role in any theoretical causal explanation, and that Minkowski "slopes" in relativity theory cannot plausibly be interpreted as making a putative reference to any structural feature of reality (Levin, 1984). Third, there are sometimes good reasons for holding that some theories are observationally incommensurable whatever our technological advances. We may sometimes have good theoretical reasons that explain why, for example, there could be no detectable difference between competing theories of the space-time metric (van Fraassen, 1980).

Thus, it is not claimed that a realist account of theory applies to all theories, or to all aspects of all theories, although neither is it to deny that a realist interpretation can be given for many aspects of fundamental physical theories (Boyd, 1985; Giere, 1985; Levin, 1984). This qualification simply reflects the more modest thesis about theoretical realism advanced in the present volume. It is argued that a realist interpretation provides the best account of theoretical development and evaluation for a great many theories in biology and chemistry, and for some theories (and some aspects of some theories) in physics and astronomy. On the basis of these arguments and examples, a realist account of theory in social psychological science is advanced and defended against some of the standard criticisms.

Theoretical Representation

It was noted earlier that the instrumentalist cannot provide an account of the explanation of causal laws by theory, or the development of theory to generate novel predictions. This is because the instrumentalist holds that theories in essence contain no more information than the sum of their observational consequences, since the meaning of theoretical postulates is essentially specified by the correspondence rules linking theoretical and observation languages. Hempel's notion of a scientific theory as a "partially interpreted calculus" *allows* for the development of theory by the development of new correspondence rules to generate novel predictions. Yet since the theory itself provides no additional information about reality, it is hard to see how it can furnish an explanation of causal or functional laws or be developed in any systematic way.

The realist can provide a rational account of theoretical explanation and development since a theory is held to provide a potentially accurate representation of the real nature of particulars and the mechanisms of causal generation. It provides potentially accurate and useful information about the nature of reality *additional* to the causal and functional laws that it explains. Thus, for example, the powers of acids are explained in terms of their electronic structure and transformations of chemical bonding by transfer of electrons. The power of female anopheles mosquito bites to generate malaria is explained in terms of the transmission of the microorganism plasmodium, and its reaction with blood cells. The heating of a gas generating expansion in the gas is explained by the fact that increasing the kinetic energy of the molecules increases molecular impacts and thus pressure.

On this conception, theoretical explanations are held to function as representations of those entities and structures that provide theoretical explanations of generative causality. When accurate, they make a direct reference to such entities and structures rather than an indirect reference to the causal and functional laws that they are introduced to explain (which is the instrumentalist claim). Indeed, it may properly be said that they directly refer to those causal and functional relations that they are introduced to explain, since they are related to these phenomena via *transformation rules* (Harré, 1970). These rules describe how the theoretical dimensions are *instantiated* in the system to be explained. In natural sciences, this often involves the specification of the composition and structure of the particulars whose causal relations are the object of theoretical explanation, and of the mechanism responsible for such relations. Thus in the kinetic theory it is not simply the case that theoretical propositions containing terms like "mean kinetic energy" are related to "observational" propositions containing terms like "temperature". Rather, the kinetic theory claims that gases are composed of molecules with kinetic energies, and that changes in mean kinetic energies are responsible for empirically discriminable changes in temperature. It is precisely by virtue of these claims that kinetic theory provides an *explanation* of the causal and functional relationships described in the gas laws, since the kinetic theory provides *additional* information about the causal processes responsible for these relationships. It is also precisely because of these claims that theoretical explanations often integrate and unify apparently discrete causal and functional laws.

The scientific empiricist conception of correspondence rules plays a major role in the justification of instrumentalism. But this conception conflates three distinct forms of linguistic relations that may be embodied in an explanatory theory. The scientific empiricist argues that the formal meaning of theoretical postulates is specified by their definitional interrelations with other terms in a theoretical system (Hempel, 1965; Scriven, 1958; Suppe, 1977). The scientific empiricist claims that such theoretical systems alone are empty formalisms. They are only factually meaningful—they only say something significant about reality—when they are related to the observational level by correspondence rules. The observational level is held to confer meaning on theoretical postulates by a process analogous to capillary action (Koergte, 1972), via an "upward seepage" of meaning from the "soil" of observational experience (Feigl, 1970).

According to the realist, theoretical propositions are descriptions of reality. Transformation rules describe how the theoretical dimensions postulated by the theory are instantiated in the systems to be explained. But although transformation rules might appear analogous to correspondence rules, they are not to be identified with them. For transformation rules, unlike correspondence rules, do not specify the factual meaning of the theory.

It may very well be the case that any theoretical term must be relatable to the empirically discriminable, if such a term is to be meaningfully employed in the description of reality. This claim may of course be disputed, but it will be assumed that this is the case for the sake of argument. For it *does not follow that the meaning of theoretical descriptions must be specified via transformation rules (or correspondence rules) that link the theoretical explanans with the causal and functional explananda.* The fact that the meaning of theoretical descriptions is not specified in this way explains why theoretical explanations provide additional information; why two competing theoretical explanations of the same explanada are not equivalent in meaning and need not be evidentially equivalent or incommensurable; and how theoretical descriptions can be developed to generate novel predictions.

According to the realist, the meaning of a theoretical description can be given by the specification of *analogical* relations between the postulated theoretical entities and some other empirically discriminable phenomenon (Harré, 1970). This enables scientists to introduce novel but immediately meaningful theoretical descriptions such as:

. . . electrical charge (on analogy with a charge of gunpowder), electric current (which flows), displacement current in aether (on analogy with electric current in conductors), curvature of space (on analogy with curvature of a sphere), and so on, by continuous steps to the most esoteric terminology of modern physics. (Hesse, 1976, p. 8)

What is known as the *positive analogy* provides the original meaning of the theoretical descriptions, by documenting those aspects of the theoretical system that are represented as analogous to empirically discriminable systems. The kinetic theory was introduced via the representation of gas molecules as analogous in certain specific respects (e.g., exchange of momentum by impact) to macroscopic spheres (like billiard balls) in motion. Bohr's theory of the atom was introduced via the representation of atomic nuclei as analogous to planetary systems.

This conception of theoretical representations or *theoretical models* as analogical or metaphorical extensions of descriptions of empirically discriminable phenomena provides an account of the explanatory force of theories. Theoretical models provide one with an intellectual insight that is more than a integrating redescription of the explananda of a theory. They provide a potentially accurate representation of a system as analogous in specific respects to a different system that is empirically discriminable (Campbell, 1921). The wave theory of light provides an explanation of the laws of reflection and refraction by representing the propagation of light rays as analogous in specific respects to the propagation of ocean waves. The clotting of blood by cholesterol deposits on the walls of blood vessels is explained by representing the flow of blood in blood vessels as analogous to laminar flow and turbulence in an enclosed and narrowed fluid system.

This also explains why a theory may provide an explanation of causal and functional laws but for a long period of time may not be testable. No observations can be made that would establish a theory or discriminate between competing explanations of the same explanada. The Ptolemeic and Copernican theories were inconsistent in their theoretical description of the relative positions and orbits of the planets. They were also inconsistent insofar as the Copernican theory predicted a stellar parallax, which the Ptolemeic theory denied. The particle (Newton) and wave (Huygens) theories of light were inconsistent in their theoretical descriptions of the nature of light; they were also inconsistent insofar as they differed in their predictions about the change in velocity of light moving into a denser medium. But they were empirically equivalent in terms of their discriminable consequences and thus incommensurable for long periods of time, until the development of telescopics enabled scientists to observe the stellar parallax some 150 years after Galileo, and until Foucault created an interferometer which enabled him to measure the velocity of light in air and water.

Since the meaning of theoretical descriptions is not specified by transformation rules (or correspondence rules), competing theories are not equivalent in meaning just because they are empirically equivalent in terms of their discriminable consequences for any period of time. Furthermore, *operational definitions* of a theory cannot be identified either with specifications of its meaning or with the transformation rules exploited in explanations of established causal and functional laws. Operational definitions may be defined as specifications of empirically discriminable phenomena that enable the theory to be tested (either to provide support for the theory additional to the minimal support provided by its accommodation of the explananda, or to provide support for a theory against its rivals).

Sometimes transformation rules can also function as operational definitions, when developments of the theory furnish novel causal or functional predictions. Thus, for example, the transformation rules of kinetic theory enabled the theory to predict that momentum and energy would be conserved in gases. But this cannot be guaranteed. Operational definitions usually specify ways in which the structures or processes described by the theory can be empirically discriminated.

Thus, the Watson-Crick theory of the structure of DNA was tested via predictions of discriminable X-ray diffraction patterns. Given the theory of X-ray diffraction, an operational definition of DNA structure in terms of discriminable X-ray diffraction patterns enabled the Watson-Crick theory to be tested and confirmed. The meaning of the theoretical descriptions employed in the Watson-Crick theory was neither specified by the transformation rules employed in explanation, nor by the operational definitions employed in the testing of the theory. The meaning of the descriptions of double helix structures was derived from descriptions of empirically discriminable double helix structures, such as the physical model built by Watson and Crick at the Cavendish Laboratory in Cambridge. The Watson-Crick theory would have been meaningful even if transformation rules and operational definitions had never been developed. It would have been meaningful and nonexplanatory if transformation rules had not been developed. It would have been meaningful and explanatory but not testable if transformation rules had been developed but not operational definitions.

The realist account of theory also provides an account of theory development and modification. This often proceeds via the development of what is known as the *neutral analogy*, by reference to the postulation of additional specific respects in which the system investigated may also be analogous to the system from which the theoretical model is derived. In the original kinetic theory, gas molecules were represented as exchanging their momentum by impact. The kinetic theory was developed by asking whether momentum and energy are conserved in molecular collisions. Bohr's original theory of the atom, which represented it as a system of orbiting electrons around an atomic nucleus of protons and neutrons, was modified and developed to account for phenomena such as the Zeeman effect that were unexplained in the original theory. The Bohr-Sommerfield theory provided an explanation of the Zeeman effect and the more complicated spectral emissions by supposing that electrons, like planets, rotate on their axes ("electron spin") while traversing orbits round a central nucleus.

OBSERVATION

A realist account of theoretical explanation is not committed to the empiricist equation of the theoretical with the nonobservable. A realist account of theoretical explanation is quite neutral with respect to the question of whether the best theoretical explanation of a generative causal relation will be given in terms of a microscopic or macroscopic explanation, or in terms of phenomena that can be more or less directly observed. For the realist, this is an entirely contingent matter. It is determined by the nature of reality and not by the general form of our theoretical explanations.

There is simply no epistemological justification for the scientific empiricist equation of the theoretical and nonobservable. Maxwell (1963) and Achinstein (1968) have convincingly argued that there is a simple progression from ordinary unaided seeing and hearing to seeing and hearing via microscopes and geiger counters. There is no essential difference *in kind* between seeing with the naked eye and seeing with the naked eye and a microscope.

It is worth noting that this is a direct consequence of the scientific empiricist adoption of physicalism in place of phenomenalism. The original constructivist analysis of discourse about physical and other theoretical objects in logical positivism was based upon an epistemological distinction between our certain knowledge of private sense data and our fallible knowledge of physical and other theoretical objects, to be found in the early phenomenalist version of logical positivism. But this distinction was simply abandoned by scientific empiricists who embraced physicalism. The scientific empiricist committed to physicalism does not claim that our judgments about physical objects are immune from error. Intersubjective agreement is taken to be sufficient grounds for objectivity at the level of observational judgment (Carnap, 1937), despite the possibility of collective delusion (Barrett, 1962). Hempel (1965, p. 127), for example, defines the observable as those features of reality which are "directly and publically observable—that is, whose presence and absence can be ascertained, under suitable conditions, by direct observation, and with good argeement among observers."

If we focus on the requirement of intersubjective agreement about what is observed, then we can say that according to this criterion, we can observe planets through telescopes and cell structures through microscopes (and hear radioactive decay and the depth of the sea via geiger counters and sonar soundings) if observers agree about what can be seen (or heard). The realist would, however, dispute this. For the realist, intersubjective agreement is a consequence and not a criterion of the observable. Intersubjective agreement about what can be observed via an instrument must itself be a product of theoretical and empirical justifications of the accuracy and reliability of the instrument.

If this is the case, then the whole burden of the empiricist distinction falls upon the directness requirement. But this requirement is of no epistemological significance. We cannot suppose that the observable/theoretical or directly observable/indirectly observable marks any difference *in kind*, for the idea that we can have certain knowledge only of observables or directly observables is already denied in physicalism: both our "observational" and "theoretical" judgments are probable at best. Nor can we suppose that a difference in kind can somehow be marked by a difference in degree of justified belief (ignoring the problem of the arbitrary nature of any selected cutoff point). For it far from obvious that our judgments of the existence and properties of objects observed by unaided seeing and hearing are any more accurate or reliable than those made employing sense-extending instruments such as telescopes or microscopes. The scientific empiricist offers no argument for the remarkable assumption that our judgments of the position and diameter of trees and tables are more accurate and reliable than our judgments about the position and diameter of planets and positrons (Musgrave, 1985).

The scientific empiricist cannot justify this claim by appealing to the fact that our perceptual judgments based upon the employment of sense-extending instruments tend to depend upon our theories of what *can be* observed via the use of such instruments. For there is no contrast here with unaided seeing or hearing. Our perceptual judgments based upon the employment of unaided seeing and hearing are equally based upon our theories about what can be seen and heard with the naked eye and ear (Churchland, 1979; Giere, 1985). There is no good reason for supposing that our theories about what can be seen with the naked eye are any less immune from error than our theories about what can be seen through a microscope. Which will require revision or modification depends on the contingent fact of the success or failure of our theories about the realities that may be possible objects of unaided or aided vision, and our theories about the accuracy and reliability of *receptors* such as the human eye and the light and electron microscope.

As a number of writers have stressed (Churchland, 1979; Shapere, 1982), the critical feature of possible objects of scientific knowledge is their *detectability* by suitable receptors, not their observability by humans. Indeed, most of the time natural scientists prefer to employ nonhuman receptors rather than rely on the limited discriminatory capacities of humans. The only reason why our science must ultimately be rooted in the observable is in virtue of the wholly contingent fact that the only receptors we humans have are our sense organs. The readings on the oscilloscope and computer printout must ultimately be read by humans if they are to contribute to science conducted by humans. Although this obviously means that unaided human observation has a special epistemological significance (all human knowledge is ultimately possible because of it), it does not mean that unaided human observation has any privileged or superior epistemic warrant. Our scientific theories about reality would not necessarily be any different or less epistemically warranted if we had been equipped by evolution with electron microscopes instead of (or in addition to) our "naked eyes" (Churchland, 1985). The *causal origin* of these different modes of our epistemic access to reality is of no significance in the assessment of the epistemic warrant of our judgments about reality. The accuracy of any form of representation of reality can be tested and is empirically discriminable so long as the represented reality can be detected by any form of receptor.

THEORY EVALUATION

For the realist, the explanatory claims of a theory can often be confirmed by direct observation. The processes of ocean wave propagation and Brownian motion can be more or less directly observed, as can the mechanics of a clock or an internal combustion engine. All that is required is that the scientific agent position herself appropriately to make the relevant observations. Sometimes intervention is required. The explanation of blood clotting in terms of laminar flow can be established by surgical intervention to display cholesterol deposits on the walls of blood vessels. Sometimes the development of sense-extending instruments is required, with or without intervention. Watson and Crick's theory of the helical structure of DNA and the mechanism of hydrogen bonding was confirmed by Rosalind Franklin's X-ray diffraction photographs.

Critical observations may be defined as observations that are possible only if a theory provides an accurate representation of reality (if the entities putatively described by the theory exist and have the properties attributed to them), or that are not possible if a theory provides an accurate representation of reality. It may be said that the observation of the stellar parallax is a critical observation insofar as this observation is possible only if the Copernican theory provides an accurate representation of reality; it is not possible if the Ptolemeic theory provides an accurate representation of reality. The X-ray diffraction data produced by Rosalind Franklin are possible only if DNA has the structure described by the Watson-Crick theory; they are not possible given other competing theories of the structure of DNA. Scientific theories can be established or refuted when such observations are made.

In this respect it may be said that *transcendental arguments* are employed in the evaluation of scientific theories. This claim, however, requires qualification in a number of ways, for our theoretical knowledge based upon critical observations will always remain provisional in a number of different respects. In the first place, our judgment that certain critical observations are possible only if our theory provides an accurate representation of reality is always made relative to its viable theoretical rivals, which rule out the possibility of such observations. But, of course, it is always possible that a new viable alternative theory will be developed that predicts such observations. Second, since many critical observations are based upon instruments, these observations will themselves depend upon theories about what can be detected by such instruments. If we are forced to revise these theories, then we may be forced to abandon some claims about critical observations. And it is not claimed that it is easy to establish such transcendental arguments on the basis of critical observations.

These epistemic qualifications are integral features of a realist account of science. Realism is not to be equated with *essentialism* (Musgrave, 1986) or *revelationism* (Ellis, 1985). The realist recognizes that certainty can never be achieved in the empirical (as opposed to the purely mathematical) sciences. All knowledge is provisional insofar as it is revisable in principle. But this is not to say that we cannot have good reasons for preferring one theory over another in terms of their representation of reality. And it is to insist that our presently established forms of theoretical knowledge should only be revised when we have critical observations that discriminate in favor of some alternative theory.

It is also important to recognize that some critical observations do not establish one theory over its presently viable rivals. Some extend or restrict the scope of a theory. The detection of viruses extended the scope of the microorganism account of diseases that was previously restricted to bacterial infections. The recent Groczynski-Steele experiment (Steele, 1982), which appeared to suggest that immunological tolerances produced by injecting foreign cells into the developing immune system of newborn animals could be inherited by future generations of offspring, would have clearly demonstrated that the "central dogma" of modern evolutionary genetics (that DNA modifies RNA, but not vice versa) is inaccurate, if it had been successfully repeated. It would not have shown that the genetic theory of Darwinian evolution by natural selection is inaccurate, or even less accurate than previously supposed. It would have simply restricted the scope of this form of explanation of the evolution of biological characteristics, by demonstrating a Lamarckian account of the inheritance of *some* acquired immunological tolerances. This would not have ruled out a neo-Darwinian account of the inheritance of other characteristics. There is no inconsistency or absurdity in supposing that neo-Darwinian and Lamarckian mechanisms both operate in the evolution of biological characteristics.

It should also be noted that many of the critical observations documented above were the product of human agency. They involved interventions in the course of nature to establish the accuracy or inaccuracy of a theory (either in the form of scientists positioning themselves to make the relevant critical observations, or by the creation of controlled experiments or instrumentation). Furthermore, it is often the case that the critical support for a theory comes from the success of interventions based upon the structures and mechanisms putatively represented by the theory. An integral part of the scientist's confidence in the accuracy of a theory often derives from the justified belief that certain interventions would be possible and successful only given the entities, structures, and mechanisms represented by the theory. Conceptual integration of "observation" laws is simply not enough, however economical or mathematically harmonious. A rocket directed to Jupiter based upon the representations of Ptolemeic theory will not reach its destination. The quarantine of yellow fever sufferers and the wearing of protective masks will not be effective against yellow fever for those who live in marshes infested with tiger mosquitos. Microsurgery employing lazers will not be effective (and may be fatal) given an inaccurate topology of brain function.

A putative reference to the "dormative virtue" or "nature" of opium is admittedly an empty explanation until it is filled out by a putative reference to the composition and structure of morphine alkeloids, and the mechanism of analgesia. Like the "unless something interferes" clause in a causal explanation, an initial reference to the "nature" of a theoretical particular is a "promissory note" (Harré & Madden, 1975), to be completed in a concrete fashion by theoretical work. A reference to the alkeloid morphine, and the presence of alkeloid molecule receptor sites in the "pain pathways" of the nervous system, provides a theoretical explanation of the analgesic power of opium. This produces a real advance in knowledge. The theory explains why opiates are effective analgesics. The theory has to be a fairly accurate representation of the structure of morphine alkeloids and the mechanism of analgesia, otherwise the employment of synthetically created morphine alkeloids would not be effective. And we must have a fairly accurate representation of these matters if we are to employ more effective synthetic alkeloids, or deploy nonaddictive alkeloids by synthetic manufacture or by the manipulation of the homeostatic mechanisms of enkephalin production (effectively reversing the process of addiction by temporarily increasing the production of enkephalins).

A more striking example perhaps is our theoretical explanation of tuberculosis. The theoretical representation of the structure of the tubercle bacillus and the mechanism of infection and bacillus production explains both how the tubercle bacillus generates tuberculosis and why an antibiotic such as streptomycin is effective in preventing the development of tuberculosis. Unless the scientist believes that the theory is a fairly accurate representation of the structure of the tubercle bacillus and its mode of operation, he has no idea of how to create an antibiotic that will be effective against the tubercle bacillus. And only if his theoretical account is in fact a fairly accurate representation of the structure and mode of operation of the tubercle bacillus, will the employment of an antibiotic such as streptomycin be effective.

To paraphrase Putnam (1975), it is not only the case that the success of science considered as a predictive discipline would be a "miracle" unless many of our theories were fairly accurate representations of reality. It is also the case that our increasingly more successful technological interventions would be miraculous unless many of our theories were fairly accurate representations of reality. In this sense, realism makes possible all the instrumental achievements of theory. An accurate theory employed by a community of scientists is a practical as well as an intellectual instrument.

THEORETICAL REPRESENTATIONS IN A SCIENCE OF ACTION

A realist approach to theory in a science of action treats theoretical explanations as potentially accurate representations of particulars, structures, and mechanisms of generative causality in the social and psychological domain. There seems little doubt that a science of action would be greatly advanced if social psychological theories were treated by practitioners as potentially accurate representations of reality. Equally, there seems little doubt that the progress that has been achieved has been a result of theorists and experimentalists not practicing their instrumental preachings.

A number of points about a realist account of theory need to be stressed to guard against misinterpretation. Realism in a natural or social psychological science is not equivalent to materialism. Michael Faraday was a realist about lines of electromagnetic force (since cutting these lines produced real electromagnetic effects), but sceptical about material substance. A realist science of action is not committed to the empiricist "unity of science" thesis that social explanations can be reduced to psychological explanations, and psychological explanations reduced to neurophysiological and biochemical explanations. It is not even committed to this as an ideal or goal. Realism is quite *neutral* with respect to the question of whether a social, psychological, or physiological theory provides the best explanation of a human power or liability.

It was noted earlier that physics is the most fundamental science. But it simply does not follow that all phenomena can be given a completely adequate theoretical explanation in terms of physics. There may be fundamental powers on the social or psychological (or biological or chemical) level that cannot be completely explained in terms of physics. The sense in which physics was said to be the most fundamental science is quite different from this.

It is a contingent fact about our reality that it is ontologically stratified with respect to enabling conditions. Physical structures and powers provide enabling conditions for chemical structures and powers; chemical structures and powers provide enabling conditions for biological structures and powers; biological structures and powers provide enabling conditions for human structures and powers; human structures and powers provide enabling conditions for social structures and powers. Because of this contingent fact, a reference to the structures and mechanisms on a lower level of stratification will always be *part* of a theoretical explanation of the powers of entities on a higher level of stratification; it will always be part of an explanation of enabling conditions. Thus, a reference to chemistry will always be part of an explanation of biological powers, and a reference to neurophysiology will always be part of an explanation of human powers.

But it cannot be assumed that our theoretical explanations will simply parallel this ontological stratification. On any ontological level of stratification, there may be powers of chemical, biological, human, or social systems that are *emergent* and cannot be wholly explained by reference to systems on a lower level of ontological stratification. In this respect, they may be as fundamental as the fundamental powers of physical systems described by physics. In fact, our theoretical explanations of some powers may precisely reverse the ontological order of stratification. Many human powers, such as the power of some persons to fail students or sentence the guilty to death, are clearly dependent upon social relations as enabling conditions. Some chemical powers, such as the powers of organic compounds, can only be manifested in biological environments.

Any theoretical explanation proceeds by claiming that the explanatory dimensions described by a theory are *instantiated* in the system to be explained. But this is not of necessity equivalent to an account of the embodiment or incarnation (Margolis, 1984) of a system in the ontological order (although as noted above, there will always be a partial overlap, since embodiment or incarnation will always furnish enabling conditions). Sometimes a reference to the instantiation of dimensions from a lower ontological stratum will furnish a complete theoretical explanation of the powers of systems on a higher ontological stratum. In this case, we have an explanation that provides a theoretical *reduction*. But it is always an empirical question whether any power on any ontological stratum can be explained in this way. It is not conceptually guaranteed by the form of theoretical explanation, and does not furnish a criterion for the adequacy of a theoretical explanation (except in the partial sense noted above).

It must also be stressed that to employ a theoretical analogy is not to assert an identity between the system explained and the source of the analogy. Explanatory theoretical models are *paramorphic* (Harré, 1970): the *source* (e.g., macroscopic objects such as billiard balls) and the *object* (e.g., gas molecules) of the theoretical representation are different. The theoretical representations of kinetic theory ascribe some but not all of the properties of macroscopic physical objects.

It is an entirely legitimate theoretical enterprise to represent many social interactions as analogous to games (Berne, 1970; Scott & Lyman, 1968) or liturgical rituals (Goffman, 1959), many action performances as analogous to the scripted performances of the theater (Goffman, 1959; Harré & Secord, 1972), many intellectual processes as analogous to computer processing (Boden, 1977), and many complex organizations as analogous to savage tribes (Turner, 1977). However, this is not to claim that social interactions *are* games, that human actions *are* theatrical performances, that men *are* computers, or that complex organizations *are* savage tribes. Some interactions cannot be avoided by refusal to participate, most action performances are not reviewed by press critics, computers are never ashamed, and savage tribes do not file income tax returns. An atomic nucleus is analogous to a planetary system and gravitational field, but is neither a planetary system or a gravitational field. Light is analogous to a wave and a particle, but is neither a wave (it is not fully continuous) nor a particle (it is not fully discontinuous). Nor does it mean that a class of interactions or an individual interaction is exclusively analogous, for example, to either a game or a liturgy. It may be analogous to both (it may involve elements of hazard and ritual). Light is something that is analogous to both a wave and a particle.

Now it might be objected that our theoretical references to psychological states such as emotion and motivation provide an exception to this general rule. It might be objected that these references are *homeomorphic*: the source and object of these representations are identical. It might be claimed that our theoretical ascriptions of psychological states to others is based upon an analogy with our own psychological states. But in fact this is not the case. Our theoretical representations of the psychological states of self and others are modeled upon a different class of entities. They are modeled upon some of the properties of propositions in language (Margolis, 1984). Our theoretical descriptions of psychological states ascribe to them specific *intensional contents* and *intentional objects*. Thus, to ascribe anger to Tom or myself is that say that Tom or I represent some action of another (intentional object[1]) as offensive to his or my dignity (intensional content). To ascribe a belief to Tom or myself is to say that Tom or I represent some property or relation as true of some particular or class of particulars.

Theoretical explanations in social psychological science, like the theoretical explanations of natural science, are provided via the employment of transformation rules. Thus, to explain some social interactions (or some aspects of some interactions) such as trade union negotiations by reference to the fact that they are also rituals is to say that these social interactions are instantiations of rituals. It is to claim that the dimensions of ritual are instantiated in the social dimensions of trade union negotiations. To explain some actions as motivated by revenge or reputation management is to say that specific representations of the point and purpose of actions are instantiated in the psychology of some persons.[2]

These social dimensions and representations often do play a role in theoretical explanations of generative causality in social psychological science. In this respect, they are not of a different logical order from the theoretical causal explanations of natural science. This is the brunt of much of the argument of the following chapters. However, it is equally critical to note that the social and psychological phenomena represented by theory in social and psychological science are of a different logical order from the entities described by theories in natural science.

Natural phenomena are constituted by their causal and physical dimensions. Oxygen, for example, is constituted by its causal and functional properties and its physical composition and structure. But social phenomena are largely constituted by social dimensions. Rituals are constituted as rituals by expressions of honor or offense according to a local social convention. Psychological phenomena are largely constituted by psychological dimensions: certain representations are constituted as motives of revenge by their content and object, and by their conceptual location within the agent's represented past biography and future projects. This is itself a consequence of the general argument of the following chapters that most social and psychological phenomena are essentially constituted by social and psychological dimensions, irrespective of whether they are referred to as theoretical explanations or the objects of causal explanations.

PSYCHOLOGICAL THEORY

References to psychological states are held to be especially problematic in social psychological science. In consequence, many theorists have been inclined to adopt an instrumentalist analysis of scientific ascriptions of psychological states. But such operationalist analyses of scientific ascriptions of psychological states are fundamental errors.

It has already been noted that the function of operational definitions in natural science is to describe empirically discriminable situations that provide critical tests for a theory. Operational definitions do not specify the meaning of theoretical descriptions. The meaning of our ascriptions of psychological states to human agents is socially defined in terms of their intensional contents and their intentional objects, modeled on these properties of propositions in language. Thus, to ascribe anger to Tom is, inter alia, to say that he represents some action of another (intentional object) as offensive to his dignity (intensional content). Our ascriptions of psychological states to human agents are meaningful and potentially accurate quite independently of whether they are testable, just as the Copernican and Watson-Crick theories are meaningful and potentially accurate quite independently of their testability. The meaning of psychological ascriptions, like the meaning of theoretical representations in natural science, simply cannot be equated with the explananda that such ascriptions and theories are introduced to explain, or with the empirical discriminations employed to critically test such ascriptions and theories.

Many theorists supportive of the "cognitive revolution" in psychology appear to provide a realist interpretation of psychological theory by treating psychological ascriptions as the positing of "internal states" that cause behavior. On this conception, to attribute anger to Tom is to ascribe to him an internal state capable of producing characteristic behaviors given suitable stimulus conditions.

But although this account does provide particular realist interpretations of particular psychological theories, it is not entailed by a realist account of theory. A realist account of psychological theory is only committed to the thesis that psychological states exist independently of our theoretical representations of them. It is not committed to the thesis that psychological states are constituted by causal dimensions.

A poison is partially constituted by its causal efficacy in generating sickness or death. Consequently, a poison is defined as any entity that will generate sickness or death (Armstrong, 1968). Anything that did not generate sickness or death would not be a poison and would not count as a poison. But to ascribe a psychological state to an agent is not to make any attribution of causal efficacy. It is to ascribe to an agent a representation of natural or social or psychological reality with a specific intensional content and intentional object. To ascribe shame to Tom is to say that Tom represents some action of his (or failure to act) as a personal disgrace. To ascribe a motive of revenge to Jane is to say that Jane represents a contemplated action as a repayment of some prior injury. But an agent may be ashamed, intend to harm another, or harbor a motive of revenge, even if these psychological states have no causal efficacy. The agent may intend to harm another or revenge herself even if she cannot bring herself to harm another or revenge herself, or if she lacks the power or opportunity to do these things (although she must *believe* she has the power to do these things to properly intend them).

This is not to say that references to psychological states cannot function in accurate causal or theoretical explanations. Of course they can and often do *when we make an additional claim about their causal efficacy*. It is rather to stress that the *identity* of psychological states is quite independent of any causal efficacy they may happen to have, and that the meaning of our psychological ascriptions is quite independent of any role such ascriptions may play in our causal and theoretical explanations of human actions.

There is no logical inconsistency or incoherence in supposing that all our psychological states are *epiphenomenal*, even though this supposition is not remotely plausible. But the coherence of this supposition does demonstrate that the identity of psychological states is wholly independent of their causal properties. My decisions would remain *my decisions* even if my decisions were totally ineffectual. There is no logical absurdity in the Freudian claim that most of our conscious and avowed reasons are rationalizations that play no causal role in the generation of human action. But whatever the accuracy of this claim (or whatever the historical accuracy of ascribing this claim to Freud), it remains true that our represented justifications of our actions are *our reasons* for our actions, even if they are not *the* reason for our actions (even if they do not figure in any accurate causal explanations of our actions).

THEORY AND OBSERVATION IN A SCIENCE OF ACTION

The above arguments do not deny the importance of testing the accuracy of our psychological ascriptions when these states are represented as playing a role in our causal and theoretical explanations of action. However, the epistemic problems of identifying the psychological states of agents are grossly overstated in the scientific empiricist and scientific psychological literature. This is largely because of the scientific empiricist equation of the theoretical with the unobservable or not directly observable, and the scientific psychological claim that psychological states are unobservable.

We have noted that it is the concept of detection rather than observation per se that specifies what kind of entities and properties are empirically discriminable in natural science. All empirically discriminable phenomena must ultimately be related to observations because of the contingent fact that humans only receive information about the natural world via the medium of their sense organs.

There is no essential difference with respect to social psychological science. Although there are no sense extending instruments that enable us to empirically discriminate psychological states, nevertheless they can be detected via critical observations that may include agent accounts.

Given our knowledge of social context and biography, we are often in a position to say that an agent would have acted in the way he did only given a specific representation of reality.[3] We can say of Captain Oates that he would have sacrificed his life only if he thought that his action might preserve the lives of others. We can say of the agent who always helps others in represented emergencies (even if she does not represent their welfare as her responsibility) that she would have refrained from acting in this emergency only if she did not represent the situation as an emergency. Very often we are in a situation where we can ask agents about their emotions and motivation. These may be honestly articulated by the agent, and received by the scientific researcher via the sensory media of sound or sight (according to whether such accounts are spoken or written).

This does not mean that a social psychological science based upon realist principles would mark a return to introspective psychology. A realist conception of psychological ascriptions does not entail that human agents have direct and certain knowledge of their psychological states. This particular philosophical dogma has its roots not in realism but in scientific empiricism. It is a peculiar historical irony that the neurotic concern of the scientific psychologist with the "observable" is historically and conceptually based upon the original empiricist thesis that psychological states (sense data) are the only possible objects of observation and knowledge.

A realist account of psychological ascriptions does not even entail that agents can provide generally accurate accounts of their psychological states. This thesis requires independent justification, and a full justification is beyond the scope of this chapter and the present volume. But a number of points are worth making in its defense.

In the first place, much of the scientific psychological scepticism about self-knowledge is just based upon empiricist and behaviorist dogma about the observable. Second, many of the contemporary doubts about self-knowledge are based upon the empirical studies of Nisbett and Wilson (1977) and Nisbett and Ross (1980), which appear to demonstrate that human agents have poor introspective access to their psychological states.

Now it should be noted that most of these studies are not concerned with the identification of psychological states at all. Virtually all the studies documented by these authors are examples of subjects' failure to correctly estimate the causal potency of experimentally manipulated stimuli. But very few theorists have ever claimed that agents can provide authoritative causal accounts of their behavior, and certainly this is not entailed by a realist account of psychological state ascriptions. More important, this evidence of our fallibility with respect to causal judgment would only undermine our general authority with respect to accounts of our own psychological states if we assume that such states are constituted by their causal dimensions, and that our accounts of our psychological states are a species of causal judgment. But this has already been denied.

Only two of the studies documented by Nisbett and Ross (1980) have any bearing upon the authority of agents with respect to their own psychological states. These are the Schachter-Singer experiment (1962) and Bem's studies of attitudes (1967, 1972). But both of these studies at most establish something about the social contextual determinants of agents' judgments about their emotions or attitudes. They say nothing whatsoever about the accuracy of such judgments, because neither provide any independent account of emotion or attitude. It is true that Schachter (1965) does suggest that emotion is itself jointly constituted by physiological arousal and the cognitive labeling of arousal. However, if this were the case (which is doubtful), then error in emotion judgment would be logically precluded. If I constitute my arousal state as anger by labeling it as "anger," then I can never be mistaken.[4]

However, this does not yet get to the heart of the matter. For our contemporary conception of psychological states and self-knowledge is still burdened by classical Cartesian and empiricist conceptions of psychological states as mysterious "inner states," and self-knowledge as a form of internal monitoring or perception.

Part of the problem is the historical empiricist assimilation of sensation and cognition. But an emotion such as shame, for example, is not analogous to a sensation such as pain. Nor is our knowledge of our shame analogous to our knowledge of our pain. Our pains occur independently of semantic representation, and we come to make correct identifications of our pain when we learn to successfully employ the publically meaningful word *pain*. But emotions and analogous psychological states do not occur independently of semantic representation. Shame does not just occur in us prior to our social learning of the usage of the word *shame*. Rather, we have to learn to *be* ashamed: we have to learn to represent certain of our actions (or failures to act) as personally degrading and humiliating.

Characteristically human emotions may be said to be socially constituted insofar as they are socially learned (and negotiated) representations of social reality. They are constituted by socially meaningful intensional contents directed upon intentional objects. Analogously, our beliefs about the natural and social and psychological world are constituted as beliefs by socially learned forms of representation of the nature of reality.

Our self-knowledge of emotion, motivation, and belief is not a mysterious form of inner perception or monitoring of internal states. Rather, it is knowledge of the intensional content of our representation and evaluation of natural, social, and psychological reality. Thus, for example, I know that I am ashamed when I recognize that I represent certain actions of mine (or failures to act) as personally degrading and humiliating. I do not more clearly recognize my shame, my motive of revenge, or belief that the value of the dollar will fall by looking inwards, as the poets say. Rather, I sharpen my knowledge by focusing upon the meaningful way I represent reality. Contra Churchland (1979), self-knowledge is not analogous to theory-informed perception. Rather, it is analogous to my knowledge of the theories I accept which sometimes do inform my perception. Self-knowledge cannot be a form of cognitive monitoring of psychological states, for such monitoring would only tell us the intensional content of our representation of our psychological states, not the intensional content of our representation of the realities to which our psychological states are intentionally directed.

This is not to claim that self-knowledge is sacrosanct. But it is to claim that agents generally can provide authoritative articulations of their psychological states, since our success in the social learning of intensional content is precisely what enables us to have emotions, motivations, and beliefs. The supposition that errors in agent accounts of intensional content are the rule rather than the exception is not just improbable, it is scarcely intelligible. This would be like supposing that agents are regularly mistaken with respect to their beliefs about what they mean by their linguistic utterances, that their interpretation of what they mean by their declarations, commands, and requests is regularly mistaken (Davidson, 1984). But this is absurd because our successful social learning of intensional content is precisely what enables us to master language.[5]

Finally, it should be noted that psychological states *must* be empirically discriminable if social psychological science is to be possible. This is not merely because psychological states sometimes legitimately function in causal and theoretical explanations, but because human actions and social practices that form the explananda of social psychological science are themselves partially constituted by psychological states via agents representations of their point and purpose. In this context, it is perhaps worth noting that self-knowledge of emotion and motivation is logically identical to knowledge of what one is doing. Thus, my knowledge that I am being aggressive is knowledge that my behavior is directed toward the injury of another. It is knowledge of the intensional content of my representation of my behavior. This provides a final reason for rejecting sceptical doubts about self-knowledge. Self-knowledge in this sense is a precondition for nonchaotic social interaction. It is "the very ontological condition of human life in society" (Giddens, 1974).

THEORY EVALUATION IN A SCIENCE OF ACTION

There is no reason in principle why transcendental arguments cannot be employed to establish theoretical explanations in social psychological science in the same qualified way that they can be employed in natural science. We can say, for example, that hysterical aphasias that reveal under hypnosis strong guilt feelings about a deceased mother would only be possible given the meaningful symptoms and repression described by Freudian theory. We can say that the cognitive dissonance account of attitude change cannot be accurate if agents change their attitudes without cognitive dissonance, or retain their attitudes despite cognitive dissonance. Analogously, we can say that a form of psychotherapy such as systematic desensitization will only be more effective in the treatment of phobias than other therapies (or control treatments) based upon other theories if phobias are the product of conditioning. We can say that a theory postulating invariant states of intellectual development cannot be accurate if educational interventions enable children to achieve intellectual skills long before they are theoretically possible.

Again, not all critical observations will establish that a theory is accurate or inaccurate. Some will extend or restrict the scope of a theory. There is no absurdity or contradiction in supposing that some instances of attitude change are produced by cognitive dissonance and others by rational persuasion; that some phobias are produced by conditioning and others via the defense mechanisms of sexual repression; or that some instances of bystander apathy are a product of failures of social perception of emergencies or personal responsibility, others a product of social anxiety, others still a reflection of the total disregard of some persons for the welfare of others. Only a dogmatic empiricist commitment to theories as unifying and integrating fictions would lead one to suppose otherwise. It will be noted presently that there are good reasons for anticipating such a multiplicity of causal and theoretical explanations in social psychological science.

The same reflections apply equally to the social dimensions of human action. The dimensions of ritual can be empirically discriminated in the forms of interaction and accounts of soccer hooligans (Marsh, Rosser, & Harré, 1978) and high court judges. The social relations of family and workplace can be empirically discriminated via social histories and social accounts of their conventions. The social rules of the Bedouin and the bedroom may be discriminated via the socially articulated sanctions against their violation. The implicit rules of familial interactions may be revealed through the disruption created by their violation (Garfinkel, 1967). Many of the theoretically articulable rules (again based upon the linguistic analogy) governing the syntax rather than the semantics of social interaction cannot be articulated by agents participating in such interactions, but they can be discriminated via their identification of artificially created sequences as anomolous (Clarke & Crossland, 1985). If the above discussion has tended to focus almost exclusively upon the ascription of psychological states, it is simply because these have been the traditional object of epistemic concern in social psychological science.

With respect to social psychological theories, there seems no reason in principle for supposing that competing theories are bound to be evidentially equivalent and observationally incommensurable. We have noted that such an argument cannot be based upon the mere fact that competing explanations share a common explanada. And the arguments advanced in favor of this thesis are not very convincing. Greenwald (1975) has claimed that this is the case with respect to the theoretical conflict between cognitive dissonance and self-perception theories. These theories are incommensurable alright, but not for the reasons commonly supposed. They are incommensurable because on a realist interpretation they are concerned with different explananda. The cognitive dissonance theory is about attitude change. The self-perception theory is about the determinants of attitude avowals. Although attitude avowals may sometimes be accurate descriptions of attitudes, they are not identical to them according to a realist analysis. It cannot be assumed that explanations of changes in our attitude avowals will always be identical to explanations of changes in our attitude. Some agents may change their avowals of their attitudes toward black persons and women, but not their attitudes.

Sometimes the claim about evidential equivalence and incommensurability is based upon familiar claims about the theory informity of observations. This argument is rejected in the following section with respect to natural science and in the following chapters with respect to social psychological science. Nevertheless, many theories in social psychological science are incommensurable in a critical respect which constitutes perhaps the greatest historical irony. They are incommensurable because of the inadequacy of operational definitions.

The problems of causal explanatory and theoretical social psychological science are not the problems of applying the realist logic of causal and theoretical explanation and empirical evaluation to the phenomena of human action. The general philosophical problem about social psychological science is the scientific psychological misconception of the essential nature and *identity* of social psychological phenomena. The practical problems of social psychological science derive from a general failure to establish the identity not only of the putative explanans but also of the explananda apparently isolated in laboratory experiments, field experiments, participant observation, developmental studies, and evaluations of psychotherapy.

These problems are a direct function of the scientific psychological conception of the empirically discriminable as restricted to the "observable" behavior or movements of human beings. The irony is that it is precisely this narrow conception of operational definitions that precludes the effective identification of human actions in experiments (or other forms of evaluation) designed to test theoretical and causal explanations of human actions. Since most human actions and social practices are partially constituted by agent representations, any operational definition of human actions and social practices must enable these psychological dimensions to be discriminated. These psychological dimensions must be reproduced and empirically discriminated in any empirical study designed as an evaluation of causal or theoretical explanations of human actions and social practices.

Observation and Theory

The greatest threat to a realist account of objectivity in science is posed by the doctrines of the theory informity of observations and the Quine-Duhem thesis, and the consequent relativist claims that competing theories are observationally incommensurable and evidentially equivalent. The initial plausibility of these *neo-empiricist* claims derives from an inaccurate and distorted conception of the relation between theory and observation that is derived from classical forms of scientific empiricism.

The doctrine of the theory informity of observations is held to provide support for a thesis about the *radical underdetermination* of theory by observational data by stressing what is held to be a particularly intimate and constitutive relation between theory and observation. A scientific-theory is held to be analogous to a gestalt that organizes the material of perception within the gestalt. In contrast, the Quine-Duhem thesis is often held to support a similar claim about radical underdetermination by emphasizing the supposedly tenuous nature of the link between theory and observation. It is claimed that theories only make contact with observations via a "network" of auxiliary hypotheses and theories. Although the implications of these theses have been much debated, most commentators simply assume that theoretical accommodations of recalcitrant data *can* always be made, by reinterpreting the evidence in terms of the theory or by the modification of auxiliary hypotheses and theories.

The increasingly popular philosophical conception of scientific theories involves the representation of a "web of belief" (Quine & Ullian, 1970), with scientific theories at the center of the web protected from direct falsification by a series of auxiliary hypotheses and theories that link the theory with observational descriptions at the periphery of the web. This conception is perhaps most explicit in Lakatos's (1970) account, in which scientific theories may be saved from falsification by the "protective belt" of auxiliary hypotheses and theories that "surround" the "hard cores" of research programs.

This conception of scientific theories is just a development of the traditional scientific empiricist account, in which theoretical postulates are held to be linked to observations by a system of correspondence rules. Since such observations are held to be explained by the deduction of their descriptions from the system of theoretical postulates plus correspondence rules, it is clear that such correspondence rules are supposed to be designed to ensure a "goodness of fit" between theory and observation.

The neo-empiricist who accepts the Quine-Duhem thesis simply develops an apparent implication of this model: correspondence rules or auxiliary hypotheses[6] can always be modified or replaced to accommodate recalcitrant observational data. Those who argue for the theory informity of observation also accept this empiricist model but reverse its traditional semantic implications. In the traditional account, the observational level of science is held to confer meaning on theoretical postulates by a logical process analogous to capillary action. According to Kuhn, Hanson, and Feyerabend the situation is precisely reversed: observations derive their significance by interpretation according to some theory (Brown, 1977).

THE STRONG PROGRAM IN SOCIOLOGY OF SCIENCE

Some relativists seem to suggest that since the concepts employed in theoretical accounts of reality are not themselves directly abstracted from reality in the manner of our concepts of "blue" and "table," then they cannot be employed as descriptive representations of reality. The strongest version of this account is to be found in Gergen (1982, 1985), who distinguishes between what he calls the *exogenic* and the *endogenic* perspectives (which are loosely identified with the philosophical positions of empiricism and rationalism). According to the exogenic perspective, knowledge is grounded in an observable reality that exists independently of our thought. According to the endogenic perspective, knowledge is grounded in human thought.

Of course, Kant showed that both were necessary, and that the constructive activity of scientific theorizing does not empirically vouchsafe any particular scientific theory. Furthermore, we have already noted that it is quite wrong to suppose that a scientific theory cannot be employed in a directly referential manner and be tested by empirical discriminations of reality, just because the meaning of theoretical descriptions is not derived from the empirically discriminable features of reality which they are introduced to explain, or from the empirically discriminable features of reality which are employed in the testing of the theory.

The Watson-Crick theory is meaningful because it ascribes a structure to DNA that is analogous to the structure of empirically discriminable physical models. Although its meaning is not abstracted from the phenomena that it is introduced to explain, it makes reference to the real structure of DNA, and the accuracy of its representations can be tested by further empirical discriminations even though the meaning of such representations is not abstracted from these discriminations. To suppose that the exogenic and endogenic perspectives are exclusive is to accept the most extreme form of meaning empiricism: that the source and object of meaningful concepts must be identical for objectivity to be possible. But our previous discussion of theory has shown this thesis to be demonstrably false.

Nor does the fact that most theories are social in origin, or that some theories are expressions of contemporary ideologies, itself undermine the objectivity of theoretical science. No doubt the Greek astronomers were influenced by their common cultural belief that the circle is the most perfect geometrical shape when they represented the motion of the planets as circular. But they quickly realized that this system of representation would not work, and adopted the complicated system of epicycles. Copernicus and Kepler also had an affection for circular orbits. But Kepler tried for about 10 years to represent the orbit of Mars as essentially circular and was eventually forced to abandon the project. Despite the possible origin of the Ptolemeic theory in deistically inspired beliefs about man and earth as the center of the universe, the theory was eventually demonstrated as inaccurate and abandoned, despite continued theological antagonism.

There is no doubt at all that sometimes scientific communities and individual scientists are influenced in their judgments by sociological and social psychological factors. No doubt Semmelweis would have been more successful in his propagation of the germ theory of disease if he had not been an antagonistic Hungarian Jew with a rather turgid prose style. No doubt Milikan's published presentation of his measurement of the charge on the electron would have been less successful if he had not neglected to mention the (intentionally) excluded data that supported Ehrenhaft's rival theory of sub-electrons (Holton, 1981). No doubt the intellectual climate was sympathetic to Darwinism in the late 19th century and hostile to field theories in the 18th century. But these and other examples are insufficient to establish the thesis of the strong program in the sociology of science (Barnes, 1977; Bloor, 1976): that the consensual decisions of theoretical scientists (and their disagreements) *can only be explained* in terms of social and psychological factors *extrinsic* to the avowed logic of theory evaluation by reference to empirical discriminations of reality.

There are, of course, all kinds of social factors that are *intrinsic* to the scientific enterprise (a shared language, effective communication, financial support for scientific institutions, the social valuation of scientific work, etc.), which enable scientific knowledge to be produced, and which promote and maintain the intellectual and experimental endeavors of working scientists. This is a proper object of social psychological research. But we are only obliged to accept the thesis of the strong program in the sociology of science if we are already committed to the thesis that the consensual theoretical judgments of scientists cannot be rationally based upon critical observations that support or refute a theory. That is, the thesis of the strong program in the sociology of science is itself based upon the relativist claims that scientific theories are radically underdetermined by observations, and that competing theories are observationally incommensurable and evidentially equivalent. Thus, the strong program is undermined if we have good grounds for rejecting the relativist arguments in favor of these claims.

THE THEORY INFORMITY OF OBSERVATION

Hanson and Kuhn are perhaps correct to criticize the traditional empiricist account of perception as the passive reception of sense data. They claim in contrast that perception is *active* and *constructive*.[7] This claim is not novel, and is historically associated with Kant. But it does not obviously follow from the supposed fact that perception is active that it must also involve cognitive construction according to theories. Gibson (1979), for example, tries to provide an account of perception that is active but *not* constructive. This issue has been much debated (Heft, 1982; Heil, 1979; Reed & Jones, 1981). Yet even if perception does involve theoretical construction, it does not obviously follow that there is any threat to objectivity. For some of these theoretical constructions may turn out to be accurate and others inaccurate, in precisely the same fashion as our constructed theories about the charge on the electron or the structure of DNA.

If the postulated theoretical component in perception is to pose any threat to objectivity, it must be the case (at least) that such theories are *constitutive* of observation. This is precisely what Kuhn and Feyerabend do claim when they liken a scientific theory to a gestalt structure: scientific theory organizes our observations in the way a gestalt structure organizes the elements of perception. According to this account, the *identity* of observations is determined by their theoretical interpretation, in precisely the same way that the elements of perception derive their identity from their location within the gestalt structure (according to gestalt theory).[8]

The gestalt analogy does not appear to obviously hold true with respect to scientific theories and observation. We can observe cells under a microscope without any theoretical knowledge of the nature of the cell or microscopy. As Hacking (1983) notes, the early pioneers of the microscope who observed cells through microscopes had no real idea of how the microscope worked and little theoretical knowledge of cells. Yet generations of practitioners have made the same observations of cells through changes in the theory of the cell and the theory of the microscope. Nor is it obvious that those observations that are the object of scientific explanations must be interpreted in terms of some theory. One does not need to represent smallpox as generated by a virus or "miasma" or by hereditary factors to observe cases of smallpox. One does not need to represent light as wave-like or particulate (or both) in nature in order to observe the reflection and refraction of light. And it would be hard to imagine how we could ever provide illuminating theoretical explanations of such phenomena if this were in fact the case.

To these criticisms it might be objected that such observations are of little epistemic value in the assessment of scientific theories. It is doubtful if this is in fact the case. The observation of the presence or absence of small-pox under various conditions, such as the vaccination of persons or animals, certainly appears to have epistemic significance with respect to the evaluation of the microorganism theory of the disease. Nevertheless, the neo-empiricist critic is correct to stress that many of the epistemically significant observations of science are based upon theories. Furthermore, there is an important respect in which it is true to say that "what we observe" is *partially constituted* by our theories. Theories often serve as *necessary* enabling conditions for observation, in conjunction with whatever is held to be the "raw data" of observation. However, this poses no threat to objectivity because "what we observe" is never *wholly constituted* by our theories. Theories never serve as *sufficient* conditions for observation (in conjunction with whatever is held to be the "raw data" of perception).

To make this clear, we should distinguish between two senses of the expression "what we observe." This may refer to the *intentional object* [9] or *intensional content* of observation. The *intentional object* of observation may be defined as the object or state of affairs that is the real object of our successful perceptual discrimination. The intentional object of observation exists quite independently of any theories we may have about it, and our theories about it and observation of it play no role in its constitution. The intentional objects of our observations of dung beetles and neutrinos are dung beetles and neutrinos, which exist quite independently of our theories about them and observations of them. Furthermore, we may be said to observe dung beetles and neutrinos if we can perceptually discriminate the small crawling creatures which are dung beetles and the tracks in a cloud chamber which are the tracks of neutrinos. We do not need to recognize *that* they are dung beetles or the tracks of neutrinos. When we describe or report the intentional object of observation, we naturally characterize it in terms that most readily identify it for our projected audience, *not* in terms that most readily identify it for the person who made the original observation. Thus, we can truly say of the child that she saw the mayor in the park and a lion at the zoo, even if she did not recognize *that* it was the mayor or a lion. We can say of Fleming and Röntgen that they observed the action of penicillin and X rays long before they came to recognize *that* it was the action of penicillin and X rays.

The *intensional content* of observation may be defined as the information gleaned about reality in the process of our observation of it. It refers not to a physical object or states of affairs, but to a propositional content expressed in a "that" clause. In this sense, we talk about Thomson observing *that* cathode rays are negatively charged. Now it is certainly true that the intensional contents of many observations in science are *partially* constituted by the observer's background beliefs and theories. This is true insofar as these background beliefs *enable* us to make scientific sense of many of the intentional objects of observation. Thus, it is generally true that an agent cannot be said to observe that X is the case unless he has the appropriate background knowledge of what it is for something to be an X and how it can be recognized (how it normally appears). The atomic physicist cannot be said to observe that there are negatively charged particles in the discharge tube unless he knows that there are charged plates in the tube and that negatively charged particles are deflected by them in a specific direction.

It is also true that it is precisely these intensional contents that have epistemic significance in the evaluation of many scientific theories. However, the background beliefs and theories employed in our observations are only *partially* constitutive of the intensional content of our observations. They are not *wholly* constitutive of intensional content. The employment of such background beliefs and theories is a necessary *enabling* condition for making the relevant observations, but it is *never* a sufficient condition.

Having the appropriate background beliefs and theories is a necessary enabling condition for observing that there are negatively charged particles in the discharge tube, but not a sufficient condition. An agent only observes that there are negatively charged particles in the discharge tube if there are negatively charged particles in the discharge tube (the intentional objects of her perceptual discrimination). If there are no negatively charged particles but there appear to be so because of some fault in the apparatus, the agent neither observes negatively charged particles (intentional object) or that there are negatively charged particles (intensional content).

Background beliefs and theories are never wholly constitutive of the intensional content of observation because background beliefs and theories may simply be wrong, and appearances may be deceptive. Priestley did not observe that phlogiston was given off in combustion and Brahe did not observe that the sun was moving. Despite employing essentially the same background beliefs and theories as those employed in the observation that X rays are diffracted through crystals, Blondlot did not observe that N rays could be polarized and refracted through a quartz prism, because there are no such things.[10]

Now it might be objected that the force of the above claims is based upon a contingent peculiarity of the ordinary language term *observes*. In normal usage, *observes* is a "success" or "achievement" word. Furthermore, it might be objected that the "success" of any particular observation can only be determined relative to our best current ontological theories about the intentional objects of our observations. Our judgments about "what we observe" are necessarily informed by what we hold to be our best current theories (Brown, 1977; Churchland, 1979; Putnam, 1981). In consequence, observers committed to different current theories will make different observations informed by different theories. Thus, in Hanson's (1958) example of Brahe and Kepler watching the sun at dawn, Brahe is bound to conclude that he sees a moving sun, and Kepler is bound to conclude that he sees a stationary sun.

Two points must be stressed in reaction to these objections. In the first place, the whole point of the previous discussion is that significant observation *is* very often a theory-informed achievement. The logic of the term *observe* is not a linguistic accident. We are very often only able to make a particular observation given certain theories: we need to have a theory about how charged particles behave in discharge tubes in order to observe them. Second, although it is true that our currently accepted ontological beliefs are (or ought to be) determined by our best theories, the observations that confirm our best theories *do not generally presuppose them*. The observations that confirm our best current explanatory theories are informed by *quite different theories* that enable us to make the critical observations that establish our best current explanatory theories. The theory informity of observation would only pose a threat to objectivity if observations are *necessarily* informed by the explanatory theory (or theories) that is (or are) the object of observational evaluation. Although it may sometimes be the case that observations do presuppose the theory that is the object of evaluation, it is patently not *necessarily* or even regularly the case (Feigl, 1970). Explanatory theories are frequently demonstrated by reference to observations informed by other previously established theories, which may be usefully characterized as *exploratory theories*, since they *enable* scientists to make observations that are critical in the evaluation of *explanatory theories*.[11]

Our present belief (which is admittedly based upon our present theories) that Brahe did not observe a moving sun (or that the sun moved) would only be epistemically suspect if the theories employed in making the observations that undermined the geocentric theory themselves presupposed the inaccuracy of the geocentric theory and the accuracy of the rival heliocentric theory. But the theories of light transmission and telescopics employed in the observation of the stellar parallax presupposed neither the accuracy or inaccuracy of either the geocentric or heliocentric theories.

The X-ray diffraction data on the structure of the DNA molecule were certainly theory informed. The observations made by Rosalind Franklin were based upon the theory of X-ray diffraction, which enabled scientists to make observations of crystalline structures. This theory did not itself presuppose the accuracy of the Watson-Crick model of the structure of DNA, any more than it presupposed the inaccuracy of the alternative models advanced by Linus Pauling or Maurice Wilkins (and many others). Why otherwise did Watson and Crick go to such elaborate lengths to get hold of Rosalind Franklin's most jealously guarded data[12] if, as Kuhn and Feyerabend suggest, they could simply be accommodated according to their own or Pauling's theoretical interpretation? The answer is surely because they could *only* be accommodated by the Watson-Crick model (and not by any other extant model).

The basic point may alternatively be expressed by stressing a significant difference between the two kinds of examples employed by neo-empiricists to support their claim that observations are theory informed. The first set of examples are the ambiguous figures drawn from gestalt psychology, such as the duck-rabbit figure popularized by Wittgenstein (1953) and Hanson (1958). In these examples, the usual additional information required to make a successful perceptual discrimination is intentionally left out, and the line drawings can be interpeted in a variety of different ways.

Notice that in these cases, although it can be said that an observer may see the line drawing *as* a duck or a rabbit, it cannot be said that any observer sees *that* it is a duck or a rabbit (since it is neither a duck or a rabbit). Lest it be thought that this claim depends upon the peculiar fact that the object of observation is in this particular example itself a representation, it should be noted that precisely the same is true of an observer who sees the shadowed head of an animal in a darkened barn. Although the observer can see the shadowed head *as* the head of a rabbit (or a duck or some other animal), she can only be said to observe *that* it is a rabbit when she has sufficient perceptual information to discriminate between rabbits and other animals (she sees the body in the light, or the shadow of whiskers and bob tail, etc.).

Kuhn and Feyerabend want to claim that the observational situation in science is analogous to the ambiguous figures of gestalt psychology. Observations informed by and apparently supportive of one theory can always be accommodated via interpretation by a rival theory. Competing theorists can always see an observation *as* supportive of their theory by interpreting it in terms of their theory. Thus, the Brahe-Kepler example is treated as analogous to the duck-rabbit figure: the observation of the sun can be interpreted according to either theory.

Let us call this postulated form of theoretical interpretation *theory informity₁*. It embodies the claim that observations can always be interpreted according to explanatory theories that are the object of observational evaluation. It is now important to notice that this claim does not provide an argument supporting the familiar thesis about the incommensurability of competing theories. To make the claim that observation in science is analogous to the observation of the ambiguous figures of gestalt psychology is simply to beg the question about the incommensurability of theories. That is, it *presupposes* that observations can never be made that enable us to objectively discriminate between competing theories. For only if this is the case, is it true that observations can always be interpreted according to different competing theories. The general argument about theory informity₁ is itself *based* upon the incommensurability thesis, *and does not provide any independent support for it.*

Furthermore, the second set of examples employed by neo-empiricists to support claims about theory informity have an entirely different implication. Far from suggesting the incommensurability thesis, they illustrate how it is often *not* possible to interpret certain observations as supportive of particular theories. The examples of Polanyi (1958) and Duhem (1906) about the observation of lung-tissue scars on X-ray plates and the observation of fluctuations in electrical resistance make the point that we often need independently supported *exploratory theories* in order to make observations that are critical in the evaluation of explanatory theories. Such theories enable us to see *that* there is a scar on the lung tissue and *that* there is a fluctuation in electrical resistance. We must have theories about how lung tissue scars appear on X-ray plates and how electrical resistance manifests itself in an electrical circuit in order to evaluate theories *about* pulmonary diseases and electrical resistance.

Let us call this form of intepretation in terms of exploratory theories *theory informity*$_2$. Now it is important to notice that the employment of exploratory theories does not undermine objectivity by *creating* incommensurability. On the contrary, the employment of exploratory theories is responsible for the observational *mensurability* and *commensurability* of competing explanatory theories. It enables scientists to make critical observations supporting one theory over its rivals. Incommensurability is not a *necessary* product of theory informity$_2$. Rather, incommensurability is often a *contingent* and *temporary* product of the *absence* of theory informity$_2$. It is a product of the absence (or temporary poverty) of exploratory theories at certain historical periods.

Prior to the development of X-ray diffraction, competing theories of the crystalline structure of proteins were observationally incommensurable, because it was not possible for anyone to make the observation *that* a protein had one particular structure rather than another. During this period, competing theorists could see the observational data as manifestations of their postulated theoretical structures. After the development of X-ray diffraction techniques, Rosalind Franklin and Watson and Crick could observe *that* DNA has the structure of a double helix, and no one who accepted the theory and techniques of X-ray diffraction could see the results *as* evidence for any other structure.

Contrary to most neo-empiricist accounts,[13] *seeing as* is not a special case of *seeing that*. Seeing as is usually a case of *not being able to see that*. Because of the poverty of the theory and technology of telescopics at the time, both Brahe and Kepler could see the sun *as* moving and stationary, respectively. Brahe could not see *that* the sun was rotating round the earth because it does not. Kepler could not see *that* the sun was stationary because he was not able to. Only the development of the theory and technology of the telescope *enabled* later scientists to do that.[14]

Seeing that is a theoretical achievement based upon exploratory theories. Our ability to observe—and consequently our ability to discriminate between competing theories—increases with the development of exploratory theories. As Shapere (1982, p. 153) notes, a developing science " . . . *learns how* to observe nature, and its ability to observe increases with increasing knowledge . . . . " This is especially true in advanced physical sciences based upon sophisticated instrumentation. Most observations employed in the evaluation of advanced theories in modern physical sciences are based upon assumptions about the effectiveness of experimental interventions and the accuracy of measurements generated by these procedures. Observations of planets through telescopes and nerve cells through microscopes depend upon the general assumptions that telescopes magnify distant objects and microscopes magnify minute bodies. Specific calculations of the position of planets and the diameter and charge of nerve cells depend not only upon these general assumptions, but also upon specific and detailed theories of light transmission and magnification in telescopes and microscopes.

This is an epistemological point of some importance, which is quite independent of the psychological question of whether perception is itself active or passive, direct or constructive, atomistic or gestalt governed. It does nothing to undermine traditional concepts of objectivity with respect to theory evaluation. On the contrary, it demonstrates that the employment of exploratory theories—theory informity$_2$—*promotes* objectivity in the observational evaluation of competing theories.

Given this argument, the only way that the theory informity$_2$ of observations could be held to undermine objectivity is by supposing that an explanatory theory can always accommodate recalcitrant observations by modifying or rejecting exploratory theories. But if this is the case, then the neo-empiricist argument for the theory informity$_1$ of observations and the incommensurability of theories is seen to be ultimately based upon the Quine-Duhem thesis.

THE QUINE-DUHEM THESIS

The version of the Quine-Duhem thesis that provides apparent support for the thesis about the inevitable evidential equivalence of competing theories involves the claim that any potentially recalcitrant observations can *always* be accommodated by the modification or replacement of auxiliary hypotheses employed in the application and evaluation of explanatory theories. There is good reason to doubt this claim with respect to exploratory theories employed in epistemically significant observations.

It is sometimes said, for example, that Prout's hypothesis about integral atomic weights could accommodate the deviant weight of chlorine at 35.5 g/g atom, by treating this as a case of experimental error due to imperfect techniques of chemical separation and purification. In fact, various committees in England and France spent many man-hours in laborious and painstaking purifications of samples of chlorine—to no avail. The atomic weight of chlorine never came close to 35 or 36 (Hacking, 1983). Worse still for this form of attempted accommodation, the weights attained did not vary much, as would be expected if the deviance was due to experimental error. Purified chlorine consistently produced a weight in close approximation to 35.5. The experimental measurement was successfully repeated. There was no indication at all of experimental error.

Consider the consequences of supposing that separation and purification techniques were unreliable. If that were the case, then measurements of the atomic weights of other elements, which produced approximately integral values and provided the *original support* for Prout's hypothesis, would also have to be dismissed as unreliable. Either such techniques were reliable or they were not. If they were not, Prout's hypothesis could not be tested by critical observations, and the original observations in support of the theory would have to be abandoned. If they were, the systematically deviant weight of chlorine demonstrated that something was seriously wrong with Prout's hypothesis. Many scientists in the 19th century dumped Prout's hypothesis for this perfectly good reason.

Or consider Hanson's example of the microscopic observation of a Golgi body. It is true that a scientist could dismiss a microscopic observation as "a cluster of foreign matter, a coagulum resulting from faulty staining techniques" (Hanson, 1958). Yet it cannot be so readily dismissed if the preparation is carefully and systematically repeated by experimentalists who are practiced in the art of staining. To persist in such dismissal in the face of such reproductions is to question the experimental techniques of preparation and staining. This is in effect to abandon an effective intervention technique for evaluating theoretical claims about microscopic particulars and structures. It is also to abandon any prior microscopic support for alternative theories of microscopic particulars and structures.

These examples, which are generally employed to demonstrate or illustrate the incommensurability of competing theories, in fact suggest two critical points that must be noted when considering the evaluation of theories by critical observations. The first is that although it is always possible to dismiss a single observation as inadequate in some form, it is not so easy to dismiss a series of critical observations, or carefully reproduced examples of the same critical observation. The second point is that with respect to the evaluation of explanatory theories, there is usually a set of exploratory theories about interventive techniques and instruments, which cannot be seriously questioned without undermining the prior support for the explanatory theory, based upon precisely these techniques and instruments.

The deviant motion of Mercury's perihelion showed that something was fundamentally wrong with Newton's theory. By the end of the 19th century most astronomers knew that (but they had nothing better to replace it until Einstein). They could not accommodate this anomaly by postulating the existence of another planet (as they had previously accommodated the deviant orbit of Uranus by postulating the existence of Neptune), because no new planet could be observed in the required position. It is true that astronomers could have easily dismissed a single deviant observation of the orbit of Mercury's perihelion, since the astronomer might have been young and inexperienced or old and tired. But carefully repeated telescopic observations of the same anomaly could not be so readily dismissed. Any attempt to accommodate such an anomaly by questioning the reliability of contemporary telescopic observations would have been counterproductive. It would have completely undermined most of the previous support for the theory based on telescopic observations. Or, if it were supposed that there was a systematic error due to intrinsic limitations of the telescope, or if a different exploratory theory was introduced, this would have created new observations that would have falsified Newton's theory (it would produce different values for telescopically calculated positions and diameters, etc.). The adoption of such strategies would make the theory *rapidly degenerating*.

Many theories do become rapidly degenerating and are abandoned by scientists. The phlogiston theory claimed that the substance phlogiston is lost on combustion. It was observed that some metals do in fact lose weight on combustion. Guyton de Morveau later demonstrated that some metals gain weight upon combustion. To have "accommodated" this anomaly by supposing that phlogiston has "negative weight" (as some theorists suggested) would have transformed the originally supporting instances into equally serious anomalies. Lavoisier introduced the theory that combustion is due to the fixation or combination of oxygen in the air with the burning substance (heat and light are products of gaseous oxygen rather than the inflammable substance phlogiston). Lavoisier demonstrated gains and losses of oxygen in different metalic combustions. The phlogiston theory was abandoned.

It is important to notice the formal similarity of all these examples. The critical observations could not be accommodated by abandoning or modifying the exploratory theories on which they depended, because the prior observational support for the explanatory theory also depended upon these exploratory theories. The dependence of observation upon exploratory theories tends to preclude rather than promote the preservation of explanatory theories by the modification of exploratory theories when faced with anomalies, if preservation is held to include the prior observational support for an explanatory theory (which seems a reasonable demand). The "web of belief" tends to reduce rather than increase the room for intellectual maneuver when faced with recalcitrant observations. Such anomalies can often only be accommodated at the unacceptable price of abandoning the prior observational support for an explanatory theory. It is worth remembering the nature of Quine's (1953, p. 43) own qualification about the accommodation of recalcitrant observations: "Any statement may be held to be true come what may, if we make drastic enough adjustments elsewhere in the system." Some modifications are simply too drastic.

They reduce rather than maintain the observational support for an explanatory theory.

This is not to deny that exploratory theories are often modified in the course of scientific development. Nor is it denied that anomalies can sometimes be resolved by the modification of other auxiliary hypotheses (e.g., about initial conditions). Both of these occurrences are common enough in the history of science. What is denied is the common assumption that exploratory theories can always be modified in the face of anomalies to preserve the evidential equivalence of an explanatory theory with respect to its rivals. For if competing explanatory theories T_1 and T_2 employ the same exploratory theories in accounting for the original support for both theories, then critical observations supporting theory T_1 over theory T_2 often cannot be accommodated by theory T_2 by exploratory theory modification, for then theory T_2 can no longer share the prior observational support with theory T_1. This explains why although there may be no logically crucial experiments, some critical observations are decisive.

It should also be stressed that although this section has mainly been concerned with the role of exploratory theories, essentially the same point applies to *any form of auxiliary hypothesis* employed in the evaluation of explanatory theories. As an explanatory theory is developed and applied via the employment of auxiliary hyptheses, it becomes increasingly difficult to accommodate anomalies by the modification and replacement of these auxiliaries without abandoning the prior observational support for the developed explanatory theory.

In one respect, this point is just a specification of the traditional requirement that scientific theories be *consistent*. Explanatory theories must remain consistent with the description of observations that provide the original support for the theory. When such observations are based upon exploratory theories and other auxiliary hypotheses, and when such theories and hypotheses are modified or replaced, the consistency requirement will be violated. What this shows is that the consistency condition is not a trivial formal requirement for explanatory theories, but exerts powerful epistemic restraints on the development and modification of such theories.[15]

EXPLORATORY AND EXPLANATORY THEORIES

The above discussion also suggests that there is something fundamentally wrong with the neo-empiricist (and original scientific empiricist) conception of the relation between explanatory theories and exploratory theories and other auxiliary hypotheses upon which many observations depend. According to this conception, explanatory theories are introduced to explain a set of empirical data or laws, and are related to descriptions of the observational data via correspondence rules and auxiliary hypotheses, which can then be replaced, modified, or added to in order to ensure a "goodness of fit" between theory and observational data. Thus, for example, Kuhn and Lakatos both talk about central "paradigms" or "hard cores" of research programs that can be protected against falsification via the modification or replacement of auxiliary hypotheses. The idea is that we start at the center of the "web of belief" with explanatory theory, and adjust our intermediary network of auxiliary hypotheses and theories to accommodate the observational data at the periphery. The clear implication of this conception is that auxiliary hypotheses and theories are selected originally and continue to be selected to favor an explanatory theory, insofar as they enable the explanatory theory to accommodate observations. In this important respect, the particular auxiliaries employed would be biased in favor of the protected theory.

Now if the Kuhn-Lakatos account was a fairly accurate account of the way in which theories are historically evaluated, one would expect that scientists adopting a new or alternative explanatory theory would adopt a quite different set of exploratory theories and auxiliary assumptions than those selected by its rival(s), in order that it might itself accommodate the observational data. Yet it is a historical fact that there are a host of exploratory theories and auxiliary hypotheses common to competing explanatory theories. The same exploratory theories about telescopics and photography were employed in the evaluation of Newton's and Einstein's theories; the same techniques of chemical separation and purification were employed by defenders and critics of Prout's hypothesis; the same theories of X-ray diffraction were employed in the testing of competing theories of the structure of DNA.

The neo-empiricist reverses the natural priority of exploratory theories and auxiliary hypotheses, and explanatory theories that are the object of observational evaluation. Rather than exploratory theories being selected to accommodate the observational data, it is competing explanatory theories that are selected by the employment of exploratory theories. It is in fact often impossible to evaluate competing explanatory theories until independently supported exploratory theories are developed. It may be said, for example, that it was simply impossible to evaluate the explanatory claims of the Copernican theory until the theory and technology of the telescope was developed. As Weinberg (1977, p. 4) comments on past cosmological accounts in relation to contemporary theory: "Throughout most of the history of modern cosmology there has simply not existed an adequate observational and theoretical foundation on which to build a theory of the early universe." Weinberg is referring to the theory-dependent discriminations of microwave radiation, radio stars and white dwarfs, and exploratory theories and techniques such as the Doppler effect and radio telescopics.

When exploratory theories and (associated) techniques are developed and independently supported, they enable scientists to produce critical observations that undermine explanatory theories that in the past provided a fair accommodation of the observational data. The development of techniques for measuring the speed of electrical discharges between neurons completely undermined the electrical conduction theory of interneuron communication. The development of surgical techniques for severing the corpus callosum (as a treatment for grand mal epilepsy) itself led to the development of experimental techniques that completely undermined theories of the symmetry of hemispheric function in humans. As Kuhn (1970, p. 181) himself notes (although he fails to draw the appropriate conclusion): "New instruments like the electron microscope and new laws like Maxwell's may develop in one discipline and their assimilation create crises in another." The development of the electron microscope completely undermined many of the previous theoretical speculations about the ultramicroscopic structures of crystals and proteins.

The above arguments suggest that we should not think of the relation of theory and observation in terms of a central core of theory related to observations by hypotheses and theories that serve to protect the theory from falsification, but rather as a developing spiral (Enç, 1976) in which previously and independently established exploratory theories are employed to produce critical observations for the evaluation of explanatory theories. As the spiral develops, more recently established theories may be employed to support corrections of prior theories upon which they were based, or modified classifications of the phenomena they were introduced to explain. But this conception enables us to recognize that the sceptical fantasy of a recently introduced theory requiring us to abandon all our previous knowledge claims will always remain a fantasy. Any theoretical development of a spiral that undermined the observational source of the spiral would automatically eliminate its own evidential support.

The relativist might object that some day we might discover that our exploratory theories are false or seriously inaccurate, which would lead to the collapse of our most developed and cherished theoretical spirals. This is admittedly always a possibility, and one that has been actualized with respect to some exploratory theories in the past (for example, background assumptions about the successful creation of a vacuum in the research prior to Thomson's discovery of the electron[16]). However, to suppose that this fact in itself undermines the objectivity of science is to engage in wholesale scepticism about the scientific enterprise. Three points are perhaps worth making about this sceptical claim.

The first point is that our exploratory hypotheses and theories have historically proved to be rather more robust than those theories that have in the past formed the pinnacle of our theoretical spirals (Feigl, 1974). The sceptical argument concerning the epistemic weakness of our present theories based upon past failures (Leplin, 1984) has much less force on the level of exploratory hypotheses and theories. Indeed, the original sceptical argument is itself contentious precisely because it is often based upon explanatory theories that were accepted by scientific communities prior to the development of adequate exploratory theories (and rejected once these had been developed).[17]

The second point is that we continue to have good grounds for preferring some exploratory theories over others. The general argument against the Quine-Duhem thesis applies equally (and perhaps with greater force) on the level of exploratory theories. Alternative exploratory theories simply cannot always accommodate recalcitrant data without themselves becoming rapidly degenerating.

Third, the putative intuition about the fragility of our current higher level theoretical achievements is based upon our feeling that our exploratory theories have more limited evidential support because of their limited scope. This is itself doubtful. The theory of electron microscopy seems to have greater scope than many of the structural theories in chemistry and biology that it is used to evaluate. Furthermore, we tend to forget that our exploratory theories not only receive support from the observational data that they are originally introduced to explain, but also precisely from their ability to support increasingly complex theoretical spirals that are successfully developed to produce novel predictions in different domains.

EXPLORATORY THEORIES IN A SCIENCE OF ACTION

Although there are no analogues of sense-extending instruments in social psychological science (which is not to say that psychological states cannot be empirically discriminated), the basic logic of the above arguments applies equally to theory evaluation in social psychological science.

It will be argued in the following chapters that causal explanatory and theoretical accounts of human actions are simply not presupposed by epistemically significant observations in social psychological science. Nevertheless, our observations must be based upon *other* theories in the following respect. We must be able to empirically discriminate the constitutive psychological dimensions of human actions if we are to be able to critically test our causal and theoretical explanations of human action.

As noted earlier, the psychological states of agents can be discriminated by reference to their past biography and the context of action. On these occasions our observations are based upon exploratory theories concerning biography and context. Since we are often in a position to say that the agent would have behaved in the way she did only if she was dishonest or acting from a motive of revenge, we may in such situations properly be said to have *observed that* she was dishonest and acting from a motive or revenge.

Sometimes biography and context are insufficient. Sometimes we have to rely on the agent's account of her psychological state. On those occasions our empirical discriminations are based upon an exploratory theory about the general accuracy and honesty of agents' accounts of their psychological states. Since we have good grounds for accepting this general hypothesis, and often have no specific reason to doubt it in specific cases, we can often properly be said to *observe that* Tom is angry with his wife when he tells us so (or when we overhear him saying this to his wife).

Anyone who denies either of these exploratory theories in order to support an alternative causal or theoretical explanation is epistemically obliged to provide superior support for alternative exploratory theories that enable us to empirically discriminate psychological states, and that enable us to make observations that count decisively in favor of this alternative causal explanation or theory. The theorist cannot simply abandon these exploratory hypotheses, without either abandoning some of the prior support for the theory based upon precisely these hypotheses, or rendering the theory untestable and incommensurable with respect to its rivals. The reason why many competing theories of attitude change are presently incommensurable is because they fail to exploit biography and context in field experiments, and agent accounts in laboratory experiments (Secord, 1987).

As ordinary agents, we regularly exploit such exploratory theories in our judgments about the thoughts, emotions, and actions of others (and occasionally ourselves). Without these exploratory theories, social life, far less social knowledge, would scarcely be possible. The reason why so many theories in social psychological science are untestable and incommensurable is precisely because theorists fail to exploit such exploratory theories in the experimental evaluation of explanatory theories.[18]

Antirealism

In concluding this chapter on theory, it is perhaps worth considering a heroic attempt to defend an antirealist position that is not to be identified with traditional instrumentalism.

Most empiricists accept ontological realism. Contemporary antirealists also increasingly accept at least some form of linguistic realism: that theories are putative representations of reality rather than conceptually integrating redescriptions of explananda. Yet out of a desire to keep ontological commitments to an absolute minimum, the empiricist might still retain a form of epistemological idealism. The empiricist might always want to resist the conclusion—whatever the evidence—that the specific entities and properties represented by individual theories really exist. The empiricist might claim, for example, that we should always restrict ourselves to the epistemologically safer conclusion that observed reality behaves *as if* it has the properties represented by an particular theory (Fine, 1984; van Fraassen, 1980). This thesis may be classified as *surrealism* (Leplin, 1987), since it appears to have all the advantages of realism without the disadvantage of making specific ontological claims that may turn out to be false. Likewise, the scientific psychologist might accept all the foregoing and still resist the conclusion in any particular case that an agent was dishonest or acting from a motive of revenge, and simply conclude that agents acted *as if* they were dishonest or *as if* they were acting from a motive of revenge. And this surely explains part of the still contemporary appeal of treating psychological theories as *mere* "constructs" that make no commitments about psychological reality (Anderson, 1981).

SURREALISM

The surrealist position is itself based upon the standard empiricist distinction between the observable and the theoretical, which has already been rejected. Given that most epistemically significant observations are informed by theories, the surrealist position collapses into realism or relativism, since the whole point of surrealism is to restrict our ontological commitments to the empirically discriminable. If one accepts that the theory informity of observations promotes objectivity by enabling one to empirically discriminate the entities and properties represented by a theory, then one is a realist. If one accepts that the theory informity of observations precludes objectivity by making empirical discriminations inherently ambiguous with respect to competing theories, then one is a relativist. If one believes that theory informity precludes empirical discrimination, one is an original idealist.

However, the epistemological position of the surrealist is worse than these remarks suggest, and much worse for the surrealist in social psychological science. For surrealism is not just parasitic upon realism. Without realism, it is wholly vacuous. The explanations of the surrealist are clearly parasitic upon the explanations of the realist. To say that light behaves as if it has the properties of a wave, or to say that DNA behaves as if it has a double-helix structure, is either to vacuously repeat the explananda of theories that make such claims, or to claim that light and the DNA molecule behave as if they *really* have the properties of a wave or a double-helix structure. Now a theory can be meaningful and explanatory long before we have empirical means of determining its accuracy, so long as it is interpreted realistically. Explanations proceed via transformation rules that state that the properties or structures described by the theory are instantiated in the phenomena that form the explananda of a theory. We can understand and, perhaps incautiously, accept such a theoretical explanation long before we are in a position to determine its accuracy. Now it might seem that an "as if" explanation is epistemologically and ontologically less committed, but in fact it is not. For to avoid vacuity, a surrealist explanation *must make much stronger epistemological and ontological claims*.

The meaning of the realist claim that light *has* some of the properties of waves, or that DNA *has* a double helical structure, is clear enough and is provided by the theoretical model. But the meaning of the surrealist claim that light behaves as if it has the properties of a wave or that DNA behaves as if it has a double helical structure is significantly different, and is not exhausted by the theoretical model. If an "as if" explanation is not simply a vacuous statement that something behaves the way it behaves, it presupposes that we know how something would behave if it really did have the properties or structures ascribed to it by the theory. But we can only know this if we have established that this is how something that has these properties or structure does behave. To say that DNA acts as if it has a double helical structure is to make a much stronger claim than to say it simply has a double helical structure. And only an epistemological realist can make the former claim without vacuity.

Analogously, to say that an agent is angry with his eldest child is to ascribe to him a psychological state with an intensional content and intentional object. To say that an agent is behaving as if he was angry is to make a quite different and much stronger claim: it presupposes that we can discriminate human anger and determine how angry people act in specific social contexts. An epistemological idealist can make the former claim (so long as he accepts linguistic realism), but only an epistemological realist can make the latter claim. Furthermore, in social psychological science this point applies equally to the actions that form the explananda of such a science. An epistemological idealist may meaningfully describe an action as aggressive, by claiming that a behavior was represented by the agent as directed toward the injury of another, while denying the possibility of determining the accuracy of such a description. But only an epistemological realist can nonvacuously claim that an agent was acting as if he was aggressive.

In the following chapters, it is argued that most human actions are partially constituted by agent representations, and that causal explanations of human action may legitimately make reference to agents' reasons and representations. In consequence, there is *no* alternative to realism in social psychological science. The only alternative is the abandonment of the scientific enterprise.

6
Hermeneutical Psychology

Explanation and Understanding

Characterizations of social psychological disciplines as *causal* sciences have been the object of sustained criticism for a number of decades, and general objections to the assimilation of the natural and human sciences have been propounded for centuries. The central claim of critics who may be classified as *hermeneutical psychologists* (Gauld & Shotter, 1977; Taylor, 1971) is that the explanation of action is essentially hermeneutic in nature. Its object is not the causal explanation of action, but rather the *explication* or *interpretation* or *understanding* of the meaning of human action.

This critical perspective has a long history deriving from the 18th century humanism of Vico (1668–1744) and Herder (1744–1803), and the theological interpretations of Schleiermacher (1768–1834). More recent developments in the sociological tradition by Simmel (1908), Dilthey (1937), and Weber (1949) embody post-Kantian articulations of the distinction between the natural world of science (governed by causal laws) and the "intelligible" world of human freedom and morality (governed by human reason and purpose). A parallel distinction is made between causal explanation (erklären) and interpretative understanding (verstehen), which is held to mark the distinction between the natural sciences (naturwissenschaften) and the human and social sciences (geisteswissenschaften). This hermeneutical tradition is well represented in the interpretative sociologies and anthropologies, and is most forcefully presented with respect to historical understanding by Collingwood (1946).

Many contemporary articulations of this tradition in the philosophy of social psychological science are extensions of Anglo-American analytical philosophy of action. These derive in the main from post-Wittgensteinian analyses of agency and reason explanations. Central to this position is the claim that explanations in the natural and human sciences are fundamentally different. Causal explanations of human action are simply inappropriate, with the possible exception of exceptional cases (e.g., nervous spasms, automatic reflexes, etc.): ". . . if we are in fact confronted with a case of genuine action . . . then causal explanations are ipso facto inappropriate . . ." (Peters, 1958, p. 12). The explanation of human action is held to be noncausal *because* it is essentially the interpretation of human action in terms of shared human reasons, values, purposes, and so forth. As this type of explanation may be characterized as the critical explication of the meaning of shared concepts, it is often held to be closely akin to the philosophical enterprise, at least in the analytic tradition (Winch, 1958).

This claim is supported by a whole battery of arguments that attempt to demonstrate that explanations of the meaning of human action and causal explanations are of a different logical order, based upon putative contrasts between these forms of explanation. Such arguments have been presented in the sociological sphere by critics such as Winch (1958), Louch (1966), and von Wright (1971), and in the psychological sphere by philosophers and psychologists such as Peters (1958), Melden (1961), Taylor (1964), Bruner (1979), and Gauld and Shotter (1977).

MEANING AND RULE-GOVERNED BEHAVIOR

Many of these arguments lay great emphasis on what has been called the "semantic dimension" (von Wright, 1971) of human action, and its symbolic and expressive aspects. The aim of the hermeneutical psychologist is to determine the meaning of a human action in terms of the agent's reasons and purposes, and intelligibly relate this to the meaningful rules governing a particular form of social life (MacIntyre, 1971; Winch, 1958). These two forms of understanding—the understanding of the meaning of an action and the understanding of its relation to social rules and practices—are not discrete. The general form of social life shared by human agents is not a molecular product of independent and atomic action types. Rather, it is the case that human action is meaningful by virtue of its relation to other human actions and social practices. For example, the act of wage payment is meaningful because of its relation to employment and financial practices in a given form of social life. For this reason, a reference to the meaning of human action is not to be identified with the subjective meaning for an agent (contra Schultz [1967] for example). The meaning of human action, like the meaning of language, is largely determined by public and social criteria (Coulter, 1979; Wittgenstein, 1953).

The dominant analogy here is with the understanding of language, and many contemporary hermeneutical psychologists lean heavily upon the later Wittgenstein's account (1953) (anticipated by von Humbolt [1836] and Saussure [1916]) of linguistic meaning in terms of rule-governed social action. The meaning of a linguistic item is determined by its relational location within a "language game," and the "form of life" in which these language games occur. Many hermeneutical accounts are in effect the application of this relational account of linguistic meaning to the analysis of the meaning of human action. The meaning of human action is also to be found in its relation to other meaningful social practices in a given form of social life. Language games, human actions, and forms of life are all governed by *rules*. This is the point of the regular emphasis on the "rule-governed" or "rule-following" nature of human action (Peters, 1958; Winch, 1958), which is held to illustrate the inappropriateness of causal explanations of human action. Thus, for example, Ryan (1970, p. 140) argues that an explanation of the actions of drivers at stop lights cannot be causal because:

The connection between the lights turning red and the cars stopping is. . . a conceptual connection, for in terms of the rules governing behaviour on the road a red light *means* stop. And it is plain that the meaning is not causally analysable, in the sense that the explanation of the way in which a red light means stop is not at all like the way in which clouds "mean" rain—i.e. they are a causally connected sign of rain; the explanation of the meaning of red lights is like the explanation of the meaning of words and other conventional symbols.

RULES AND REGULARITY

One aspect of this line of argument may be readily granted. It is true that an understanding of the meaning of human action is not, or not simply, the recognition of a correlation, causal or otherwise. Understanding that the transfer of pieces of paper (called *cash* or *checks*) means wage payment is not simply the recognition that such a transfer is regularly preceded by one type of behavior (work), or regularly followed by another (payment for goods and services).

The identification of a behavioral regularity is neither necessary nor sufficient for the understanding of a socially meaningful practice. It is not necessary because one may perfectly well understand the meaning of a social action such as oathtaking or marriage without any inkling of the actual incidence of consequent committed actions or divorces. It is not sufficient because one might perfectly well determine the degree of behavioral regularity underlying some social psychological phenomena, but have no insight into the rules governing their meaning, like the proverbial martian or anthropologist faced with a completely alien culture.

In fact, behavioral regularity is not itself necessary or sufficient for the existence of a meaningful social practice. It is not necessary because there are social rules and values that are frequently violated. Not everyone stops at traffic lights, and few may actually avoid premarital sex or littering. Behavioral regularity is not sufficient for a rule-governed meaningful social practice since there are regularities that are not obviously rule-governed, such as drinking coffee in the afternoon, or visiting the bookshop on a Saturday morning.

These are legitimate arguments against theorists such as Mill (1866), who equated rule-governed meaningful action with behavioral regularity, and Weber (1949), who considered the identification of such regularity a necessary but preliminary step to a proper causal analysis. Such putative causal analyses of social meaning are certainly incorrect. Yet it has already been argued in detail that regularity (or "statistical probability") is neither necessary nor sufficient for the existence of causal relations or confirmation of causal explanations. In consequence, these points are only directed against the empiricist account of causal explanation (Bhaskar, 1979), not against the realist account advanced in this volume. In any case (as will be presently noted), these arguments confuse the quite separate issues of the identity and explanation of meaningful human actions. By themselves, they provide no reason for supposing that one cannot causally explain an action as produced by the agent in accord with (or for the sake of) socially meaningful rules.

According to this analytic version of hermeneutical psychology, the explanation of human action is simply the explication of the rule-governed meanings in a given form of social life. This tradition is fairly strongly committed to the thesis that there is such a thing as *the* social meaning of human actions and social practices, and that this can generally be established by appeal to public contextual criteria.

Social Constructionism

ACTION AS TEXT

There is, however, another hermeneutical tradition. Contemporary articulations in the philosophy of social psychological science are extensions of Continental European philosophy of history, culture, and art. In this tradition, human action is held to be not so much analogous to language, as to a completed written text or texts (Ricoeur, 1977). In fact, this is the original tradition, since early theorists were concerned with "reconstructing" the integrated unities of fragmented texts, disparate historical events, and inevitably incomplete works of art. The hermeneutics of Schleiermacher, for example, was primarily concerned with the interpretation of biblical texts. For Schleiermacher and Dilthey, hermeneutics involved a reconstruction of the "inner reality" of the text(s) or historical action(s), by which was meant a kind of empathetic understanding of the meaning of the events described by the author *for* the author (what the events described by the disciples of Jesus meant for the disciples), or the point and purpose of a historical action for the historical agent (what the crossing of the Rubicon meant for Caesar). Thus, Dilthey characterized hermeneutical sciences as "sciences of the spirit."

Later theorists denied the importance and indeed the relevance of the author's interpretation of the meaning of the text, or the agent's interpretation of the meaning of a historical action. A completed text or historical action is an autonomous entity (Ricoeur, 1977). Its meaning can be con-structed and reconstructed anew in different historical periods, or in different contemporary cultures. Thus, the Bible or Plato's *Republic* mean something different to readers in different historical ages. Shakespeare's plays mean something different for London or New York theater audiences and the Tiv tribe of the African bush (Bohannan, 1966). Interpretations of the storming of the Bastille are continually revised or reconstructed by generations of historians. The invasion of Afghanistan or the Falklands means different things to different nations.

No doubt some Christians, classical scholars, literary and drama purists, historians, and nations would disagree. However, the main point of this hermeneutical analysis is the claim that the meaning of a text or historical action is quite independent of the author's or agent's intentions (or in-tended meaning). Many would agree with that, even if they dispute the legitimacy of multiple interpretations. This brings continental develop-ments closer to the Wittgensteinian developments in analytic philosophy, treating meaning as a public matter with at least the possibility of a unitary and objective interpretation within any specific culture or historical period. Indeed, some writers in the continental tradition seem to believe that the meaning of a text or action can be more or less objectively specified. Ricoeur (1977), for example, argues that the text or action itself excludes certain interpretations. He claims that if hermeneutical disciplines are to achieve the status of sciences, they must be modeled on human sciences such as linguistics. Habermas (1970) also argues that a critical theory can establish "objective frameworks," which cannot always be discriminated by social participants.

Alternative developments of the continental tradition deny this. Heideg-ger (1962) at least suggested that there is no reality (text or action) inde-pendent of interpretations that can be accurately represented by them. In-terpretations of the social world are held to be *constructions* of that world. When interpretations of the social world are transformed (e.g., by reading a text such as the Bible or Plato's *Republic*, or by historical events or every-day social interactions), the world is itself transformed. This conception is fairly explicit in the work of Gadamer (1975), who completely rejects the idea that interpretations of the social world are "grounded" in any form of "objective reality." Competing interpretations are simply equally possible and legitimate constructions of social reality. None can be preferred be-cause they are all equally "prejudiced" by specific cultural and historical categories of interpretation. There can be no method for determining an "objective" interpretation since there is no objective social reality to be discriminated. Interpretations based upon Marxist theories and historical economical research, or psychoanalytic theories and techniques, or indeed natural or social scientific theories based upon the methodologies of natu-ral science are equally legitimate. None are privileged since there can be no effective method if there is no independent social reality.

SOCIAL CONSTRUCTIONISM

Gadamer tends to restrict his account to the analysis of texts, with little explicit discussion of the implications for a putative social psychological science. Nevertheless, the relevant implications can be easily drawn (Hekman, 1984, 1986), and are clearly expressed in *social constructionist* versions of hermeneutical psychology (Berger & Luckmann, 1966; Gergen, 1977, 1982, 1985; Gergen & Davis, 1985; Henriques, Hollway, Urwin, Venn, & Walkerdine, 1984). Gergen (1985), for example, explicitly claims that there is no social psychological reality independent of human interpretations. Social psychological theories are not reflections of social psychological reality but constructions of it. They are "artifacts" of discourse, like the "logical constructions" of the scientific empiricist. Since different societies, different groups within society, different historical eras, and "folk" and "scientific" psychologies employ different concepts of social psychological reality, they construct quite different ontologies of mind and action.

There can be no observations independent of these theoretical constructions, for observations are themselves theoretically constructed, like the theory-informed observations of relativist natural science. There can be no "scientific method" because there can be no observational "foundation" of such a method. Indeed, theories in folk and scientific psychology are not descriptions of reality at all, but forms of the "social negotiation" of reality in which competing images and ideologies vie for social domination.

Like Gadamer, Gergen "queries" the concept of truth in social psychological disciplines. Experiments in social psychology are simply useful "illustrations" or persuasive "vignettes" in the process of social negotiation. This is as legitimate as any other form of social persuasion, but has nothing to do with the discrimination of the causal processes of an independent reality.

RELATIVISM

This radical version of hermeneutical psychology is strongly relativist and idealist. Despite the traditional hermeneutical antagonism to scientific empiricism and scientific psychology, it is in fact identical in critical respects to scientific empiricism and scientific psychology, when the observation base is held to be theory informed. That is, it is identical to relativized versions of scientific empiricism and scientific psychology. Both adopt an instrumentalist account of theories, differing only with respect to their account of theoretical utility (in terms of prediction of observational reality versus social negotiation).

This radical form of hermeneutical psychology suffers from the standard problems of idealism and relativism, not least of which is the intelligibility of such accounts (one of the few elements left "sacred" in the constructionist account). For example, Gergen bases his claim about the social construction of gender, emotion, and self on the argument that "changes in conception do not appear to reflect alterations in the objects or entities of concern" (Gergen, 1985, p. 267). It is hard to see how this claim can be warranted if there are no "objects or entities" independent of conceptions, and if conceptions construct different ontological items such as genders, emotions, and selves.

The social and moral significance of this form of hermeneutical psychology is supposed to lie in the recognition of the negative social psychological consequences of certain forms of social psychological theorizing, such as the damaging effects on children of certain applications of theories of child psychology (Walkerdine, 1984). It is hard to see how anyone could be convinced of this if they really believed that social psychological theory and research are ideological constructions. For the same reason it is hard to see how this feature could be used to justify social constructionism. Gergen, like Kuhn and Gadamer (1975), wants a "kind of truth." But he can't have it.

Hermeneutical psychology derived from the analytic tradition may seem less extreme, but is held to have equally radical consequences:

> But we cannot hide from ourselves how greatly this option breaks with commonly held notions about our scientific traditions. We cannot measure such sciences (moral and hermeneutical ones) against the requirements of a science of verification: we cannot judge them by their predictive capacity. (Taylor, 1971, p. 51)

One very important consequence is the view that experimental techniques in social psychology, which aim to delineate causal relationships, are not merely presently inadequate, but are wholly inappropriate.

MEANING AND SCIENTIFIC PSYCHOLOGY

These hermeneutical critiques have made little impact upon the practice of social psychological science. Nor is this surprising, since philosophical arguments stressing the meaningful nature of human action have been historically tied to the claims that explanations of human action are explications of meaning, that human actions are theoretical constructions, and that the classification of human action presupposes some purposive explanation in terms of human agency. Practicing social psychologists committed to a causal explanatory science of action justly perceive the first claim as tantamount to a denial of a *causal* science of action, the second claim as tantamount to the denial of an *objective* science of action, and the third claim as tantamount to a denial of an *empirical* science of action. Conversely, the hermeneutical psychologist sees the commitment to a causal science as the denial of meaning, purpose, and human agency.

This leads to a bifurcation of psychologies accepted by both scientific and hermeneutical psychologists. Thus, Richer (1975, p. 344) suggests that:

. . . there are two types of psychology. One is within the broad scientific tradition which studies behaviour and when and where it occurs. . . . The other . . studies private states, mental phenomena, verbal reports, agency, meanings, feelings, intentions and the like.

The scientific psychologist often accepts that hermeneutical enquiries are socially useful but insists that they form no part of a scientific psychology. Knowledge of the meaning of human action is: ". . . of immense value to the novelist, the teacher, and the social worker, and to each of us in his handling of his everyday affairs. But it is not science." (Lunzer, 1968, p. 178).

This remains a common view among practitioners. It does enormous damage because it assumes that a causal explanatory science of human action can proceed independently of the determination of social meaning and human purpose.

In the following chapters, the traditional contrasts that appear to support this unfortunate view are denied. In Chapter 7, it is argued that the meaningful nature of human action does not preclude the causal explanation of human action. In Chapter 8, it is argued that the meaningful nature of human action poses no threat to scientific objectivity. In Chapter 9, it is argued that explanations in terms of human agency are neither precluded by a causal science of action nor vouchsafed by the meaningful nature of action.

7
Causal Explanation and the Meaning of Human Action

The standard scientific psychological account of social psychological science is inadequate because it is a direct mapping of an inadequate scientific empiricist account onto the social psychological domain. The critical arguments of the hermeneutical psychologist are vitiated because they are based not upon real contrasts with causal explanations in natural science, but upon contrasts between explanations of human action and scientific empiricist accounts of causal explanation in science. Some of these arguments were noted in Chapter 4. The absence of empirical invariance and the limits on prediction cast no more doubt upon the adequacy of causal explanations in social psychological science than they do upon the adequacy of causal explanations in natural science. According to a realist account, empirical invariance and predictability are not criteria for the adequacy of a causal explanation.

The central argument of the hermeneutical psychologist is the "conceptual connection" argument. This argument does not establish that explanations of human action are noncausal, because it is also based upon the scientific empiricist account of explanation. However, it does indirectly illustrate some important truths about social psychological phenomena.

Rules and Relations

THE CONCEPTUAL CONNECTION ARGUMENT

Many hermeneutical psychologists in the analytic tradition argue that explanations of human action in terms of social rules, reasons, purposes, and values cannot be causal because they are not *contingent*. They violate this basic requirement of the Humean account of causality and the deductive-nomological account of causal explanation. It is argued that there is a "conceptual" or "logical" connection between the descriptions employed in explanations of human action. For this reason, it is often called the *conceptual connection* or *logical connection* argument (Stoutland, 1970). Explanations of human action cannot be contingent because they are true by virtue of the meaning relations between the descriptions employed in such explanations. In contrast, causal propositions such as "all acids turn litmus paper red" and "tin will act as a superconductor at very low temperatures" are held to describe contingent facts about the world. There is no contradiction or absurdity in supposing that things might have been different.

Thus, it is argued that there is a close conceptual connection between "criminal actions" and "punishment" (Ryan, 1970), "commands" and "acts of obedience" (Winch, 1958), and "intentions to harm another" and "aggressive actions" (Taylor, 1964), such that it would be absurd or unintelligible to suppose that such phenomena might not have been regularly correlated. The meaning connections between the descriptions "criminal action" and "punishment," "authoritarian commands" and "obedience," and "desire to harm another" and "aggression," for example, are such that it is absurd or unintelligible to suppose things might have been otherwise. For there could not be criminal acts without legal and penal systems legitimizing punishment for rule violations, commands without effective authoritarian systems, or intentions to harm without recognition of the ability to cause harm.

Part of the meaning of "criminal acts" is that they are regularly punished. Part of the meaning of "commands" is that they are regularly obeyed. Part of the meaning of "intention to harm" is that such intentions can be successfully executed. Explanatory propositions relating such phenomena cannot be contingent and thus cannot be causal. For the hermeneutical psychologist, explanations relating such phenomena simply explicate the meaning of concepts such as "criminal action," "obedience," or "aggression." The task of the hermeneutical psychologist is to provide a more detailed and integrated account of human action by relating such concepts to the wider context of rule-governed and meaningful social practices in a particular form of human life.

CAUSALITY AND CONTINGENCY

However, all the hermeneutical critic points out is that the meaning of many social psychological concepts is relational in nature. The meaning of a social psychological description such as "command" derives from its relation to associated descriptions such as "request," "supplication," "authority," "superior," "obedience," "refusal," "cooperation," and so on, via interrelated meaning rules that characterize particular forms of social action. But there is no contrast here with the language of science. The meaning of natural scientific concepts also (in part) derives from their definitional interrelations with other concepts. This is true of theoretical concepts according to the classical scientific empiricist account (Hempel, 1965). Hesse (1970) has demonstrated that it is equally true of those concepts classified as observational in the empiricist account. According to the realist, natural phenomena such as acids and sulfur are defined in terms of their causal powers and their composition and structure. Consequently, it is a conceptual truth in natural science that acids are corrosive, and that sulfur burns in oxygen and has atomic number 16.

Thus, in whatever sense it is true to say that there is a conceptual link between criminal acts and punishment such that it would be absurd or unintelligible to suppose that there might have been criminal acts without acts of punishment, it is equally true to say that there is a conceptual link between protons and electrons such that it would be absurd or unintelligible to suppose that there might have been protons (positively charged particles) without electrons (negatively charged particles). The mere fact that it is part of the meaning of "authoritarian commands" that they are usually obeyed does not entail that Milgram's (1974) studies of destructive obedience are noncausal, any more than the fact that it is part of the meaning of "acids" that they react with alkalis to form salts entails that the manifestation of this power is not a bona fide causal sequence.

This does not mean that natural scientific propositions are true by definition in an objectionable fashion. Developing classifications and theoretical definitions are the product of empirical (and usually experimental) discriminations of the real powers and structures of natural phenomena. What is contingent about natural scientific truths is that *there are* natural phenomena with such powers and natures, not that such phenomena have these constitutive powers and natures. It is a contingent fact that there are acids and the element sulfur. It is not a contingent fact that acids are corrosive and proton donors, or that sulfur burns in oxygen and has atomic number 16.

Precisely the same is true of social psychological concepts and phenomena. It may not be a purely contingent fact that criminal acts are regularly followed by punishment, authoritarian commands regularly followed by obedience, or intentions to harm regularly followed by aggressive behavior. But it is a purely contingent fact that *there are* phenomena such as criminal acts and punishment, authoritarian commands and obedience, and intentions to harm and aggression in any particular form of human life. There is no contradiction or absurdity in supposing that these phenomena might not have existed. Indeed, this is more clearly revealed with respect to the conceptual truths of social psychology. Some social psychological phenomena in some forms of social life, such as voting or witchcraft, are in fact not manifested in other forms of life. Some presently cherished social psychological phenomena, such as marriage or private property, might no longer exist in possible future forms of social life (for example, in an extreme form of totalitarian communism).

The fact that social psychological and natural scientific concepts form a relational system, comprised of interrelated meaning rules, has no ontological implications for the types of interactions that can take place between the entities designated by such concepts. Specifically, it does not preclude the possibility of causal relationships between such entities. Nor does it preclude in any way the investigation of quantitative relationships between entities whose causal relationship is expressed in conceptual truths. The conceptual truth relating acids and corrosion says nothing about the degree of concentration required for specific degrees of corrosion. The putative conceptual truth relating authoritarian commands and obedience says nothing about the relation between physical proximity of authority figures and degree of obedience.[1]

Constitutive and Regulative Rules

Many of the arguments concerned with the causal status of explanations of rule-governed social action are considerably obscured by a general failure to distinguish between *constitutive rules* (defining what counts as a social situation or practice) and *regulative rules* (prescribing or prohibiting actions in situations defined by constitutive rules).[2] The constitutive rule for a "try" in rugby, for example, specifies that the grounding of the ball in play in the opponents' in-goal area is what counts as a try in rugby. Regulative rules relating to tries in a game of rugby would prescribe strategies for players to achieve tries for their own team and prevent those of their opponents (Collett, 1977).

Consider the constitutive and regulative rules involved in the social practice of trial by jury. The constitutive rules would include something like the following: "A trial by jury is the examination of evidence by a body of persons comprising a judge, jurors, learned counsel, defendant, and officers of the state and court, and the determination by the jury of the guilt or innocence of the defendant accused of some civil or criminal offense"; "A juror is a member of a body of 12 men or women who comprise a jury in a court of law, who take an oath to render a decision on a judicial question," and so forth. The regulative rules for a trial by jury might include something like the following: "Jurors should not let their own prejudices influence their judgment"; "Judges should not intimidate witnesses," and so on.

The constitutive rules for a trial by jury specify conditions that must be satisfied for a social action to count as a verdict, an individual to fulfill the role of juror, or a social formation to constitute a court of law. Anyone who tried to specify such rules would quickly become convinced of their relational nature. A trial by jury is defined by its relation to legal, judicial, and penal systems, and their legislative, bureaucratic, and executive agencies. A juror is defined by her relation to the judge, defendant, and other jurors within the institutional setting. Furthermore, to fully understand what it is to be a juror, for example, one must understand how this role relates to the practice of trials by jury, and the relation of this practice to wider social and institutional contexts. Such rules provide criteria for the identification of social psychological phenomena, such as trials by jury, in our own or other forms of life. Social psychological phenomena that do not satisfy the relational definition of a trial (according to the constitutive rule) would not constitute or count as a real trial. We classify social psychological phenomena that bear a superficial resemblance to trials but fail to satisfy such relational requirements as "ritual humiliations" (as in Nazi or Soviet "mock trials") or "lynchings."

Regulative rules do not define constitutive conditions for social psychological phenomena, but rather regulate actions and situations defined by constitutive rules. The constitutive rule relating to the social role of "juror" specifies relational criteria that must be satisfied for an individual to occupy the role of juror. The regulative rule to the effect that jurors should not allow their personal prejudices to influence their judgment, prohibits a course of action for an individual who occupies the role of juror in an organizational setting constituted as a court of law. One most significant difference between constitutive and regulative rules is that social psychological phenomena retain their identity under regulative rule violation, but not constitutive rule violation. For example, if an individual is not a member of an appointed jury, that individual is not a juror. But an individual who satisfies such constitutive criteria remains a juror even if he violates the regulative rules governing the role of juror (he is only a bad juror if he lets his prejudices influence his judgment).

There has been some debate about whether this distinction is relative or absolute (Black, 1962; Gumb, 1972). One point is, however, quite apparent. Within the Humean causal framework in which these questions are discussed, it is only references to regulative rules that are remotely plausible candidates for interpretation as causal explanations. A reference to an agent following the regulative rule prohibiting traffic movement when lights are red at least looks like a causal story (it appears to support counterfactuals like "if the light had not been red, she would not have stopped"). Constitutive rules are definitional rules for classifying and identifying social psychological phenomena, and as such are clearly not plausible candidates for interpretation as causal explanations[3]. An explication of the meaning of red traffic lights does not even look like a causal story. However, it should be clear from the previous section that the arguments of the hermeneutical psychologist relate essentially to constitutive rules.

It is true that the understanding of constitutive rules in social psychological science is not an identification of causal relations. However, this is equally true of the understanding of constitutive rules in natural science. This is because both types of understanding are the understanding of the semantics and logic of classificatory descriptions of social psychological and natural scientific phenomena. The social psychologist's understanding of social psychological phenomena is not on a logical par with the natural scientist's identification of causal powers. However, it is on a logical par with the natural scientist's understanding of the classificatory rules accepted by members of the scientific community in which he practices.

RELATIONS AND IDENTITY

At this point a very important qualification must be made. It has already been noted that the meanings of classificatory descriptions in natural and social psychological science are relational in nature. Their meaning is derived (inter alia) from their relation to other classificatory descriptions via systems of interrelated meaning rules. Constitutive rules in natural science in general make reference to the causal powers and composition and structure of the natural phenomena defined, as in the case of acids and tin. In contrast, the constitutive rules for human actions and social practices make reference to social relations.

The reason of this is quite straightforward, but quite independent of the point about the relational nature of meaningful descriptions in natural or social psychological science. *Social psychological phenomena are themselves relational in nature.* Human actions and social practices are partially constituted by social relations, such as group membership, status, cooperation, employment, government, marriage, authorization, legitimation, and so forth. Judges and jurors are judges and jurors by virtue of their relation to the social practice of trial by jury. A trial by jury is a trial by jury by virtue of its relation to legal and penal institutions. Anyone who did not satisfy these relations would not be a judge or juror. Anything that did not satisfy these relations would not be a trial by jury. The nature and identity of social psychological phenomena is determined by their relation to other social psychological phenomena within the wider social contexts of a form of human life.

Two points are worth stressing to avoid confusion. The first is that the relational nature of actions and social practices does not follow from and is quite independent of the relational nature of linguistic meaning. The meanings of natural scientific classificatory descriptions are relational in nature, but most natural scientific phenomena are *atomistic* in nature. They retain their natures and identity quite independently of the existence of other natural scientific phenomena to which they may be causally related. An acid remains an acid when it is not reacting with an alkali to form a salt. A sample of tin remains tin when it is not conducting (or superconducting) electricity. But an individual is not a juror in the absence of constitutive relations to the social practice of trial by jury. An organizational setting is not a trial by jury in the absence of legitimizing relations to judicial and penal institutions. Of course, there may be some natural scientific phenomena that are relational in nature, such as quarks and magnetic fields, but again this neither follows from the relational nature of the meaning of classificatory concepts, nor does it preclude the existence or investigation of the causal powers of quarks and magnetic fields. Furthermore, it should be noted that the relational nature of any entity does not follow from the causal dependence of the existence of some entities on the existence of others. Quarks and kings are not relational in nature *just* because their existence may depend upon the existence of other quarks and court doctors. Although all identity conditions are also existence conditions, not all existence conditions are identity conditions. The presence of oxygen is a condition of the existence but not the identity of human agents.

The second point is that although most natural scientific phenomena are relational in nature, they are constituted by relations different in form from those that are constitutive of social psychological phenomena. The nature and identity of most natural scientific phenomena is determined by their internal composition and structure, and these relations among *intrinsic* components are described in theoretical definitions. However, the nature and identity of human actions and practices is determined by their relations to other actions and practices that are *extrinsic* to them. For convenience, these relations will be classified as *intrinsic relations* and *extrinsic relations*, respectively. It should be recognized, however, that according to the traditional philosophical usage, both intrinsic and extrinsic relations are a species of *internal* relations, insofar as they are partially constitutive of the *identity* of natural phenomena and human actions and practices.[4]

Some examples may make this distinction between intrinsic and extrinsic relations clearer. The nature and identity of tin and sulfur is partially determined by their internal composition and structure (intrinsic relations). The nature and identity of a magnetic field is partially determined by its directional relations to other fields (extrinsic relations). The nature and identity of a particular example of the biological species Homo sapiens is partially determined by its anatomical and biochemical composition and structure (intrinsic relations). The nature and identity of the prime minister of the United Kingdom is partially determined by his or her relation to other key members of the executive and legislature (extrinsic relations).

A natural or social psychological phenomenon retains its identity if such constitutive conditions are satisfied. Most natural scientific phenomena are partially constituted by intrinsic relations. Most human actions and social practices are partially constituted by extrinsic relations. It is, of course, true that some human actions and social practices are partially constituted by intrinsic as well as extrinsic relations: the nature and identity of an employment interview is partially constituted by the asymmetric relations between the participants as well as its location within an institutional setting. The extrinsic relations are stressed because of their methodological significance.

Most human actions and social practices are only partially constituted by these forms of social relations, for another critical relation that is partially constitutive of many human actions and practices is the relation of representation by human agents. This marks another critical difference between the phenomena of natural and social psychological sciences, for although acids, tin, sulfur, quarks, magnetic fields, and so forth can exist independently of human agents' representations of them, human actions and practices such as dishonesty and aggression do not exist independently of human agents' representations of them.

In this critical respect, the theoretical representations of the social psychological scientist must "presuppose" the representations of the human agents whose actions and social practices are the explanatory object of enquiry (Winch, 1958). However, we should be very careful in our statement of this claim. This does *not* mean that the theoretical definitions and causal explanations provided by social psychologists must be restricted to those employed by participants in a form of social life. Nor does it mean that we are methodologically obliged to accept agents' classifications of their actions. Ignorance is no defense in a court of law, and social incompetents and unwary anthropologists may unknowingly insult their colleagues (e.g., by asking about details of their sex life) and marry their native informants (e.g., by accepting gifts).

Explanation and Description

The conceptual connection argument does not establish the noncausal nature of explanations of human action. It does, however, indirectly illustrate the social relational and representational nature of human actions and practices. That is, this argument embodies an important truth about the *explanada* of social psychological science. It does not demonstrate the noncausal nature of any theoretical *explanans*. Nevertheless, the same point can be extended to cover the theoretical explanans in social psychological science.[5] Rituals and motives are not constituted by their causal dimensions, but by their social relational and representational dimensions. That is why there is no logical inconsistency or absurdity in supposing that all the social relational and representational dimensions of the world are *epiphenomenal* with respect to human actions and social practices, even though this supposition is not remotely plausible. Yet this point about the constitution and identity of rituals and motives does nothing to suggest that references to rituals and motives cannot figure in causal explanations of human actions and practices.

Constitutive rules do not furnish causal explanations of human action. They specify the constitutive social relational and representational dimensions of human actions and practices. This is not to say that a reference to constitutive and regulative rules cannot function in causal explanations of human action. Our causal explanations of why many persons stop at traffic lights may legitimately refer to the fact that they recognize that a red traffic light means stop. Our causal explanation of why our country cousins or foreign visitors do not stop at red traffic lights may legitimately refer to the fact that they do *not* recognize that traffic lights mean stop. Our causal explanations of human actions may legitimately refer to the fact that agents may be mistaken in their representations of social reality, either because they do not understand the constitutive rules or fail to discriminate instances of the phenomena defined by them. Thus, agents may be dishonest at times precisely because they do not represent their actions as dishonest. Agents may fail to invervene in an emergency precisely because they do not represent the situation as an emergency.

The accurate description and discrimination of human actions and social practices is critically important for any social psychological science. The hermeneutical psychologist is correct to insist upon its importance, but it is the beginning and not the end of social psychological enquiry.

The hermeneutical psychologist will regularly claim that a wholly adequate explanation of human action can be provided by the description or classification of behavior (Lukes, 1968; MacIntyre, 1958; Peters, 1958; Winch, 1958). It is argued that the descriptive classification of a behavior as an instance of aggression or dishonesty provides a wholly adequate explanation of it. However, this fact is somewhat of a red herring in the debate about the possibility of a causal science of human action.

In an ordinary everyday sense of explanation we can provide an explanation of a natural phenomenon or human action by descriptively identifying it as an instance of "yellow fever" or "suicide." These identifications provide us with information about physical properties and social relational and representational dimensions. It is also true that such identifications do not provide causal explanations of yellow fever or suicide. However, the fact that some identifications provide us with information that is not causal explanatory does not preclude the possibility or illustrate the inappropriateness of causal explanations of yellow fever or suicide in natural and social pychological science.

It is also true that many descriptive identifications of natural scientific phenomena also provide causal explanations of them (we provide causal explanations of phenomena by classifying them as instances of "tuberculosis," "oxidation," and "metal fatigue"), whereas this is rarely the case with respect to our identifications of human actions and practices (actions are not causally explained by classifying them as instances of "aggression" or "dishonesty"). However, this is simply a consequence of the fact that human actions and social practices are constituted by social relational and representational rather than causal dimensions. Nothing prevents us from providing causal explanations of human actions and social practices that are constituted in this fashion.

It is also precisely at this point that the textual analogy breaks down. It is, of course, as important to determine the social meaning of human action as it is to determine the literary meaning of a text. But again this is the beginning and not the end of social psychological science. The explanation of human action is not so much analogous to the interpretation of the literary meaning of a text as it is to our causal explanation of the author's production of a text (for example by a biographer).

The fact that the author's reasons for producing the text or its intended significance cannot be identified with the literary significance of the text does not mean that we cannot provide a causal explanation of its production in terms of the author's reasons and intended significance. It may be the case that Shakespeare wrote for money and Hume wrote for fame, whatever the literary and philosophical significance of their work. Analogously, the fact that the social significance of a judge's decision or an employment interview is independent of the judge's reasons for making the decision or an agent's reasons for attending the interview does not mean that we cannot provide a causal explanation of the judge's decisions or the agent's attendance in terms of their reasons or any other causal factors.

Although the accurate description of actions and practices cannot be treated as a substitute for causal explanation, the social psychologist concerned with advancing an explanatory science of human action cannot afford to ignore the social meaning of human action. She cannot afford to do this because she is *necessarily* concerned with the identity of human actions and practices. The social relational and representational dimensions of play, aggression, and interviews, for example, must be identified by empirical discrimination in laboratory experiments, field experiments, developmental studies and so forth if such forms of investigation are to legitimate causal explanations of play, aggression, and the social dynamics of interviews. If such dimensions are not reproduced and established in causal forms of enquiry in social psychological science, explanations based upon these forms of enquiry cannot be treated as empirically warranted explanations of play, aggression, and the social dynamics of employment interviews.

8
The Social Constitution of Action

The critical claim of social constructionism is that social and psychological reality is an intellectual construction according to the linguistic conventions of a culturally and historically specific form of life: "Social constructionism views discourse about the world not as a reflection or a map of the world but as an artifact of communal interchange" (Gergen, 1985, p. 266). Two radical consequences are held to more or less immediately follow from this. Ths first is that there can be no objectivity with respect to individual or collective representations of social reality, since there is no independent reality that serves as the putative object of such representations. The same physical behaviors can be constructed as diverse actions or practices according to the different definitions of different individuals or social groups. The police officer or police community may construct the officer's behavior as an arrest. The black youth and the black community may construct the officer's behavior as harassment. Analogously, different historical periods and cultures may construct different ontologies of the social world. A behavior such as homosexuality may be sacreligious in some medieval communities but a normal human relationship in ancient Greek and some contemporary societies, and a mark of divinity in some Indian tribes. The second consequence is that there can be no objectivity with respect to causal explanations of actions and practices, since socially constructed actions and practices may not be reidentifiable cross-culturally and transhistorically.

The fact that theoretical concepts of reality are not "reflections" of reality—their meaning is not abstracted from the phenomena they are introduced to explain—does not entail that they cannot provide accurate (and inaccurate) representations of that reality which can be empirically evaluated[1]. However, there is a more fundamental objection to social constructionism. If human actions and social practices are socially constructed in the sense proposed by social constructionist theorists, then it must be the case that our classifications of human actions and practices are *sufficient conditions* for their existence (Hamlyn, 1982).

But this is plainly *not* the case. It is patently not a sufficient condition of a

trial by jury, employment interview, or communion service that the participating agents or nonparticipant observers represent activities as instances
of trial by jury, employment interview, or religious communion. Without
the constitutive social relations of a trial by jury, employment interview, or
religious community, no activity would count as a trial by jury, employment interview, or religious communion. Men and women do not become
slaves or servants just by representing them as such. Slavery and servitude
are essentially constituted by social relations of dominance and exploitation. Although social relations are the outcome of purposeful human actions (as well as an enabling condition for them [Bhaskar, 1979]), they are
not constituted by the purposes that motivate them. Cooperation may be
the product of entirely selfish individual motives. The actions of communist
states and committees enforcing reverse discrimination may promote social
inequality rather than social equality. Although there is a sense in which
some human actions and practices are intellectual *creations*, it is never the
case that individual actions or social practices are even partially constituted
by individual or collective representations of them. In order to demonstrate this, we must first determine the various respects in which human
actions and social practices may be said to be *socially constituted*.

The Social Constitution of Action

Most human actions and social practices are socially constituted insofar as
they are partially constituted by social relational dimensions. An employment interview is partially constituted by its relational location within an
organization. Most human actions and social practices are also partially
constituted by representational dimensions. Acts of aggression and dishon-
or are partially constituted by the representations of individual agents and
social collectives. Without these social relational and representational
dimensions, there would be no human actions or social practices: human
behavior would have no meaning or significance. These are conceptual
facts about human actions and social practices that are on a logical par with
the conceptual fact that physical reality has physical dimensions (shape,
solidity, etc.).

It is also true that actions and practices are socially constituted in the
sense that the agent and collective representations that are partially constitutive of human actions are *social representations*. That is, they are
shared representations that are socially learned and negotiated by participants in a form of social life. In this respect, the representational dimensions of human actions and practices are also social dimensions. It is also
true, although this point must be carefully distinguished, that the descriptive and theoretical representations employed by social agents in their classification of actions and practices are also social in nature in precisely the
same respect. They are socially learned and negotiated by participants in a
form of social life.

It is crucial to note that the social dimensions of actions and practices are not a conceptual consequence of the social dimensions of the descriptive and theoretical representations employed by social agents in their classification of actions and practices. The descriptive and theoretical representations employed by natural scientists in their classification of physical reality have social dimensions insofar as they are socially learned and negotiated by the scientific community. But it simply does not follow that physical reality has any social dimensions. Although there is, of course, a more intimate connection between representation and ontology in the case of human actions and practices, nevertheless, actions and practices do not have social dimensions by virtue of the social dimensions of their consensual definitions. And only if this were the case would individual and collective definitions determine the ontology of the social world in the ways that are conventionally held to undermine objectivity and causal explanation.

REPRESENTATION AND OBJECTIVITY

The representational dimensions of human actions and social practices mark a significant respect in which the phenomena of social psychological science are different from the phenomena of natural science. For unlike the physical phenomena of natural science, which are generally recognized to exist independently of natural scientists' representations of them, there is an important respect in which it is true to say that human actions and social practices do not exist independently of human representations. We do not attribute slavery or trials by jury to sticks or stones, because the movements of sticks and stones have no social relational or representational dimensions. We do not attribute these practices to members of the animal kingdom, because their social worlds lack the relevant representational dimensions.[2]

Yet we should be very cautious in our statement of this important truth. In the first place, it is far from obvious that all human actions and practices have representational dimensions. Sexual activity and ritualized violence would appear to be rather obvious exceptions. Although it is true that these actions and practices are transformed when they come to be represented as socially meaningful by church fathers and British soccer fans, it is also true that there were social entities and relations such as kinship systems and maternal bonding which predated our historically developed cognitive capacities for representing them (Sade, 1965) (some of which were probably necessary conditions for the development of symbolic thought [Bruner, 1975]).

The second point to note is that participant agent *classifications* of actions and practices are never even necessary conditions for human actions and practices (far less sufficient conditions, as suggested by the social constructionist theorist). Thus, an agent in any form of life may be aggressive, dishonest, in debt, and legally or morally obligated without representing his or her behavior or situation as an instance of aggression, dishonesty, indebtedness, and legal or moral obligation. Indeed, this fact may furnish a plausible causal explanation of why some agents are aggressive and dishonest, and fail to honor their debts and fulfill their legal and moral obligations, although this is a separate and empirical question.

Nevertheless, this articulation is somewhat misleading, since it tends to camouflage the degree to which many human actions and practices are partially constituted by agent representations. For although it is not a constitutive condition of aggression or dishonesty, for example, that the agent classifies her behavior as an instance of aggression or dishonesty, still it is a constitutive condition of these forms of action that the agent represents her behavior in a particular way. A behavior is not aggressive *unless the agent represents her behavior as directed toward the harm or injury of another.* A behavior is not dishonest *unless the agent represents goods removed or services received as rightly belonging to another.*

That is, agent representations of actions *as instances of aggression and dishonesty* are neither necessary nor sufficient to constitute a behavior as an instance of aggression or dishonesty. Rather, individual *behaviors* of agents are constituted as aggressive or dishonest *actions* by being represented by them as directed toward the harm or injury of another or involving the removal of goods or receipt of services rightly belonging to another, which may then be correctly classified by participant agents or nonparticipant observers as instances of aggression or dishonesty. Human actions and practices are not constituted *as actions and practices* by participant agent or nonparticipant observer *classifications* of them. Human *behaviors* are constituted *as actions and practices* by participant agents' representations of their meaning and purpose. *Classifications* of actions (by actors and observers) are accurate or inaccurate classifications of actions that are *preformed as actions* by agents' representations of the meaning and purpose of their behavior (and by its relational location within a social context).

This has the immediate and significant consequence that the crosscultural or transhistorical identification of phenomena such as aggression or dishonesty is quite independent of the question of whether there is a word in the language of that other place or time that can be translated as "aggression" or "dishonesty." It certainly does not follow that there is no aggression or dishonesty in societies that do not have concepts *of* aggression and dishonesty (i.e., classificatory terms for these *forms* of human action). Such a question entirely depends upon whether agents in these forms of life represent their behaviors as directed toward the injury of another, or as the removal or receipt of goods and services that rightly belong to another. It is not the case that the limits of social action in a certain historical period can be identified with the "stock of descriptions current in that age" (MacIntyre, 1964, p. 60; cf. Winch, 1964). The limits of social action at any time are determined only by the available forms of representation of human behavior (and social relations). The same point applies equally to other cultures.

This reflection also enables us to immediately and directly answer some of the doubts about the objectivity of classifications of actions and practices in social psychological science. For a particular behavior counts as an instance of aggression or dishonesty quite independently of whether the actor or observer represents the action as aggressive or dishonest, in precisely the same way that a physical phenomenon counts as an instance of an acid quite independently of whether any scientific observer represents it as an instance of an acid. The only difference so far noted is a difference in the constitutive dimensions of physical phenomena and human actions: between causal powers and intrinsic relations, and extrinsic social and representational relations.

Some of these points can perhaps be clarified by considering in a little more detail the diverse ways in which human actions and practices may be partially constituted by participant agent and collective representations.

PARTICIPANT AGENT REPRESENTATIONS

A great many human actions and social practices are partially constituted by participant agent representations of behavior and social context, in the sense that such representations, in conjunction with social relations, are sufficient to constitute diverse behaviors as forms of human action and social practice. Diverse behaviors are constituted as the same forms of action and social practice by their intentional direction and social location. Thus, throwing a switch on an electric shock generator and striking with a blunt instrument may both be instances of aggression, and keeping the wrong change and syphoning the neighbor's gasoline may both be instances of dishonesty. Human actions are never wholly constituted by agent classifications of actions, since agent classifications are never sufficient conditions for their existence (an agent's representation of her behavior as dishonest is not sufficient to constitute her behavior as a dishonest action). Human actions are never even partially constituted by agent classifications, since agent classifications are never necessary conditions for their existence (it is not necessary that an agent represents his behavior as aggressive for the behavior to be constituted as an act of aggression).

In fact, many of the participant agent representations that are partially constitutive of actions and practices are not descriptive representations of behavior, far less classificatory ones. They cannot properly be characterized as accurate or inaccurate representations. They are closely analogous to the class of speech acts that J.L. Austin (1962) originally classified as "performatives." Austin distinguished between "constative" utterances, which attempt to describe some state of affairs and are properly characterized as true or false (such as "he promised to pay me five dollars" or "there is a bull in the field"), and "performative" utterances, which perform some speech act (other than describing), such as promising or warning, and which cannot be properly characterized as true of false (such as "I promise to pay you five dollars" or "watch out for the bull"). Just as the utterance "I promise to pay you five dollars" does not describe any internal or external, present or future state of affairs, but partially constitutes my utterance as a promise, so too my representation of my behavior as directed to your injury is not an attempt to characterize accurately any present internal psychological state of myself or future state of another, but partially constitutes my behavior as aggressive. Analogously, my representation of goods or services received as rightfully belonging to another is not primarily an attempt to characterize accurately any state of affairs, but partially constitutes my receipt of these goods and services as a dishonest action.

There is a special class of such nondescriptive representations that may be said to be symbolic or hermeneutical: they involve the representation of something as a symbol for some other thing (Harré, 1979). Thus, in some forms of holy communion in some religions, the wafer and wine are represented as the body and blood of Christ. This form of participative representation is partially constitutive of the social practice of communion. Analogously, a soldier's representation of a flag as a symbol of his country partially constitutes his action of saving the flag as patriotic. Such representations are not themselves descriptive of an independent reality, but rather constitute the symbolic meaning of such actions according to some local convention.

Not all constitutive agent representations have this feature. Some constitutive representations are clearly putative descriptions, and others involve beliefs about the world that may be properly characterized as true or false. For example, my behavior cannot be properly characterized as an instance of prayer or witchcraft unless I represent my behavior as at least an attempt to communicate with spirits or deities. Certainly, most people who engage in such practices have such beliefs. However, the accuracy or inaccuracy of these beliefs *makes no constitutive difference*. It is not a constitutive condition of witchcraft or prayer that any agent in fact communicates with a spirit or deity. The most wicked spells and most hopeful prayers are wicked spells and hopeful prayers quite independently of whether they are supernaturally efficacious. Analogously, an act of aggression or dishonesty involves the descriptive representation that the behavior has some chance of harming another or that certain goods or services belong to another. However, an agent may still be said to be aggressive or dishonest even if these descriptive representations of their behavior are false.

It is worth noting at this juncture that complex interactions and practices involve differential combinations of constitutive agent representations. In an interview, the interviewer must represent his activity as the evaluation of potential personnel, although the interviewee need not. This may be contrasted with the situation in which one person is employed by another. Someone who revenges himself on another must represent his action as the repayment of some prior injury, but the victim of the revengeful act need not represent matters in this way. In a trial by jury, the judge, jurors, and counsel must represent their activities in appropriate ways, but the defendant need not. In a seminar, the chairperson and some of the participants must represent the activity in the appropriate way, but not all the participants need do so.

COLLECTIVE REPRESENTATIONS

This leads us to recognize a class of actions for which the participant agent's representation is not a constitutive relation, but which are constituted as actions by collective representations of a class of behaviors. A good example is an insult. One agent can insult another even if neither the insulter nor the insultee identifies the behavior as an "insult," or recognizes that it is offensive to another's honor and dignity.

Once again many of the collective representations that are partially constitutive of human action are not descriptive. Many are representations of dimensions of status, honor, dignity, power, reputation, and human welfare that are partially constitutive of the moral order of the social world. Furthermore, many are symbolic or hermeneutical in the sense noted above: a certain class of behaviors are treated according to a local convention as an expression or violation of human dignity or respect, or as the exercise of social rights and responsibilities.

There are also collective descriptive representations of these actions, which are themselves preformed as actions by collective constitutive representations of a class of behaviors as manifesting conventional moral dimensions. Thus, certain actions are classified as "insults," "humiliations," and "obligations," according to the local conventions about the constitutive rules for these forms of action. Such characterizations will be accurate or inaccurate according to whether such behaviors satisfy the consensual constitutive rule (or idiosyncratic variants of it). Thus, whether a particular action or group of actions in our own or another culture are instances of insults, humiliations, or obligations (financial or moral) depends upon whether the relevant dimensions are instantiated in our own or the other culture. A man can be financially or morally obligated to another even if neither recognizes that this is the case.

It is worth noting that the social constitution of action does not entail the general accuracy of collective classifications of particular actions. The majority may simply be mistaken or inconsistent with respect to particular judgments (and indeed with respect to many particular judgments). The majority are only an authority on the constitutive rule: they are only an authority on what counts as an insult, obligation, or humiliation. Their consensus about the rule is no guarantee of their consistency of discrimination in applying the rule: it is no guarantee that they will be successful in identifying the criterial dimensions specified by the constitutive rule.[3]

Thus, we may be inconsistent and inaccurate with respect to our judgments about the behavior of the Soviet nation or our Asian neighbors. The same forms of action (behaviors with the same intentional direction and social location) may be classified as a humiliation or insult when practiced by them, but not by ourselves. We may be quick to remind them of their "obligations," but slow to recognize our own. One need not, of course, suggest that this is a regular occurrence, but its logical possibility is sufficient to show that majority *classifications* of individual actions are not themselves constitutive of human action, and thus sufficient to show that it is an objective matter in any form of social life, whether a particular behavior counts as an instance of an insult or obligation (according to the local constitutive rule). Once again, such descriptive inconsistencies and inaccuracies may have explanatory relevance, although this is a separate and empirical question.

In the following respects then it may be said that human actions and social practices are socially constituted. Human behaviors are constituted as actions and practices jointly by their relation to extrinsic social entities, and by participant agent or collective representations that are socially learned and negotiated. Socially learned and negotiated classifications of actions and practices are not in any way constitutive of actions and practices. Accordingly, classifications of actions and practices are accurate or inaccurate according to whether the criterial dimensions of a social definition (of the society engaged in social psychological science) are instantiated in the society that is the object of study.

Ontology and Explanation

The above analysis suggests the possibility of real ontological diversity with respect to human actions and practices across different cultures and historical periods. This is simply a consequence of the fact that there may be different social relations and representations to be found in different cultures and periods. Undoubtably there is real ontological diversity cross-culturally and transhistorically. There are no parental duties to biological aunts in European cultures (as opposed to African cultures, where biological aunts are represented as mothers), and there are no longer any feudal duties. There can be no acts of dishonesty in societies without property relations, or employment interviews in societies where everyone is an equal cooperating member of an agricultural collective. This is no artifact of discourse, nor is it determined by thought or discourse alone. It is rather a reflection of the presence or absence or difference of social or representational dimensions.

In particular, it is worth stressing that ontological diversity is not itself a product of different social definitions of human actions and practices, since social definitions play no role in the constitution of human actions and practices. It is always an objective question according to a consensual constitutive rule if there are any instances of aggression or employment in other cultures, or any instances of racism or exploitation in our own. We should be especially careful to note that the employment of different social definitions (according to different local constitutive rules) does not itself guarantee ontological diversity. Ontological diversity of actions and practices is solely a product of different social relational and representational dimensions. Descriptive taxonomies of actions and practices in different cultures or historical periods may differ either because of different social relational and representational dimensions, or because identical social relational and representational dimensions are differentially combined in constitutive rules to produce different definitions.

This is precisely analogous to the point that it does not, of course, follow that the ontology of the physical world is different for different scientists just because they differ in their definition of an acid, according to whether they employ the Bronsted-Lowry definition of an acid as a "proton-donor", or the Lewis definition of an acid as an "electron-pair" acceptor. It is assumed (at least according to present physical theory) that there are entities that are proton-donors and electron-pair acceptors (and many entities that are both). The ontological items of the physical world are determined by the causal and structural dimensions of the physical world, not by our more or less useful definitions. Analogously, the ontological items of the social world are determined by the social relational and representational dimensions of human behavior, and not by our more or less useful and perhaps diverse definitions of them. The real difference is that whereas the constitutive causal and structural dimensions of the physical world remain largely invariant across time and space, this may very well not be the case with respect to the social relational and representational dimensions of the social world. It must, however, be stressed that this question is entirely empirical, as it is in the case of physical reality.

The possibility of ontological diversity in the social world often leads to familiar doubts about the universality and objectivity of causal and theoretical explanations in social psychological science (Gergen, 1973). Such knowledge appears to be rather rigidly bound to specific historical periods or cultures. Our explanation of the actions of feudal serfs and 19th century samurai seem to have no obvious bearing on our understanding of the actions of 19th- and 20th-century British trade unionists. This may very well be the case with respect to many of our social and psychological explanations. However, they are never inadequate for this reason alone.

To suppose that ontological diversity poses a special explanatory problem is to confuse the *universality* of an explanation with the *frequency* of the manifestation of the phenomenon explained. A causal or theoretical explanation is universal if it applies to each and every instance of a reidentifiable phenomenon, no matter how frequent or rare is the actual manifestation of that phenomenon. Causal explanations of plutonium sickness, evolutionary reversal, the creation of solar systems, and continental drift may be universal even though such phenomena are rarely manifested. There is no reason in principle why social psychological explanations of infanticide or cannibalism cannot also be universal despite their relative infrequency. It is true that instances of some actions or practices can no longer be reidentified because they no longer exist (such as human religious sacrifices and feudal duties), but again this poses no special threat to universality and is not unknown in the natural sciences. The explanation of the behavior of dinosaurs or the medieval strain of the bubonic plague is no less universal because these phenomena are presently nonexistent.

In any case we cannot simply assume cross-cultural and transhistorical diversity in the ontology of the social psychological world. It has already been noted that we must be especially careful not to mistake differences in social taxonomies with real ontological diversity: the same basic social and representational dimensions may be described in quite different social taxonomies. We must also be very careful not to mistake differences in symbolic conventions with real differences in social and representational relations, since the same fundamental social relations may be conventionally expressed in multifarious ways in different cultures and historical periods.

Thus, the relations of dominance and exploitation may be manifested in the relations between Roman freedmen and their slaves, between feudal lords and their serfs, between company directors and their employees, and between husbands and wives. Relations of power and social status may be negotiated through the actions and interactions of salesmen and their clients, management and unions, the sultan and his harem, the king and his witchdoctor, and husbands and wives. Reputations may be gained and lost by university exams and academic publications, violence or gentility, rain-dancing or breakdancing, promiscuity or chastity, or preservation or destruction of life. Furthermore, as these examples suggest, such constitutive relations may also play a role in causal explanations, which have more than a local historical or cultural application.[4]

SOCIAL THEORIES AND THEORY INFORMITY

The above denial of the constitutive role of many descriptive representations of actions and practices is not a denial of their causal role in the generation, maintainance, and extinction of constitutive social and representational relations. Our thought and discourse about action is a basic mechanism for ontological stability or change insofar as the constitutive social relational and representational dimensions of action are the product of actions and interactions which may themselves be strongly influenced by our thought and discourse about action. In this respect, some of our actions and practices may properly be said to be social and intellectual *creations*. Our thought and discourse about the significance of life originally transformed some interpersonal relations into the practices of marriage and baptism, and continue to sustain them. We may create new forms of trials (where the jury decides the sentence as well as the verdict) or crimes (driving without a seat belt) as a result of thought and discourse about present forms of action. Our thought and discourse about action may lead to the attenuation and eventual elimination of some social relations and values. There are no longer any feudal duties and fewer bastards these days.

All that is denied is that such actions and practices are constituted by descriptive classifications of actions and practices (by participating agents or collectives), and that is sufficient to preserve objectivity at the descriptive level. There are no longer any feudal duties because there are no longer any feudal property relations, and not simply because people no longer think or talk about feudal duties. There are fewer bastards because birth out of wedlock is no longer collectively represented as such a shameful thing, and not simply because people no longer think and talk about bastards. Analogously, such phenomena were not originally created simply by the use of the terms *feudal duty* or *bastard*. The presence or absence of a classificatory concept of an action or practice is usually a consequence of the presence or absence of actions and practices and not a constitutive condition of them. Such classificatory concepts are concepts of actions and practices that are preformed as actions and practices by social relational and representational dimensions.

The same is true with respect to our causal and theoretical accounts of action and social practices. It may very well be the case that many forms of action are sustained or promoted by accurate or inaccurate causal beliefs about them. Many religious practices such as prayer and baptism are certainly sustained by accurate or inaccurate beliefs about their efficacy; certain forms of dishonesty may be promoted by accurately or inaccurately low estimates of detection rates or degrees of social approbation; the practice of marriage may be sustained by accurate or inaccurate beliefs about the emotional and financial security that marriage brings; the practice of punishment may be sustained by accurate or inaccurate beliefs about its remedial or deterrent efficacy; and the institution of democracy may be sustained by the accurate or inaccurate belief that it is the most equitable and representative political system. Nevertheless, an agent needs to have none of these beliefs in order to pray, be dishonest, get married, or punish another; most of the members who form a democratic state may have a serious preference for a heredity monarchy. Analogously, some actions may be promoted by inappropriate estimates of social value. Some agents may commit suicide in the face of financial ruin, although this is no longer considered to be socially appropriate; some men may marry their pregnant girlfriends in order to give their child a "name," although this is no longer a social obligation. Nevertheless, an agent does not need to have such beliefs in order to commit suicide or get married.

One of the major sources of doubt about the objectivity of action descriptions in social psychological science is the argument that descriptions and observations of human action are theory informed. This argument is partly based upon the relativist argument that descriptions and observations in any science are invariably theory informed, and partly based upon the correct intuition that the relation between representation and action is especially intimate in social psychological science.

The latter point has already been dealt with at some length. Since human actions and practices are not even partially constituted by actors' or observers' classifications of them, there is no special threat to objectivity. We have also noted that although it is true that some observations in natural science, and particularly those technically advanced areas of natural science, are theory informed in an epistemically important sense, this poses no threat to objectivity because the theory that informs the description or observation is simply not the theory that is the object of evaluation. Our observation or description of X-ray diffraction data does not presuppose the accuracy of any theory about the structure of DNA. In precisely the same way, our classifications and observations of human actions and practices do not presuppose any causal explanations of them.

This point can be clearly established by reference to the conceptual fact that we may without inconsistency or contradiction provide quite different and exclusive causal analyses of particular instances of aggression, dishonesty, marriage, "bystander apathy," and "attitude change," which we could not do if such accounts presupposed the applicability of any particular causal explanation. There is no inconsistency or contradiction involved in accepting that people may be aggressive for a variety of reasons and causes, which there would be if aggression was defined in terms of a particular reason or cause. Some acts of aggression may be performed by agents to seek revenge, others may be caused by "violent stimuli" (Berkowitz & LePage, 1967), and some may result from a failure to represent the action as "aggressive." No doubt, people are also dishonest and get married for a variety of reasons and causes. It may very well be the case that some instances of bystander apathy are a product of failures of social perception (Latané & Darley, 1970), while others are the product of social anxiety. Some instances of attitude change may be a product of cognitive dissonance (Festinger & Carlsmith, 1959), others a product of rationalizing inference (Bem, 1967), while still others a product of rational reflection or negotiation.

The same point may be alternatively expressed by noting that the successful identification of actions and practices tells us *nothing* of their cause. My successful discrimination of a behavior as an instance of aggression or dishonesty tells me nothing about its cause or reason. This is simply a consequence of the fact that actions and practices are constituted by social relational and representational dimensions, and not by any antecedent causal or motivational states.

This point also undercuts one version of the conceptual connection argument, according to which descriptions of action embody descriptions of the motivating reason for action (Louch, 1966; Melden, 1961; Peters, 1958). The social constructionist theorist employs this claim to demonstrate that classifications of action are informed by causal theories: "On the present account when a behavior is named (viz. reading, playing, helping), one has simultaneously specified its motive or reason" (Gergen, 1982, p. 85). But the argument of this section demonstrates that the premise of this version of the conceptual connection argument is simply false. It is not true that descriptions of actions embody descriptions of the motivating reason for action. It is simply false to claim that the classification of an action as an instance of reading or play involves a specification of its reason or motive or any other cause. No motive or reason is in fact specified. People read and children play for a wide variety of reasons.

THE INTENTIONALITY OF HUMAN ACTION

In recent times many analytic philosophers have rejected the noncausal implication of the conceptual connection argument. Many now argue that reasons are causes, and that a reference to agents' reasons can provide a perfectly adequate causal explanation of their actions (Davidson, 1980; Locke & Pennington, 1982). But they still maintain that there is a conceptual connection between descriptions of human actions and agents' reasons. It is argued that a behavior is a human action if and only if it is intentional, and that a behavior is intentional if and only if it is caused by the agent's reasons, or produced by the agent for the sake of reasons (Goldman, 1970; McGinn, 1979). According to this view, a behavior does not count as an action unless it is caused by the agent's reasons.

But this is also a mistake. Many human actions are intentional: they have a represented point or purpose. To claim that many human actions are partially constituted by agent representations is to claim that many human actions are intentional. But not all actions are intentional. The domain of the social relational is more extensive than the domain of the socially meaningful, and both are more extensive than the domain of the intentional. Not all actions are intentional because some actions are wholly constituted by social relations. A mother or boss may dominate her son or employee, although neither has any inkling of it. Not all actions are intentional because some actions are constituted by collective rather than agent representations. By waving to a friend entering the auction rooms, I may unintentionally make a bid for a painting I thoroughly despise. Of course, many actions constituted by social relations and collective representations are intentional under some description (Anscombe, 1957). I may unintentionally bid for the painting by intentionally waving to my friend. But not all are. I may unintentionally make a bid for the painting by unintentionally stretching my arm. I may unintentionally insult my colleagues or foreign guests by my flatulence or absent-minded nose-scratching.

No doubt many human actions are a causal product of agent reasons for action. Yet the intentionality of most actions does not vouchsafe this. My behavior is intentional if it has a represented point or purpose: my behavior is an act of aggression if my action is directed toward the injury of another. My intentional act of aggression *may* be causally produced by my motive of revenge or for the sake of it. But it might also be generated by my uncontrollable aggressive drives or violent stimuli. Certainly, there is no logical inconsistency or absurdity in supposing the latter is at least sometimes the case. Analogously, my intentional act of dishonesty may be produced by or for the sake of my avowed desire to avoid bankruptcy, or produced by some kleptomanic drive.

Agent representations of the directed purpose of their behaviors are forms of constitutive representation. They do not vouchsafe any causal explanations of human actions, far less any explanations in terms of agent reasons. One of the reasons we may be liable to be confused about this distinction between *constitutive purposes* and *causal explanatory reasons* in the realm of intentional action is because constitutive representations of the nature and intended outcome of actions *can* also function as reasons for action, although there is no logical guarantee that they do in any particular case. To take Gergen's earlier example of helping, an agent's behavior may be said to constitute an act of helping another if and only if the agent represents his behavior as directed toward the relief of the distress or discomfort of another. But the discrimination of the agent's behavior as an act of helping another tells us nothing whatsoever about the agent's reasons for helping another, or the causes that impelled him toward it. Some agents may help another in distress in order to impress their girlfriends or colleagues, or in the hope of receiving some financial reward; others may be moved by overwhelming emotions of pity and sympathy. No doubt there are also some agents who act for a pure Kantian reason: they help another in distress for that reason alone. In this case, the constitutive purpose of the action is held to be a sufficient reason for acting by the agent. Sometimes our constitutive purpose of harming another is also our sole reason for our aggressive action. But there is no reason to suppose that this is inevitably or even regularly the case. Certainly, it is not entailed by the correct classification of a behavior as an act of helping another or aggression.

This perhaps explains the correct intuition behind the original conceptual connection argument: a reference to the agent's intention often does not causally explain an action (Taylor, 1964). For a reference to the agent's intention in the classification of a behavior as an aggressive action is not causal explanatory. But it does not follow that a reference to agent *reasons* cannot provide causal explanations of actions such as aggression, or that a reference to constitutive purposes can never provide a causal explanation of actions such as aggression.

It might be maintained that although a reference to constitutive purposes may not provide a full causal explanation of intentional actions (it may not specify causally sufficient conditions), it will always form part of the causal explanation of an action: constitutive purposes are always causally necessary enabling conditions. This does not undermine the main point of this section: as representational dimensions of human action, constitutive purposes are logically necessary conditions, but cannot be presumed in any case to function as causally sufficient conditions. No doubt constitutive purposes are often also causally necessary conditions. An agent's representation of her behavior as directed toward the injury of another may often be a causally necessary condition as well as a constitutive condition for her aggressive action. But it is not obvious that this will always be the case. The agent who acts dishonestly may only recognize that the money belongs to another as he uses it to purchase a bottle of wine (he suddenly realizes that the previous salesperson gave him $10 rather than the $5 due to him from his previous purchase, but makes no attempt at restitution and returns home with the wine).

Natural and Social Psychological Kinds

The above arguments suggest that different societies may often properly be said to employ different concepts and theories *of* aggression, dishonesty, marriage, and other social actions and practices, and indeed may follow different regulative rules in relation to these activities (e.g., in some societies it may be prescribed that marriage partners should be decided by parents, in others by the participating agents). It is, of course, true that scientific communities may also employ different theories about the same class of physical entities. There were, for example, a great many theories explaining the causal powers of acids and electricity during the past centuries. Yet most of these theories are now recognized to be incorrect, whereas this does not appear to be automatically the case with respect to different causal or theoretical accounts of aggression, dishonesty, and marriage in different historical periods or in different cultures.

This finally leads us to recognize a significant difference between causal and theoretical explanations in natural science and social psychological science. There is in the end an important reason why causal explanations of human action cannot be presumed to be universal. Causal explanations of the properties of physical objects are presumed to be universal in the sense that such explanations will apply so long as the physical object retains its identity. Thus, we always give the same explanation of the corrosive power of acids or the conductive properties of metals in terms of their composition and structure. Furthermore, we presume that ontological differences between different events and processes such as different diseases are to be explained in terms of their different causal histories.[5] But we simply cannot presume that this will prove to be the case with respect to our explanations of human action. The social relational and representational dimensions that enable some agents to exploit others, sentence some to death, and financially reward others, or that promote productive or destructive obedience may be quite different in different historical periods and cultures. The reasons for and causes of medieval aggression and dishonesty may be entirely different from the reasons for and causes of contemporary Western aggression and dishonesty, which may in turn be quite different from Far Eastern reasons for and causes of *the same forms of action.*

This has led some writers to conclude that there cannot be a genuine science of human action, since human actions do not form "natural kinds" (Rosenberg, 1980; Wilkes, 1984). But this poses no threat to the objectivity or adequacy of causal explanations of human action. The possible non-universality of causal explanations of human actions and practices is simply a consequence of the fact that actions and practices form *social psychological kinds* rather than natural kinds. That is, it is simply a consequence of the fact that actions and practices are constituted by social and representational dimensions rather than causal and internal structural dimensions. We have the logical right to presume that our causal explanations of the powers of any physical object X will be universal precisely because physical objects are constituted and defined in terms of those intrinsic structural dimensions which centuries of scientific experience has taught us play an important role in causal explanations of their powers. We have no such right to presume the same with respect to human actions, since such phenomena are constituted and defined in terms of extrinsic social relations and representations that may play no role in the causal explanation of them.

But, of course, they might. The present point is simply that we have no reason to presume that this will be the case. For neither can we say that such explanations cannot be universal. There is no a priori reason for supposing that this is the case. The recognition of the special mode of constitution of social psychological kinds of action and practices is *completely neutral with respect to this empirical question.* Furthermore, some of these explanations may be *general* as well as universal. They may provide adequate causal explanations of a variety of ontologically different kinds of action and practices. Thus, we may provide causal explanations of some instances of dishonesty, aggression, and witchcraft in terms of reputation management. We may explain the outcomes of some marriages, interviews, and human sacrificial rituals in terms of power negotiation.

These points serve to explicate the sense in which Durkheim (1895) was correct to claim that human actions and social practices are "sociopsychological" in nature. This is true insofar as human actions and social practices form sociopsychological kinds that are constituted by social relations and participant agent and collective representations. These constitutive dimensions do nothing to undermine the objectivity of classificatory descriptions and causal explanations of human actions and social practices. Such phenomena and their explanation may or may not vary transhistorically and cross-culturally, although that is an entirely empirical question for which there is no reason to suppose that there is not an objective answer, however difficult it may be in practice to achieve it.

It should also be recognized that the claim that human actions and practices have social relational and representational dimensions is quite independent of the empirical question as to whether any individual action or practice is best explained in terms of social or psychological factors. Although acts of aggression are partially constituted by participant agent representations, the best explanation of some acts of aggression may be in terms of social relations. The social context of some institutions, for example, may provide a better explanation of some acts of aggression than any putative explanation in terms of agents' avowed reasons and psychological biographies (Milgram, 1974). Although the practice of trial by jury is partially constituted by social relations, the verdicts of juries may be best explained in terms of individual psychological biographies. The social relational and representational dimensions that are constitutive of human actions and social practices do not vouchsafe *any* causal explanations in terms of social relations and representations, including those constitutive dimensions themselves. It is perhaps the failure to recognize this important point that has led to much of the confusion in post-Durkheimian debates about holism and individualism.[6]

THE FUTURE OF FOLK PSYCHOLOGY

To argue these points is not to claim that the "folk psychological" classifications of actions and practices made by social agents are particularly accurate, or that there is sufficient consensus to provide universally agreed articulations of constitutive rules. All that is claimed is that any adequate classification of human actions and social practices must make reference to the social relational and representational dimensions of actions and practices, since it is precisely these dimensions that constitute diverse behaviors as the *same forms of action* (diverse behaviors are constituted as instances of aggression, play, helping, etc.). Nevertheless, this point is worth stressing. It is precisely because many behaviors are intentionally directed and socially located that we require a classification system for actions and practices based upon these dimensions. To deny the relevance of these dimensions is to deny the basic ontology and explanadum of social psychological science.

Thus, it cannot be correct to say that our present classificatory system for human actions and social practices could or should be replaced by a radically different system based upon purely behavioral or neurophysiological dimensions, for any such system would not be a classification of socially meaningful human action.[7] Some have argued that since our present classifications of human actions are theory informed by folk theories about their causal explanation, they could or should be replaced by more accurate classifications based upon superior theories, the most favored candidate being some form of neurophysiological explanation (Churchland, 1979; Feyerabend, 1963; Rorty, 1965; Sellars, 1963). This argument is vitiated by the fact that our folk psychological classifications of human action are simply *not* theory informed by folk theories about their causal explanation. Although we might discover that most acts of aggression are produced by excitations of our hypothalamus which are not represented as our reasons, rather than produced by or for the sake of our represented reasons, this would not oblige us to abandon or revise our definition of aggression. For any behavior produced by these neurophysiological states, which was not directed to the injury of another, would not be an instance of aggression. Consequently, any reference to such states could not provide an explanation of aggression unless this representational dimension was established with respect to any behavior. For the same reason, we would not be obliged to abandon or revise our folk psychological classifications of action even if the Freudian claim that most of our actions are a causal product of unconscious rather than conscious reasons was established.

In this respect our folk psychology is conceptually fundamental. In another respect it is not. The social and psychological dimensions of human action do not vouchsafe any social or psychological explanations of them. All or most of the common and cherished causal explanations of folk psychology in terms of agents' reasons, and all or most of the current explanations of our social psychological science (and depth psychology, etc.) may turn out to be false. There is no logical contradiction or absurdity in supposing that no human actions are the causal product of agent reasons or social relations. The social relational and representational dimensions of human actions and practices *may* be entirely epiphenomenal. This supposition is not remotely plausible, but its logical possibility does demonstrate that *no* form of causal explanation is conceptually guaranteed by the social relational and representational dimensions of human actions and practices.

It is, of course, entirely legitimate for a developed social psychological science to reclassify and redefine instances of human actions such as aggression and dishonesty in terms of their causes, once these have been established, in much the same way as medical researchers reclassify or define different forms of a disease in terms of different etiologies. However, if such a system of classification is to discriminate different forms of human aggression, for example, based upon different causal explanations, then the causal dimension simply discriminates actions *preformed* by social psychological dimensions (that is, such a system causally discriminates different forms of behavior directed to the injury of another). This essentially *supplements* rather than supersedes the original classificatory dimensions.[8]

EXPLANATION AND DEFINITION

The scientific social psychologist is not obliged to blindly accept any social definition of actions and practices provided by participating agents in a form of life, if for no other reason than the fact that social agents will regularly disagree about some of the details of their definitions of aggression, dishonesty, and employment interviews. However, the absence of complete consensus is no impediment to objectivity or causal explanatory inference in social psychological science, so long as the practitioner provides a clear articulation of the social meaning of the actions studied.

Experimental studies may suggest that violent stimuli tend to promote aggressive actions, defined by the experimenter as behaviors represented by the agent as directed to the injury of another. Such an account may be legitimately employed to explain everyday instances of aggression which satisfy this definition and are preceded by violent stimuli. Such an account cannot be presumed to apply to any instances of aggression according to a different definition, for example in terms of the actual or probable harm to another. But whether it does or not is an entirely empirical question, which can be established by experimental or other empirical enquires in which these different dimensions are reproduced. The point of a clear articulation of the social meaning of human actions such as aggression or dishonesty is to facilitate communication, replication, and explanatory inference in social psychological science, not to ensure consensus or concordance with any privileged definition.[9]

Furthermore, the divergence of social definitions should not be exaggerated. The consensual nature of social definitions is conceptually guaranteed within limits by the social nature of the meaning of social definitions. Social definitions of aggression and dishonesty are not "free to vary with the predilections of those who use them" (Gergen, 1985, p. 268). I simply cannot make the linguistic description "aggression" mean something radically different, no matter how strong my predilection to do so. Descriptions are only meaningful and communicable precisely because of the (albeit limited[10]) social consensus about their definition.

The scientific social psychologist is not obliged to accept any social definition of human actions and practices. Nevertheless, definitions of actions such as aggression, dishonesty, and obedience employed by experimentalists and other researchers must be a *close statement* of the consensual social definition. For otherwise, experimental studies or any other forms of enquiry cannot be presumed to empirically support causal explanations of what *most people mean* by aggression and dishonesty.

Too often, the experimental definition is deviant, and radically so. Too often, experimental definitions of aggression and dishonesty do not specify constitutive representational and social relational dimensions. Too often, the experimenter employs purely behavioral definitions for manipulative convenience, but then employs the social consensual definition when making causal explanatory inferences to everyday instances of aggression, dishonesty, and obedience.

For example, the experimenter will operationally define aggression in a laboratory experiment as the movement of a control switch on a shock generator,[11] or dishonesty in a field experiment as the receipt of currency belonging to another.[12] Causal explanations of these behaviors are then promoted as causal explanations of aggression and dishonesty according to the consensual social definition. But such explanatory inferences are only warranted if the constitutive dimensions of aggression and dishonesty are discriminated in laboratory or field experiments. Only if it can be determined in laboratory experiments that agents represent their behavior as directed to the injury of others, or determined in field experiments that agents represent money received as rightly belonging to another, can explanations based upon such experiments be extended to cover everyday instances of aggression and dishonesty. For only then are we justified in assuming that instances of aggression and dishonesty have been reproduced and reidentified in laboratory experiments. The satisfaction of an operational definition solely in terms of behavior can *never* justify the assumption that this is the case.

This is not to deny the fact that real differences in the social definitions of different groups or idiosyncracies of individual variants may themselves have explanatory significance. Differences in collective or individual definitions may causally explain some aggressive actions and reactions to them. But we must be careful to distinguish the constitutive dimensions of human actions from the causal explanatory implications of variance in social definitions.

The experimenter's critical articulation of the constitutive dimensions of dishonest actions and trials by jury *is* analogous to the philosophical enterprise (Winch, 1958). It is essentially a conceptual enterprise designed to produce a close statement of the consensual social definition for the purposes of communication, replication, and explanatory inference. Nevertheless, an empirical enquiry is required if references to differences in social definitions and idiosyncracies of individual definitions are to figure in causal explanations of differences in the production of dishonest actions or jurors' decisions by different social groups or individuals, or their differential reaction to them. There is no paradox or absurdity in the empirical investigation of different interpretations of constitutive and regulative rules, which are nevertheless our common conceptual coinage in the social world. Empirical investigations of differences in social criteria for judgments about dishonesty, profit, and punishment, or causality, blame, and punishment are not illegitimate just because of the close conceptual connection between these concepts, as Shotter (1981) has recently claimed. Differences in collective and individual criteria for judgments about dishonesty, blame, and punishment may very well provide a causal explanation of some acts of dishonesty and the judgments of some jurors, or some agents' reactions to them.

SOCIAL NEGOTIATION OF REALITY

The social constructionist often claims that social reality is negotiated by negotiation of definitions (Gergen, 1982). Thus, it is argued, for example, that the car salesman and the shopper negotiate the reality of their situation (Brenner, 1982). It is true that social reality is negotiated, and it is also true that social reality is sometimes negotiated via the negotiation of definitions. Yet social reality is not itself transformed by differential social definitions, for actions and situations are not constituted by anyone's definition of them.

The car salesman and the reluctant window-shopper do negotiate the definition of the reality of the situation, but the reality of the situation is not established by one or the other finally accepting one social definition over another by negotiation. Rather, it is determined by actions and reactions in attempts to create or avoid constitutive social relations and representations. The car saleman tries to shift the window-shopper into the *position* of buyer, by promoting interest, by drawing up a financing agreement ("no obligation to sign sir, but just see how easy the terms would be!"), by ensuring partial commitments difficult to revoke (e.g., test drives and a free bottle of champagne, thrust in your hand to keep even if you do not buy), and so forth.

The window-shopper tries to avoid being manipulated into this *position*, by trying not to get too interested, by avoiding the partial commitments (i.e. refusing the test drive and champagne), and so on. The social reality is not determined by the accepted social definition. Indeed, the salesman may manipulate the original window-shopper into the position of buyer precisely by carefully convincing the buyer that he is still just a window-shopper. In this way the man who still thinks he is a window-shopper may find himself the somewhat proud but rather confused owner of a new car. His consequent negotiations of social definitions are unlikely to convince his wife, who is looking forward to the long-awaited (but now financially impossible) holiday.

Social agents negotiate social reality via the creation and destruction of relations and representations through action and interaction. Some of these are a consequence of their own plans and choices, others are not. None are a consequence of just representing matters according to a social definition. You cannot make her love you just by thinking that she does. You cannot eliminate an obligation to repay a debt by pretending it does not exist. You cannot make everyone your enemy just by representing this as the case. People can, of course, do these things by creating and destroying constitutive relations and representations. You can (perhaps) make her love you through your actions toward her and others. You can eliminate the obligation by repaying the debt in cash or in kind. You can make everyone your enemy by giving them good cause.

AMBIGUITY

The justification of causal explanatory inferences from laboratory or field experiments (or any other form of empirical enquiry) requires the successful reproduction or identification of the form of action studied. The scientific psychologist restricts the operational definition of actions and social practices to "observable" behavior and stimulus events, because he mistakenly believes that only these phenomena can be empirically discriminated. Any other type of definition is held to be hopelessly subjective and subject to multiple interpretations. It is true that without operational definitions, which enable us to discriminate the constitutive dimensions of actions and practices, human behavior would be inherently ambiguous. But the scientific psychologist's attempt to achieve objectivity by restricting the empirically discriminable to the observable plays directly into the hands of the hermeneutical critic. The hermeneutical critic correctly points out that any behavior can be an instance of a wide variety of different forms of action (e.g., the raising of an arm can be a signal, a salute to a dictator, a bid, or a vote), and that many different behaviors can be instances of the same form of action (e.g., different behavioral forms of dishonesty and marriage). If no attempt is made to discriminate social relational and representational dimensions in laboratory and field experiments, then the behavior of agents in such experiments *is* inherently ambiguous.

Human actions and social practices cannot be classified solely in terms of behavioral criteria, because they are constituted by social relational and representational dimensions. However, it simply does not follow that all behavior is inherently ambiguous, or that any form of behavior can be interpreted as any form of action (contra Gergen, 1982). This is, of course, precisely what the scientific psychologist fears if she ventures beyond the simple description of observable behavior. But this fear is quite unjustified. Although it is true that we can always conceive of a situation in which any form of behavior *might* count as an instance of some form of action (e.g., we can think of all the possible ways in which aggression and dishonesty might be behaviorally manifested), it is not true that any particular behavior can be legitimately interpreted as any form of action in specific contexts, any more than it is true that any piece of evidence can be legitimately held to support any theory in science.

Ambiguity arises for any observer when relevant information is lacking. A Wittgensteinian example may be useful. A matchstick figure on an inclined plane can be interpreted as either a man walking up a hill or sliding backwards down a hill. The drawing is ambiguous because the information required to discriminate between the two interpretations is lacking. The single drawing does not itself determine which interpretation is correct.

However, if the first drawing occurs in the middle of a sequence of draw-ings, in which the figure is first seen lower down the inclined plane and finally seen higher up, then only one interpretation is possible. Analogous-ly, the placing of a cardigan in a bag is not itself an instance of dishonesty. In some contexts, where a woman places her own cardigan in her bag be-fore leaving the house (in case it gets colder later on), it is plainly not. But the woman who places a cardigan in her bag in a department store is usual-ly being dishonest.

To determine that the woman's action is an act of dishonesty, we must also determine that she represented these goods as rightly belonging to another. However, for many actions the agent's representation of her ac-tion can be effectively determined by social context, since the agent would not normally act in such a fashion unless she represented her action in the appropriate way. Someone standing at the taxi stand and waving her arm is plainly hailing a taxi. Someone kicking another violently in the head is plainly aggressive.

Not all actions partially constituted by agent representations are so transparent. Nevertheless, the representational dimension can be easily determined via the agent's account or the account of a close friend or col-league. In this way we can determine whether the agent was signaling a taxi (away from the taxi stand) or waving goodbye to a friend, or whether she was searching or simply clearing her desk.

Of course, there will be situations in which we are inclined to distrust the agent's account. The dishonest person is unlikely to admit to dishonesty by agreeing that she represented the goods as belonging to another. Thus her behavior in the department store may be ambiguous. The woman may have placed the cardigan in her bag as an innocent error, or simply because her arms were filled with other packages. Or she may be a thief. But the determination of the nature of the case is not beyond the scope of human powers and ingenuity. Nor is the store detective bound to passive observa-tion. Direct confrontation inside or outside the store may distinguish the innocent from the amateur thief, but not the innocent from the profession-al. The discovery of two dozen missing cardigans in her car trunk does.

Difficult situations may require further information and intervention to determine the nature of action. Equally it is worth stressing that just as often this is not the case. The constitutive representations may be dis-played by the social context without any need for intervention or atten-tion to agent accounts:

We tell a man who has driven his car over a curb, up a steep bank, and down the sidewalk, thus running down a man who was blackmailing him, that his car was not out of control. Such cases lead us very readily to think of intentions as "imbedded in human customs and situations" (Wittgenstein, *Investigations*, para 337). (Louch, 1966, p. 112)

The identification of any action is "infinitely revisable" or "infinitely negotiable" in a logical sense. It is always possible that we are mistaken. The same is true in natural science. Any theory may be revised if critical observations can be demonstrated as inadequate in some way (e.g., by establishing that a vacuum had not in fact been effectively created in the experiment). But here the onus is on the critic to demonstrate that the critical observation was unsound. We might eventually become convinced that the woman with the cardigans or the man driving over the curb is innocent. But this would require a special justification backed by evidence of further relations and representations that established the special and peculiar nature of the situation. It is not established by wishful thinking. Juries are justifiably unconvinced by defense lawyers who simply deny that their clients represented their actions in the obvious way.

The satisfaction of a behavioral criterion is not sufficient to establish an action as an instance of aggression or dishonesty, or a sequence of actions as an employment interview or a trial by jury. This is because behavior is not itself constitutive of forms of human action. But actions can be identified by discriminations of the social relational and representational dimensions of behavior, because many behaviors are constituted as specific forms of action by social relational and representational dimensions. The explanatory inferences of experimental social psychology are justified precisely when the social relational and representational dimensions of behavior are discriminated.

9
Agency, Causality, and Meaning

Although the concept of human agency is central to our everyday under-standing and explanation of human action, it is often held to be anathemic to a properly scientific study of human action (Sheldon, 1982). The scientific psychologist treats human agency as, at best, a prescientific superstition (Skinner, 1974), and at worst, an objectionable piece of metaphysics. The hermeneutical psychologist does little to discourage this conception by appearing to remove the question of agency from the domain of legitimate empirical enquiry.

In this chapter, it is argued that those concerned with advancing a causal explanatory science of human action should take very seriously the supposition that many actions are the product of human agency. This is argued in the strong sense that many actions may be sui generis self-determined by agents, and not determined by any conditions, including the psychological states of agents. It is argued that there are no good reasons why this possibility should be conceptually excluded from a science of human action, and a fairly good reason for supposing that agency explanations may play a central role in such science. The only objectionable metaphysical positions in this debate are the scientific psychologist's a priori rejection of human agency and the hermeneutical psychologist's a priori avowal of it.

Agency and Causality

Unfortunately, the present debate about human agency is largely vitiated because it is usually presented in the guise of an entirely spurious conflict between scientific psychology and hermeneutical psychology. The scientific psychologist sees the goal of social psychological science as the explanation, prediction, and control of behavior via the identification of its causal determinants. The hermeneutical psychologist sees the goal as the explication of the meaning of human action in terms of purposes and reasons. The scientific psychologist committed to a causal science often sees this commitment as ruling out the possibility of human agency. The hermeneutical psychologist believes, more often than not, that a commitment to human agency rules out the possibility of causal explanations of human action.

This spurious conflict arises because both parties are committed to the Humean account of causal explanation in terms of conditions that are ontologically sufficient for the production of an effect.[1] The scientific psychologist is committed to the claim that all human actions are determined by such conditions. The hermeneutical psychologist denies that explanations in terms of agent reasons make reference to stimulus conditions sufficient to produce action.[2]

The hermeneutical psychologist is right to complain that references to agent reasons cannot be presumed to provide explanations of action in terms of ontologically sufficient conditions. But the hermeneutical psychologist is wrong to claim that agency explanations are not causal explanations. An agency explanation is a characterization of an action as self-determined for the sake of reasons. It is a causal explanation that conflicts with alternative causal explanations in terms of stimulus conditions because it makes a claim about the *generation* of action. An explanation of an aggressive action as a self-determined act of revenge directly conflicts with alternative causal explanations (of the same action) in terms of internal or external stimulus variables, such as aggressive drives or environmental stimuli. The agency explanation entails the denial that the action was determined by any stimulus variables sufficient to produce the action, including the psychological states of the agent.[3]

Causality and Determinism

The thesis of universal causal determinism may be defined as stating that for every physical event or human action there is a set of conditions that are ontologically sufficient for the production of that event or action. This should be immediately distinguished from the thesis of universal causal generation, which states that every physical event or human action has a causal explanation. An agency explanation of an individual action makes the claim that the action was causally generated by the agent, but that there were no conditions sufficient to determine the agent to do one thing rather than another.[4] The agency account is thus inconsistent with the principle of universal causal determinism, but not with the prinicple of universal causal generation.

It is often said, however, that the thesis of causal determinism is a presupposition of all scientific enquiry. It is significant that this is usually said to be the case by social psychological rather than natural scientists, for this presupposition has long been abandoned by many natural scientists with respect to some physical phenomena (e.g., the subatomic phenomena of quantum mechanics). However, it is doubtful if this is in fact the primary reason why practicing natural scientists are not committed to causal determinism, even though they are concerned with providing causal explanations of natural phenomena. The natural scientist is not a universal causal determinist because he believes that many physical processes can be brought within the *control* of the scientist, as a result of scientific interventions based upon theory. He believes this not only in the sense that he believes that many of his experimental and technological interventions are effective, but also in the sense that it is up to scientists to choose whether such interventions will or ought to be made. The medical researcher and physicist are, like most of us, determinists about death and the expansion of the universe. Yet they are rarely determinists with respect to most diseases and the expansion of toxic gases, because they believe they can effectively intervene and have the choice to intervene. Indeed, the ability to intervene in the physical, social, and psychological realm is a presupposition of any form of scientific enquiry. This is what makes science possible for human agents (Bhaskar, 1975). Only an empiricist rhetoric forces the practicing psychologist to deny the presupposition of agency in her own scientific activity (Heron, 1981).

One of the reasons why many argue that universal determinism is a presupposition of scientific enquiry is because they believe that this doctrine follows from the standard empiricist account of causal explanation as deduction from laws that are logically sufficient for successful prediction (Hempel & Oppenheim, 1948). Now it is true that when there are ontologically sufficient conditions that can be discriminated, then events and actions can be successfully predicted in closed (usually experimental) systems. This is how many causal explanations are tested in natural and social psychological science. It has already been noted that it does not follow that a successful predictive correlation furnishes an adequate causal explanation, far less the best causal explanation. The correlation between abnormal animal behavior and earthquakes may be an excellent predicive instrument, but a wholly inadequate and inaccurate causal explanation. It has also been noted that it does not follow that an adequate causal explanation is an adequate predictive device in open systems. A reference to microorganisms may provide the best explanation of a disease even if it serves as a much poorer predictive instrument than a reference to early symptoms (Harré, 1972).

More significantly for the present purpose, it simply does not follow from the fact that human actions are predictable on the basis of reasons that there are ontological conditions sufficient to produce them on each and every occasion. The actions of perfectly rational agents, such as Kant's angels, for example, may be entirely predictable yet at the same time be genuine exercises of human agency. There is no contradiction in supposing that purely rational agents have the power to refrain from rational actions. Analogously, the fact that my actions can be regularly predicted on the basis of my inclinations and desires (e.g., I normally go to the movies when I am inclined to and eat when I am hungry) does not entail that I cannot refrain from any of these actions.

Conversely, it does not follow from the claim that human actions are products of agency that they are therefore unpredictable. Indeed, if many actions are products of agency for the sake of reasons, they will be predictable to a very high degree.[5] Thus, I may always stop at traffic lights and give up my seat to elderly citizens on buses, even though there are no conditions that are ontologically sufficient to produce these actions.

There is some historical irony here, for the scientific empiricist account of explanation is derived from the empiricism of Berkeley and Hume, who respectively denied and doubted the existence of generative causality. According to Berkeley and Hume and later generations of logical positivists and scientific empiricists, putative causal propositions are descriptive of empirical correlations that are *nonexplanatory*. In the Hempel-Oppenheim account, this empiricist doctrine is simply twisted into a stipulative definition of "causal explanation" in terms of the description of the constant or regular conjunction of empirical events. Conditions sufficient for prediction and generation were *never* equated in empiricist accounts,[6] and only the latter type of conditions pose any threat to human agency.

KANT AND THE PRESUPPOSITIONS OF SCIENCE

The only substantive attempt to argue that causal determinism is a presupposition of any scientific enquiry is the critical philosophy of Immanuel Kant. Kant argues that we must conceive of causal sequences as necessarily connected if epistemic experience—and thus scientific knowledge—is to be possible. Kant's argument fails to establish causal determinism, but it is instructive to note why.[7]

Kant argues that we must conceive of categorical principles such as the causal principle as necessary—in the sense that they hold *without exception*—if objective knowledge is to be possible. For it is the employment of such principles that enables us to unify our experience in an objective time order, by enabling us to distinguish the objective order of the objects of our experience from the merely subjective order of our experiences themselves. The causal principle enables us to locate events in an objective time order by specifying that some events must precede others because some events constitute causal conditions for other events.

The employment of the causal principle rules out the conceptual possibility of events that are wholly spontaneous in the sense that other conditions in space and time play no role in their generation. It is also important to note that this conceptual condition is at the same time an ontological condition. The content of our experience of the world must conform to some empirical concepts of individual causal relations. The basic ontological requirement for knowledge of causality may be expressed by stating that nature must be systematic and stable. The experienced world must be able to be represented in terms of discriminable empirical conditions for the generation of empirical effects. Furthermore, as Kant clearly recognizes, it is an entirely contingent fact that our experience of the world conforms to the causal principle. A chaotic world may not be an epistemic possibility, but it is a real possibility nevertheless.[8]

Let us grant these Kantian claims, if only for the sake of argument. For it simply does not follow that we must represent reality in terms of ontologically sufficient conditions. Consider the real possibility that radioactive decay and the firing of the nerve cell are not determined by ontologically sufficient conditions, that as a matter of contingent fact there are no empirical conditions that are sufficient to generate radioactive decay or the firing of the nerve cell. These phenomena would appear to violate Kantian conditions for epistemic experience, since they would appear to be instances of purely spontaneous events. But they do not, precisely because they are not purely spontaneous events. Some elements will emit beta particles and transmute to other elements *only if* they are of the requisite composition and structure. The nerve cell will fire *only if* it achieves a certain electrical potential. Precisely the same will be true of human actions if some of these are self-determined. A man can only intervene to save another from drowning or sentence another to death if he has the physical powers of a strong swimmer or the social powers of a judge. Contrary to many accounts of agency and human freedom (including Kant's), their products are simply not independent of *all* empirical conditions.

That is, it is sufficient for the construction of an objective time order and empirical knowledge that we represent events as having only necessary enabling conditions. Consider what this would mean in the case of the nerve cell. Kant's basic principle would still hold. We cannot suppose that the firing of the nerve cell is uncaused in the sense of a purely spontaneous event unrelated to empirical conditions, for this would be to abandon the principle that enables us to locate empirical phenomena in an objective time order. But if we represent the event as causally dependent upon prior enabling conditions, such as the attainment of a specific electrical potential, then we can locate the firing of the nerve cell in an objective time order. It always follows the attainment of this potential because it must, since the attainment of this potential is a necessary enabling condition of the firing of the nerve cell. Furthermore, we can give a perfectly adequate causal explanation of the firing of the nerve cell by reference to the fact that the achievement of a certain electrical potential enables the cell to fire.[9] Analogously, we can explain the judge's power to sentence a man to death by reference to social relations and representations, even if these or any other conditions are not sufficient to produce any particular act of sentencing.

It is a well-established but, nevertheless, a wholly contingent fact that most physical events can be given causal explanations in terms of conditions sufficient for their generation. It is not conceptually guaranteed by any form of philosophical argument. There is no contradiction or absurdity involved in the supposition that for some physical events there are no conditions that are sufficient to generate them. It follows from this that there is no conceptual guarantee that there will be discriminable empirical conditions that are sufficient for the generation of human actions.

There is a temptation to suppose that if this is the case, then our causal explanations of action and (consequently) our social psychological science will be inadequate. One might be tempted to object that causal explanations in terms of necessary enabling conditions are not fully adequate until these conditions are included in a set of sufficient conditions. But this is simply to beg an ontological question. Such explanations will be fully adequate if there are no ontologically sufficient conditions for the generation of the relevant events or actions. In any case, our explanation of self-determined action does not end with the specification of necessary enabling conditions for the exercise of human agency. It also includes a specification of the agent's reasons.

Causal Powers and Human Powers

The empiricist account of causality precludes agency explanations because it stipulates that only events that are sufficient to produce other events can be causes. This is because traditional empiricist philosophy is wedded to a Humean ontology of events (Madden, 1971), which ultimately derives from the *phenomenalism* of the classical empiricists. The inadequacies of this account have already been discussed. The realist conception of causality is based upon an ontology of enduring "powerful particulars" in causal interaction (Harré & Madden, 1975), and locates the generative power of physical particulars in their intrinsic natures (their composition and structure) and local enabling and stimulus conditions. Thus, the superconductive power of tin is explained in terms of long-range electron coupling, given a very low temperature (enabling condition) and application of a potential difference (stimulus condition).

Now it is true that many physical powers are conditioned by extrinsic stimulus conditions. Dynamite, for example, will explode if and only if a charge is applied. Nevertheless, it is an empiricist myth to suppose that there are extrinsic stimulus conditions for every physical power. Some physical particulars will manifest their power given the satisfaction of enabling conditions (e.g., the sea will exert pressure and crush any submarine that dives too deep; phosphorus will burn on exposure to the air; ammonium triiodide can explode anytime) (Harré & Madden, 1975).

Thus, we simply cannot presume that there will be such conditions in the case of human action. Human powers such as the ability to solve mathematical problems or speak Russian are more closely analogous to the power of the sea than the superconductive power of tin. Significantly, it is extremely artificial to construct putative stimulus conditions for the manifestation of such powers. The presence of a mathematical problem or another Russian speaker are more naturally conceived as *opportunities* for the exercise of such powers (or further enabling conditions), rather than stimulus conditions that are sufficient for their manifestation. We are not usually determined or driven to solve mathematical equations or speak Russian.

This is not, however, to claim that human powers are logically identical to the natural powers of physical objects, or that human agency can readily be accommodated by a realist account of physical causality. For a realist account of physical causality has come to treat the intrinsic nature and extrinsic enabling and stimulus conditions for physical powers as ontologically sufficient conditions for the production of physical effects, in the absence of interference. Thus we say that tin will act as a superconductor at very low temperatures when a potential difference is applied and in the absence of interference, because it *must*, given its physical nature and local conditions. We also say of a submarine that dives too deep that it will be crushed because it *must* be crushed, given the joint natures of the sea and the submarine. However, we do not hold this to be the case with respect to human powers. We only say of the man with the power to solve mathematical equations or speak Russian that he *may* exercise this power when presented with a suitable opportunity (Ayers, 1968). Equally he *may not*. He may choose not to exercise this power because he does not wish to show off or to blow his cover as a spy.

The critical difference between natural and human powers is that the exercise of a human power is within the *control* of the agent. The power of the sea to crush the submarine is not within the control of the sea, and indeed it makes no sense to talk this way. The power of an agent to solve a mathematical equation or speak Russian is entirely within the control of the agent if he has this power (and is given the opportunity): the agent can act or *refrain from acting* according to his personal reasons.

Nevertheless, the above analysis of human powers and agency can be accommodated by a realist analysis of causality and power. For the attribution of a generative power to a physical or human particular is not the attribution of ontologically sufficient conditions, far less the attribution of constant or regular correlation. The concepts of ontologically sufficient conditions and regular sequence are not intrinsic to the concept of power. It is only commonly supposed to be so by those who accept Hume's prescriptive definition and later variants of it. To say that a physical or social or human particular, X, has the power to generate a state of affairs, Y, is just to say that it has the ability to do it. It is simply to say that it can bring about this state of affairs, not that it will or must. What is true is that our developed understanding of how physical particulars are enabled to produce physical effects by their natures and local conditions leads us to believe that these conditions are usually ontologically sufficient for the production of physical effects, and this tried and tested conception of physical nature has been enormously useful in enabling human agents to explain, predict, and control the natural world. But again it must be stressed that this is a contingent fact that we have discovered to be true of most objects in the natural world. It is not vouchsafed by the concept of causal power. Accordingly, the concept of causal power does not vouchsafe any explanation of human action in terms of ontologically sufficient conditions.

This is not to deny that we may discover (or have already discovered) that some human actions are determined by various environmental or psychological conditions that are sufficient to generate them. We already have empirical and experimental reasons to suppose that some human actions are ontologically conditioned in the fashion of many natural powers. The presence of violent stimuli may be sufficient to produce aggression in some persons (Berkowitz & LePage, 1967), and the presence of other bystanders may be sufficient to produce apathy in some persons faced with an emergency (Latané & Darley, 1970). In some cases, agent reason representations may also be sufficient to generate action. The agent may be driven to act and may be unable to desist from acting when she represents her intended act as a justified act of revenge. But it is simply a philosophical act of faith to presume that all human actions can be explained in this way.

It is surely also significant that it is precisely with respect to such actions that we are inclined to talk about human *liabilities* rather than human powers, because they are not within the agent's control, but are stimulus bound by conditions sufficient to generate them. We say that some agents are liable to become apathetic in an emergency when other bystanders are present, even if they have good reasons for intervening. We say that some persons are liable to become aggressive when presented with violent stimuli, even if they have good reasons for desisting. We say that some agents are liable to revenge themselves, even though they may try everything in their power to prevent themselves.

The degree to which human actions can be successfully analyzed in terms of ontologically sufficient conditions is an empirical question, and the proper object of a realist science of action. The postulation of sufficient conditions for action is a useful methodological goal in social psychological science, and this form of enquiry should be pressed to its limit. The present point is that there is no conceptual guarantee that this form of explanation will be successful. Furthermore, there is an important corollary to be drawn. If we do not find social or psychological or neurobiological conditions that are sufficient to generate forms of human action, then we have to take very seriously the possibility that many actions are in fact not determined by such conditions, just as we may be forced to accept that radioactive decay and the firing of the nerve cell are not determined by any empirical conditions, when all our isolative experiments fail to locate any.

Causality and Meaning

Many writers in the hermeneutical tradition lay great stress on the concept of agency. Few give it a central role in a causal science of action, although most writers stress that agency explanations play an intrinsic role in the explanation and understanding of meaningful action, in the strong sense that any alternative explanation in terms of ontologically sufficient conditions would not constitute a legitimate explanation of human action. This leads to the most unfortunate impression that anyone committed to the meaningful nature of human actions must also accept the accuracy of some form of agency explanation of them.

It is often claimed that our commonsense conceptual scheme employed in the description and classification of human action presupposes the applicability of agency explanations for the sake of reasons. It is argued that only those human behaviors that are the product of human agency are genuine actions. It is not conceptually possible that any action could be explained in terms of ontologically sufficient conditions, for to advance such an explanation would be tantamount to denying that a behavior was a human action (Louch, 1966; Melden, 1961; Peters, 1958).

It is a common assumption that all human actions are the product of human agency. But it is a mistaken assumption nevertheless. The reason why it is mistaken has already been noted. The social meaning of human action is quite independent of any causal explanatory considerations. The fact that many human behaviors are constituted as meaningful human actions by their social relational and representational dimensions does not vouchsafe any causal explanations in terms of social relations and agent representations, far less any causal explanations in terms of self-determination for the sake of reasons. There is no logical inconsistency in supposing that no human actions are the product of reasons, or the product of human agency. This is not to claim that this is the case, nor even to claim that it is a plausible supposition. But its logical coherence does demonstrate that the social relational and representational dimensions of human action do not vouchsafe any explanation of particular actions in terms of self-determination for the sake of reasons.

This surely matches our everyday intuitions about explanations of human action. There seems to be no paradox or contradiction involved in supposing that some aggressive actions are determined by violent stimuli and others determined by uncontrollable aggressive drives, and that still others are self-determined by agents in order to repay a prior injury. Analogously, there is no paradox or contradiction involved in supposing that some persons cannot refrain from acting dishonestly when given the opportunity, and that others can, but are dishonest nevertheless.

It might be objected that human actions cannot be determined by ontologically sufficient conditions, for otherwise we could not be held responsible for them. But it is far from obvious that we can be held responsible for all of our actions, or that all of the behaviors that we are responsible for are human actions. It may be an empirical fact that some agents are not responsible for their aggressive and dishonest actions, because it is literally true of them that they could not have refrained from their aggressive and dishonest actions. It also seems to be the case that we can properly be held responsible for some behaviors that are not actions, such as our careless movements that cause destruction in the china shop. Again this surely matches our intuitions. It is only once we have established that a behavior is an instance of aggression or dishonesty that we raise scientific questions about its cause or moral questions about responsibility. One could, of course, redefine human actions as those behaviors that are the product of human agency. But then the present point could be simply restated by noting that there is no conceptual guarantee that the class of human actions so defined has any members, and that an empirical enquiry is required to establish whether it has or not.

Agency and Meaning

A causal science of action does not preclude the possibility of explanations of human action in terms of agency. The meaningful nature of human action does not vouchsafe any agency explanation. The degree to which human actions are self-determined by human agents or determined by stimulus variables is an open and *empirical* question. Nevertheless, the meaningful nature of action does provide the first premise of an argument, which suggests the *plausibility* of some explanations in terms of agency.

It is not even remotely plausible to suppose that the structure and order of the social world is a product of neurophysiological processes that operate independently of the conventional rules and reasons that appear to govern many human actions in the social world. Our neurophysiology must enable us at least to be able to act in accord with rules and reasons—even if we do not always act for the sake of them—and to do so on a significant number of occasions. For otherwise, neither the mundane order of our traffic systems nor the complex structure of our social life could be maintained. That is, the fact that we can and do act in accord with rules and reasons seems to be an ontological condition for the creation and maintenance (and occasional transformation) of the social world in which meaningful human actions are generated.

This thesis is surely uncontroversial. Part of the reason it is uncontroversial is because many contemporary philosophers and psychologists simply explain such actions in terms of want-belief matrices embodying rules and reasons that are held to function as ontologically sufficient conditions for the generation of action (Atkinson & Birch, 1970; Davidson, 1980; Kruglanski, 1979; Locke & Pennington, 1982). Human actions are held to be a product of the "vector forces" of interacting basic and sophisticated wants, and beliefs about the most effective means to their satisfaction (Alston, 1977). Such explanations proceed by articulating reason, rule, and value representations, which are held to be necessary and sufficient conditions for the generation of action, since such internal representations are themselves held to determine action. Thus, for example, Fodor (1975, p. 74) claims: ". . . a representation of the rules they (i.e. organisms) follow constitutes one of the causal determinants of their behavior."

Yet it is far from obvious that all actions can be explained in these terms. Although such an account may be adequate for the productions of robots and computers, which operate on a regimented system of syntax and semantics, it may not so easily extend to all human performances. For social rule, reason, and value representations exist in the real world only in the form of "partially interpreted rules," as do the theories and concepts of natural science (Hempel, 1965), and for precisely the same reason. Such representations must, by their nature, be partially indeterminate or "open-horizoned" (Waismann, 1945) in order that potentialities of meaning change and development can be actualized to accommodate novel facts or features of reality. This is especially true with respect to the social world, in which the realities may be themselves modified and transformed through historical time.

Social representations of constitutive and regulative rules do not themselves specify "how to go on" beyond the standard situations that form the basis of consensus and provide for the possibility of social learning (Wittgenstein, 1953). The consensus prescribes the limits of legitimate transformations, and a new consensus develops through social negotiation to accommodate novel forms of social life (Margolis, 1984; Rommetveit, 1978). One-parent "families" may be accepted as families but homosexual "marriages" may not be accepted as marriages. Such transformations of social meaning are only possible given the possibility of agent developments to accommodate novel and difficult cases, which then become the object of social negotiation.

The open-ended nature of social representations does not only provide for the development of social meaning in reaction to novelty and change. It also provides for the dynamic development of personal meaning to create possibilities of action. The consensual element defines the standard situations, but the agent must decide for herself how to act in novel and difficult situations. The agent must decide for herself whether an action is aggressive, dishonest, or disobedient in nonstandard situations (e.g., when the policeman appears unduly antagonistic; when the worker removes the office stationery for personal purposes; when the schoolchild is frozen in terror at the principal's command), and act in ways she considers to be appropriate to her judgment. She must decide for herself how to interpret social rules in difficult and novel situations, as in the case of a traffic warden faced with a traffic violator who looks sick, or a teacher faced with a brilliant essay submitted beyond the deadline. Such partially interpreted rules can and must be developed by agents in the light of their own personal experience. It follows from this that representations of reasons that may be treated as sufficient reasons by agents are not, in general, themselves sufficient conditions for action, since such reason representations do not invariably specify determinate action outcomes, even in fairly specific circumstances. Human action is often underdetermined by reasons because various courses of action may be held to be in accord with the agent's reasons.

Perhaps the clearest examples of this are moral dilemmas, such as the case of Jean Paul Sartre's student who was faced with the choice of going off to fight for the Free French or remaining at home with his invalid mother (Sartre, 1948). The agent both feels that he ought to fight for the Free French and that he ought to look after his invalid mother (he has reasons that he considers sufficiently justify both forms of action), but he can choose only one alternative. His justificatory reasons may, of course, incline him to favor one course of action over the other. The agent may be inclined to fight for the Free French if he has specialized military and intelligence skills and independent means of supporting his invalid mother. He may be inclined to stay with his invalid mother if his lame leg would be a military liability but allowed him to do useful household and farming chores to support his mother.

Yet within such a spectrum of potential justificatory reasons derived from the particular circumstances, there will be a logical area in which either course of action can be seen as in accord with justificatory reasons. Two different persons with the same reason representations and (hypothetically) the same relevant moral experience may decide on different courses of action, and each would equally be self-determined in accord with reasons. It is true that such a situation requires a decision concerning evaluative orderings (of duties and commitments) and would be explained in such terms. However, the main point of the example is that different agents may produce different evaluative orderings of reasons because reason representations plus experience do not themselves determine evaluative orderings and consequent actions. Moral rules and reasons do not themselves determine decisions about conflicts of rules and novel and difficult situations. As Sartre notes, there is a sense in which we are condemned to be free agents, since we must develop such reasons in our own ways if we are to act in such situations.

Yet contra Sartre, such a decision is not arbitrary (Taylor, 1977). It is precisely in such situations that we create the personal significance of actions by developing personal meaning in the form of committed actions. In such situations we create our own personal identities by moving through indeterminate meanings in determinate ways. We determine the personal worth and significance of actions by the development of personal meaning.

The agent's decision is not a random outcome of conflicting vector forces of inclination which reach equilibrium. The man who makes a judgment of the intrinsic worth of one action in relation to another acts out of considerations of deep personal significance. Furthermore, the indeterminacy of reasons is not simply a function of the balancing of inclinations. All the relevant considerations may incline a man to one course of action, but he may still choose the alternative, because at the end of the day he represents one course of action as having greater intrinsic worth. Like the captain in Melville's *Billy Budd*, he may wish that he was another man who could value things in a different way and act in accord with his inclinations, since he recognizes that his own decision is a matter of personal value not dictated by morality and circumstance (Winch, 1972). The man with the lame leg may at the end of the day go off to fight for the Free French, and the skilled fighter may remain with his mother.

The indeterminacy of some reason representations is not restricted to cases of moral conflict, although these perhaps provide the clearest illustration. It is, rather, a pervasive feature of representations and rules that provide reasons for action. An accepted regulative rule such as "never lend money to strangers" does not itself determine whether one should lend money to a colleague at work. It depends upon whether you consider him a stranger or not. A consensually accepted rule such as "always help members of one's own family" does not itself help family members decide whether it is best to help the sexual offender by providing an alibi to the police or informing the social services. Nor does the motive of revenge itself determine between physical or verbal violence or betrayal; the emotion of disappointment does not determine between renewed or redirected effort; and the sex drive does not determine partner or position.

Indeed, the indeterminacy of reason representations may extend to the representation of the situation itself and surrounding circumstances. While another's action may be objectively an insult, threat, or act of dishonesty, an agent is not always in a position to determine this herself. Often the agent has to act upon her faith in her own intuitions. In this respect, she is not unlike a natural scientist working at a time when there are no critical observations in favor of one competing theory over another (according to some people this is the position most of the time). The scientist's decision to continue working on one theory rather than another can only be a matter of faith in his own intuitions. Yet he must make a decision if he is to continue as a scientist. In general, the agent must simply have faith in her own intuitions and judgments of personal worth and significance if she is to act at all. We have to move through indeterminacies of social meaning to determine personal meaning if we are to make personal passages in the social world. One may bemoan the fact that moral and social rules do not always resolve our moral and social problems. Yet we determine our own personal identities by the individual ways we develop personal meaning to resolve such conflicts, or refuse to face them.

There is another respect in which the position of the ordinary agent is analogous to the natural scientist. Scientific theories and theoretical models do not themselves determine the way in which theories and models are developed (partially interpreted theoretical systems do not themselves determine the ways in which they are further interpreted), although they do provide restraints on possible or plausible developments. The development of metaphor and analogy, which forms the basis of much scientific investigation and discovery, is a creative exercise of the scientific imagination that provides richer and novel representations of reality. Likewise, personal meaning and value are often not simply a matter of selecting alternative interpretations of partially indeterminate social meaning, but a personal extension of social meaning by imaginative developments of analogy and metaphor.

Thus, the agent may see her kidney dialysis machine as a friend (Rosser, 1982), his workplace as a place of quasi-religious devotion or a circus (Gergen, 1982), her relations with family and friends as theater or Machiavellian manipulations, and his whole career as a crusade or western movie. Such personal meanings may, of course, be unrealistic and inappropriate, and even pathological. Nevertheless, a man's actions may very well be self-determined in accord with such representations of personal meaning (e.g., his western symbolism may explain his clothing and conduct at a critical interview).

Many human actions do appear to be self-determined by agents against a background of created personal meanings which embody their faith in and commitment to social, moral, religious, and scientific intuitions that extend by analogy, metaphor, and creative imagination way beyond the information given in the form of sensory inputs and cognitive rules. It would, of course, be unreasonable to deny that sometimes our actions are determined by internal or external stimulus variables, and it would also be unreasonable to deny that this is sometimes the case in conditions of representational indeterminacy. But it is grossly implausible to suppose that all such cases can be explained in this way. For any general explanation would either make reference to factors that are themselves representational in nature (such as unconscious motivations), in which case the indeterminacy would simply be relocated. Or it would make reference to factors (e.g., neurophysiological factors) that generate behavior independently of reason and rule representations, which is not remotely plausible (although logically possible) with respect to social action in general or cases of representational indeterminacy in particular. This salient feature of our social psychological life at the very least requires the serious attention of a scientific social psychology, either to provide an empirical demonstration of the inaccuracy of what appears to be the most intuitively plausible explanation in terms of self-determination, or provide a theoretical account of how human agents are *enabled* to determine their own actions for the sake of reasons.

Indeterminacy and Explanation

It might be objected that the indeterminacy of reasons poses some threat to the objective evaluation of agency explanations, since explanations making reference to this indeterminacy will not license specific predictions about action outcomes (in the sense that they cannot function as premises from which a description of action outcome can be deduced).

It is true that actions based upon indeterminate reasons will be unpredictable in principle, and it is important to recognize why this is the case. It is not due to a lack of any possible knowledge on the part of the observer, who may know all there is to know about the relevant details of the situation and the agent's representation of it. The observer's difficulty in predicting what the agent will do is simply a reflection of the difficulty the agent has in *deciding* what to do. That is, their problems derive from the same source: the fact that represented rules and reasons do not invariably specify determinate courses of action in all possible situations. This point may be expressed by noting that representations of rules, reasons, and situation do not always admit of *rational closure*.

Nevertheless, this poses no threat to the objectivity of experimental or quasi-experimental evaluations of causal explanations in terms of agency. In the first place, not all reasons and situational representations are indeterminate. Often enough our reasons and represented circumstances are only too determinate. Sometimes there is only one viable option open to us (e.g., to admit we are wrong, resign, or commit suicide). Second, it has already been noted that successful prediction in open systems is not the measure of the adequacy of causal explanation in any science.

Although it is true that representational indeterminacy may also manifest itself in conditions of experimental isolation, this does not mean that an agency account based upon the exercise of personal powers for the sake of (indeterminate or determinate) reasons cannot be shown to be the best explanation. For such explanations are always evaluated in relation to alternative liability explanations in terms of sufficient stimulus conditions, which do license very specific predictions in experimental settings. When these are consistently rejected, the agency account remains as the best available explanation. And like any other causal explanation confirmed in experimental circumstances, it can be extended to provide retrospective explanations of actions in open systems that would have been difficult to predict in practice (because of the difficulties of anticipating conditions of generation and interference) or impossible to predict in principle (because of representational indeterminacy). Indeed, the latter case provides the most extreme illustration of the asymmetry of explanation and prediction. Although we cannot in principle predict the actions of the person faced with the Sartre dilemma, we can provide a wholly adequate explanation of his eventual action as self-determined for the sake of reasons.

This is not to deny the difficulty of establishing individual explanations of human actions for the purpose of legal judgments or therapeutic assessment. It may be difficult to determine in many cases, for example, whether an aggressive action was the product of a liability or self-determined malice. But it is not impossible. The exploitation of resources such as biography, social context, agent accounting and intervention can often demonstrate, or at least strongly support, one explanation against its rivals. As noted earlier, additional information gleaned from observation or intervention generally tends to delimit the range of viable explanations rather than increase explanatory ambiguity (contra Gergen, 1982). A woman who regularly beats her children for even the most trivial offenses is not normally really concerned with moral discipline—despite her avowal to the contrary—and is not likely to be suffering from a liability if she never beats her children for offensive and aggressive behavior toward other children or adults. A woman who is normally loving and considerate and who only rarely disciplines her children for serious and dangerous offenses is clearly suffering from some liability if she is suddenly and spontaneously violent toward them, for no good reason avowed by her or apparent from the context.

These are practical matters of some social significance to be determined by social agents. Yet it ought to be stressed that these questions are *not* the proper object of social psychological science. It is simply unreasonable to expect such a science to furnish individual explanations of individual actions, and quite unrealistic to imagine that it can determine agent reasons in every individual case. The position of the social investigator is more analogous to the insurance company investigator than the natural scientist. Both exploit specific information about historical circumstances to establish specific causal explanations of individual motor accidents and fires, and acts of aggression and dishonesty. In both cases, the evidence sometimes clearly establishes only one account as viable over its possible rivals. Sometimes, the available evidence is insufficient to discriminate between two or more plausible explanations. Sometimes, the knowledge gained from natural scientific or social scientific research may aid the practical investigator in discriminating between competing explanations. Knowledge of the combustion temperature of some materials may eliminate some causal explanations of some fires in terms of discarded cigarettes or short-circuiting. Knowledge of social or neurophysiological determinants of aggression may strongly suggest that some mothers are suffering from a human liability when they beat their children.

It ought, however, to be stressed that the epistemological problems of the practical investigator are not the epistemological problems of the social psychological scientist. The practical investigator attempts to establish particular causal explanations in *open systems* on the basis of available evidence. The social psychological scientist creates or discriminates experimental and natural closures to determine human powers and liabilities, and their enabling, stimulus, and interference conditions. In fact, there are no special epistemological problems for the practical investigator who attempts to establish the causal explanation of individual actions. The effectiveness of practical investigation is delimited by moral concerns about manipulation and invasion of privacy long before the epistemological resources of the investigator have been exhausted. De Waele (1971) and his colleagues have demonstrated the power of rigorous studies based upon detailed biography and constant monitoring of the agent in discriminating between competing explanations of the actions of murderers. No doubt jurors and psychoanalytic therapists could be more objective if they had a complete video-recording of the agent's past, if they could intervene to require justificatory commentary at any point, and if they could require the agent to act in specific ways or refrain from specific actions in specific circumstances. But this is justly considered to be morally objectionable by social investigators and their subjects.

A realist philosophy of social psychological science does not suggest that there are easy answers to these questions. It only insists that there is a determinate answer to these questions, however difficult it is to achieve in practice. It denies that competing causal explanations of individual actions are invariably incommensurable because of the unobservability of psychological states or the theory informity of observations, while recognizing that some competing explanations of individual actions may remain incommensurable because of the moral restraints on our epistemological resources.

We should, however, be careful to distinguish cases of insufficient evidence from cases of genuine indeterminacy with respect to an agent's reasons for action. There may be some cases in which agents act in accord with a whole variety of reasons (including unconscious reasons), but for the sake of none in particular. The self-determined action may be simply congruent with a wide range of generally motivating representations. The question of *the* reason for an action may not arise for the scientific observer because it may not arise for the agent. This may in fact prove to be the best explanation of some of our actions. Yet although there is indeterminacy about the detailed specification of the set of relevant reasons in such cases, this does not mean there is a similar indeterminacy about the explanation or its evaluation. If all other explanations fail, then the best explanation may prove to be that the action was self-determined in accord with an indeterminate set of reasons. This may prove to be the objective fact of the matter in some cases.[10]

10
Explanation, Prediction, and Control

One of the philosophical virtues of realism is that it is theoretically *neutral*. Other philosophical "paradigms" do not share this virtue. The methodological prescriptions of the behaviorist deny the legitimacy of psychological explanations. The doctrines of scientific psychology deny the legitimacy of agency explanations, via the commitment to the Humean account of causality. The doctrines of hermeneutical psychology deny the legitimacy of explanations of human action in terms of ontologically sufficient conditions.

Realism makes no such explanatory commitments. For the realist, it is an entirely contingent matter whether any form of human action is best explained in terms of social relations or agent representations, or in terms of environmental stimuli or neurophysiological states. The realist can consistently hold that human actions are sometimes self-determined by agents for the sake of reasons, and sometimes determined and frequently influenced by situational, emotional, motivational, hormonal, neurophysiological, biological, physical, geographical, social, and political factors.

A realist science of meaningful human action does not prejudge any properly empirical questions. However, it does require some considerable modification of the traditional scientific psychological statement of the goal of social psychological science as the explanation, prediction, and control of human behavior.

Explanation

According to realism, a causal explanation of an action is not the description of a constant conjunction or regularity. Causal explanations make reference to the generative powers of human agents, and their enabling, stimulus, and interference conditions. Some of these explanations make reference to human powers of self-determination; others make reference to human liabilities determined by all kinds of ontologically sufficient conditions. Realism makes no prior commitment to the best theoretical explanation of these powers and liabilities.

In fact it can be anticipated that most theoretical explanations of human powers and liabilities will make reference to enabling conditions on a variety of ontological strata. Thus, the specific powers of a judge and the generic powers of language speakers require explanation by reference to biological, neurophysiological, psychological, and social enabling conditions, both local and developmental (Manicas & Secord, 1983).

These *causally* necessary and sufficient conditions must be carefully distinguished from the social relations and representations that are constitutive of human actions and social practices. Qua constitutive dimensions, these features are *logically* necessary and sufficient conditions for actions. These social relations and representations may sometimes also function as causally necessary and sufficient conditions, but this is an entirely separate empirical question. Like realism, the *social constitutionist* analysis of human actions and practices is theoretically neutral. It does not vouchsafe any explanations in terms of social relational or representational dimensions, or in terms of human agency.

Nevertheless, the social relational and representational dimensions of human action must be insisted upon against the scientific psychologist. The scientific psychologist does not in fact restrict the goal of social psychological science to the explanation, prediction, and control of *behavior*. Her causal explanations based upon experimental and other empirical studies are advanced as explanations of socially meaningful actions such as aggression, dishonesty, risk taking, and destructive obedience. Unless the social relational and representational dimensions of such actions are reproduced in experimental and other empirical studies, explanatory inferences drawn from them will not be empirically warranted. The successful reproduction of behavior is insufficient to establish that this is the case.

There is no reason in principle why the realist logic of experimental isolation and explanatory inference common to all causal sciences cannot be reproduced in social psychological science. The central methodological problems of social psychological science are problems of *identification*, which themselves derive from the scientific psychologist's neglect of the relational and representational dimensions of human action. The scientific psychologist's failure to establish that behaviors are instances of play, loneliness, dishonesty, aggression, obedience, attitude change, friendship, and risk taking in experimental studies and other forms of empirical enquiry is a consequence of his failure to discriminate the social relational and representational dimensions of human action in these forms of empirical enquiry. His failure to do so is a direct consequence of his methodological decision to restrict his empirical enquiries to the observation of behavior.

Nevertheless, there are two qualifications that ought to be made about explanatory inferences in social psychological science. It was noted earlier that if experimental studies demonstrate that some acts of aggression are caused by violent stimuli, then this explanation can be extended to cover everyday instances of aggression preceded by exposure to violent stimuli.

However, it cannot be presumed that every act of aggression preceded by exposure to violent stimuli can be causally explained in these terms. Some acts of aggression may be best explained as self-determined acts of revenge or determined by neurophysiological states, even when violent stimuli are present (i.e., in some cases violent stimuli are not causally potent).

It has already been noted that we have reason to expect multiple causal explanations of the same form of action, since human actions form social psychological rather than natural kinds. We would only have grounds for supposing that explanations true of some agents would be true of all others if human agents themselves formed a natural kind. Yet although human *beings* do form a natural biological kind (and some universal features of their behavior may be explained by biological theories), it cannot be presumed that human *agents* form a unitary social psychological kind. The form and content of individual psychologies and social skills may be different for some participants in a form of life, and for different cultures and historical periods.

This is, of course, an empirical question, and there may very well be some social and psychological dimensions shared by all human agents. Yet all the available empirical evidence counts against the notion that all agents are qualitatively identical with respect to their personal natures. It is very rare in social psychological experiments or everyday life to find all agents reacting in the same way to independent variables or to everyday situations and actions, whereas this is the norm with respect to the natural kinds of natural science (all samples of sulfuric acid behave in identical ways in identical circumstances). Some of these differences can be explained in terms of interference, but it is not remotely plausible to suppose that they can all be explained in this way. It seems fairly obvious that some priests are simply not liable to engage in destructive obedience, even when all impediments are removed; that some policemen are simply not liable to be dishonest, even in the face of the strongest temptation and without any chance of detection; and that some doctors are simply not liable to fail to recognize an emergency.

This obviously places limits on the explanation and prediction of individual human actions. However, it has already been noted that this is not a realistic goal for social psychological science. This is not to deny that practical investigators can often enough successfully establish the correct causal explanation of individual human actions, or to deny that the fruits of social psychological research can greatly aid them in doing so. However, this is not the sole utility of causal knowledge gleaned from social psychological research. Even if such knowledge cannot always be exploited to provide explanations of individual actions, it can be exploited via social intervention to promote or deter various forms of human action. Our knowledge of the enabling conditions for human powers, and the stimulus and interference conditions for human liabilities, enable social agents to encourage or discourage various forms of action in the social world. Thus, we may promote mathematical and social skills in children and adults by creating conditions that enable them to be developed. We may deter acts of aggression by reducing exposure to violent stimuli (via media regulation or gun control) or by demonstrating our public willingness to punish acts of aggression (either collectively or individually).

This may sound objectionably manipulative, but in fact it is not. Most of the time we can only promote or deter, or encourage or discourage, rather than *control* human action. For the second qualification that needs to be made is that it is doubtful if there really are many genuine human liabilities. It seems extremely doubtful that there are many actions that are strictly determined by ontologically sufficient conditions. A great many personal liabilities can be overcome through personal effort. Many persons are liable to be aggressive and offensive through lack of effort and attention. Many liabilities can be simply surmounted though knowledge of the liability. I may be liable to ignore my wife and family when under stress, but being aware of this is half the battle. Agents who come to learn of the phenomenon of "bystander apathy" regularly intervene in future emergencies (Beaman, Klentz, & McQuirk, 1978). No doubt some agents who read Milgram's (1974) study will be better able to resist some of the more objectionable demands of some authorities. Some genuine liabilities will remain resistant to personal effort and education, notably those human misfortunes that form the subject matter of clinical psychology. Yet their elimination or attenuation is the hope and promise of psychological therapy. In this light it is perhaps best to talk most of the time of stimulus variable *influences* rather than *determinants* of human action.

It should be stressed that the surmountability of human liabilities does *not* render causal explanations based upon them historical and thus unscientific (contra Gergen, 1973). The elimination or alleviation of bystander apathy, dishonesty, or depression by personal effort, education, or therapy does not undermine our causal explanations of these phenomena. In fact it serves as further support for them. The elimination or alleviation of these human liabilities is logically analogous to the elimination or alleviation of diseases when a prophylactic or antidote has been identified and distributed. In both cases, successful intervention is based upon causal knowledge of the mechanism of the liability or the disease. The success of the intervention only provides further support for the independently established causal account. The perhaps rare and residual instances of the liability or disease are still legitimately explained in terms of the original causal account, even if they occur only once in a blue moon. We may still explain the perhaps very rare cases of bystander apathy (after an intensive educational campaign) in terms of (failed) social perception, if this account has been independently established in laboratory and field experiments. We may still explain the perhaps very rare cases of tuberculosis in terms of exposure to the tubercle bacillus, if this has been independently established by medical research as the cause of tuberculosis.

Prediction

For the realist, the prediction of individual actions is an inappropriate and unrealistic goal for social psychological science, as the prediction of individual events is an inappropriate and unrealistic goal for the natural sciences. Few causal explanations in any science serve as efficient instruments for the prediction of individual actions and events because of the enormous difficulties of anticipating conditions of generation and interference. The proper place for prediction in any science is the testing of the implications of causal theories in conditions of experimental or natural closure. Enabling conditions can be discriminated by the successful prediction of the absence of human powers and abilities given the absence of local or developmental conditions. Stimulus determinants and influences can be determined by the prediction of correlations under conditions of experimental or natural closure.

It was noted in the last chapter that the partial indeterminacy of reasons does not preclude the objective and experimental evaluation of causal explanations in terms of self-determination in accord with reasons. Alternative stimulus variable accounts do license specific predictions under conditions of closure, and agent reasons can be established as rationalizations if stimulus variables correlate with actions in conditions of closure. Thus, it can be established that the presence of other bystanders, or violent stimuli, or proximity of authorities determine or influence bystander apathy, aggression, and destructive obedience, respectively, if these conditions and actions are closely correlated under closure, and if agents' justificatory reasons bear no systematic relation to consequent actions. Conversely, if the opposite proved to be the case, only the most dogmatic empiricist would deny that such actions were self-determined exercises of personal powers for the sake of reasons.

It is worth stressing, however, that the limits imposed upon prediction by the partial indeterminacy of agent reasons applies in general only to a very-fine-grained analysis of action. In real life and social psychological science, this limitation is more than compensated for by the predictability of human action in terms of more general categories. We may not be able to determine precisely what the agent will represent as the demands of duty, what precise form of revenge the injured man will take, what precise form of nourishment the hungry man will seek, or what specific symptoms the neurotic will manifest. Yet we can and do successfully predict that the agent will do what he represents as his duty, that the injured man will take his revenge, that the hungry man will eat, and that the neurotic will display ineffective and exaggerated responses to supposed threats. Furthermore, the meaningful and rule-governed nature of human action renders it predictable for agents and observers in a fashion that goes far beyond what is normally achieved in the natural sciences. Nor is this a surprising fact of social psychology. It is rather a condition of coordinated and integrated social interaction.

By ignoring fine-grain details of action and concentrating on the structure of interaction, we can develop and integrate a whole series of connected predictions covering a temporally extended process of action and interaction (Dennett, 1981). For many persons, we can predict a good deal of their consequent actions when they discover that their spouses have been unfaithful, when they have won a substantial amount of money in a lottery, or when they have been made redundant. This is especially true when agents occupy conventional social and political roles. We know very well the actions that will be taken by trade union officials when they are presented with an insultingly low wage offer, and we know very well the steps that will be taken by treasury ministers when faced with a financial crisis.

It is also worth stressing the extent of such everyday predictive achievements. Such successful and extended open-system predictions are far in excess of the degree of open-system prediction that can usually be achieved in the natural sciences. This is because regularities of action and interaction are maintained by social conventions rather than accidental distributions of conditions of generation and interference. Such regularities are maintained in the social world by "covering institutions" (Margolis, 1983), which are culturally and historically specific but function as very efficient predictive devices in specific cultures or historical periods. In terms of open-system prediction, it is quite wrong to say that the social psychological sciences are the poor cousins of the natural sciences.

Control

It is apposite to ask in what sense a causal science of action can mark an advance over our common and highly developed capacities for the successful and extended prediction of the actions and interactions of others. Certainly, a knowledge of stimulus determinants and influences may enable the scientist to maintain a temporary advantage over the agent. Yet such a predictive advantage can often only be maintained if knowledge of such stimulus variables is withheld from agents, for many liabilities can be surmounted through effort, education, and therapy. The elimination of human liabilities and the consequent extension of human powers in general renders human action less predictable, since it opens up new possibilities of action for agents. The only way in which a causal science of action could more closely approximate the empiricist goal of ever-increasing predictive adequacy is by controlling the dissemination of social psychological knowllege, by manipulating the stimulus and interference conditions of human liabilities, and by intervening to delimit the opportunities and options for self-determined action.

There is no doubt that a causal science of action and associated technologies could, by selective control of social psychological knowledge and the manipulation and control of stimulus and interference conditions, create or eliminate actions in the everyday world via the application of causal knowledge gleaned from experimentation. No doubt social psychologists could create more regular instances of destructive obedience in the everyday world by isolating agents from their peers (who might provide moral support for disobedience) and victims (who might engage their sympathy), and by limiting the information available to them.

Few would, of course, naturally suggest that social psychological knowledge should be employed in such a malevolent fashion. It is, however, generally assumed by those concerned with the ethics of applied social psychology that "potentially beneficial" regularities identified in laboratory experiments should be manipulated in the real world (Henschel, 1980). Yet by focusing exclusively on the moral and political questions of who should exercise the necessary control or make the appropriate identifications of benefit (social psychologists, politicians, parents, educators, or committees of such persons), writers in this tradition (Skinner, 1974) simply foreclose the question of *whether* such external control of the actions of fellow humans should be exercised.

Yet there is no intrinsic reason why this should be the case. A realist science of action that accepts the possibility of human agency may have a quite different conception of the social role of causal knowledge. Causal knowledge gleaned from experimental and other empirical enquiries may be employed and exploited to extend human powers and self-determination, and eliminate or alleviate human liabilities. This does not involve the prediction and control of others. Rather, it involves the transfer of control of action from stimulus conditions to human agents. It implies, for example, that the goal of moral education and much psychotherapy is the promotion and maintainance of human agency and *self-control*, and not the "engineering" of specific cognitions and emotions which themselves determine human action (contra Brehm, 1976). It is the promotion of the enabling conditions of principled action and self-determination, and not the inculcation of rules and reasons that determine specific performances.

This is, of course, an explicitly *moral* position. It is not entailed by a realist philosophy of science, which is morally as well as theoretically neutral. How we employ and exploit the causal knowledge gleaned from natural and social psychological sciences is a separate question, to be determined by social ethics and individual conscience. Nevertheless, it is worth nothing that a realist philosophy of science can easily accommodate the often honorable and humanitarian concerns of hermeneutical, existential, and humanist critics of a scientific social psychology.

The empiricist analysis of social psychological science simply assumes that the goal of a science of action is the prediction and control of human action via the manipulation and control of its causal antecedents, as a consequence of its commitment to a stimulus variable conception of causality and its consequent denial of human agency. A realist analysis of social psychological science illustrates that the employment of social psychological knowledge for the prediction and control of others is itself the product of a moral or political decision (or philosophical error). A causal science of action provides no special warrant for such decisions.

This is not to say that there cannot often be good moral or political reasons for intervention, especially when antisocial and dangerous actions threaten the moral order and individual lives. It is simply to insist that these moral and political decisions must be supported by moral and political reasons. They are not vouchsafed by any philosophy of science.

11
The Experimental Analysis of Human Action

The "Crisis" in Experimental Social Psychology

Traditional experimental techniques in social psychological science have been the object of vigorous and sustained criticism during the past quarter century. A variety of writers have drawn attention to problems such as "experimenter bias" (Rosenthal, 1976), "demand characteristics" (Orne, 1962), "evaluation apprehension" (Rosenberg, 1969), and the unrepresentative nature of many (usually volunteer student) experimental subjects (Rosnow & Rosenthal, 1970, 1976; Schultz, 1969). Others have focused on more fundamental issues, and have questioned the very rationale of experimental techniques on methodological (Adair, 1973; Orne & Holland, 1968), moral (Baumrind, 1964; Kelman, 1967), and philosophical grounds (Deese, 1972; Harré & Secord, 1972).

This has led some commentators to talk of a "crisis" in social psychology (Elms, 1975; Gergen, 1978). Nevertheless, despite some genuine appeals for a pluralistic approach to research (Tajfel & Fraser, 1978; Eiser, 1980), and a shift of emphasis from the laboratory to the field (McGuire, 1967; Silverman, 1977), these critiques appear to have had little effect on practice (Cochrane & Duffy, 1974; Suls & Gastorf, 1980). Indeed, according to some recent surveys, there has been an increase in the number of published laboratory studies in relation to other forms of empirical enquiry (Freid, Gumper, & Allan, 1973; Higbee, Millard, & Folkman, 1982; Potter, 1981).

The reasons for this recalcitrance are no doubt many and multifarious. It may be in part because many of the more radical critiques have been produced by professional philosophers rather than psychologists, although this is by no means exclusively the case (see, for example, Bruner, 1979; Gauld & Shotter, 1977; Gergen, 1982). It may also be in part because in the literature methodological points tend to be conflated with moral objections, which probably explains the common view among practitioners that experiments, and especially deception experiments, are "unfortunate but necessary" (Miller, 1972).

However, possibly the central reason lies in the fact that such critiques of experimentation in social psychological science are often but an aspect of more fundamental hermeneutical objections to a causal science of meaningful human action. It is regularly complained by such critics that experiments that investigate causal relationships in a science of action are not merely presently inadequate or problematic, but are totally inappropriate. This results in the wholly justified perception by practicing psychologists that the acceptance of such critiques would be to effectively abandon a scientific social psychology, and eliminate experimentation as a legitimate research strategy.

It is, however, most unfortunate that the practicing social psychologist rejects these hermeneutical critiques altogether. For it has been noted that although such arguments do not demonstrate that explanations of human action are noncausal or nonobjective, they do embody important truths (albeit implicit and often misrepresented) about the relational nature of social psychological phenomena, including the often critical relation of participant agent representation. In consequence, the commitment of the practicing psychologist to empiricist analyses of explanation and experimentation leads her to neglect or ignore the critical problems of experimental social psychology that arise because of the meaningful nature of human action. Most of the present inadequacies of experimental social psychology can be traced to philosophical misconceptions about the nature and role of experimentation in a causal science, and the neglect of the social relational and representational dimensions of human action.

The Artificiality of Experiments

The ubiquitous complaint about experiments in social psychology concerns the "artificiality" of the laboratory experiment in social psychology (Babbie, 1975; Borgatta & Bohrnstedt, 1974; Campbell & Stanley, 1966; Harré & Secord, 1972; Kelman, 1972; McClintock, 1972; McGuire, 1967; Tajfel, 1972). It is often complained that the results of such experiments have little or no relevance to real-life situations: "The greatest weakness of laboratory experiments lies in their artificiality. Social processes observed to occur within a laboratory setting might not necessarily occur within more natural settings" (Babbie, 1975, p. 254).

However, there are a variety of senses in which the laboratory experiment in social psychology may be said to be artificial. These are not always clearly distinguished, and are regularly confused in empiricist accounts. In particular, it is critical to distinguish the sense in which experiments are artificial insofar as active steps are taken to *isolate* the investigated system from alternative generative or interference conditions; the sense in which experiments may be artificial as a result of external and peculiar *contaminants* that are introduced as unwanted (and unintended) conditions of generation and interference as a product of experimenter-subject interactions;

and the crucial sense in which experimental techniques may *alter* or *transform* the very nature of the system investigated.

This is worth stressing, since there has been a considerable reaction to such critiques within the profession, in the form of defenses of the status quo. Berkowitz and Donnerstein (1982) and Kruglanski (1975, 1976) have argued that most criticisms have been overstated, and that the artificiality of experiments is a common characteristic of any science. Henschel (1980) and Mook (1983) have argued that even the grossest artificiality may be of scientific value, and Dipboye and Flanagan (1979) have questioned the assumption that field studies are more generalizable than laboratory experiments, pointing out that both are limited in terms of the subjects, settings, and behaviors sampled.

There is certainly some point to these reactions, which recognize that the isolation of social psychological phenomena is characteristic of any experimental analysis of human action. Yet by focusing on this common form of artificiality, and by treating experimental contaminants as relatively unproblematic technical interferences, such commentators simply avoid the special problems of experimental social psychology that are a product of the meaningful nature of human action. In consequence, by failing to appreciate the special difficulties of reproducing social psychological phenomena in laboratory (or field) experiments, experimentalists fail to achieve the form of artificiality of experimental analysis that is characteristic of sound scientific practice. They fail to achieve the effective isolation of hypothetical causal and interference conditions with respect to human powers and liabilities.

Experimental Isolation

It was noted in Chapter 4 that there is nothing objectionable about the *artificiality of isolation*. Indeed, it is essential to the logic of experimentation in any causal science. Experimental closure by ontological or control isolation enables the experimentalist to determine the enabling, stimulus, and interference conditions for human powers and liabilities. Causal knowledge gleaned from such experiments can be employed to provide explanations of human actions in real-world open systems. Thus, for example, if it can be established by experimental closure that aggressive actions are determined or influenced by violent stimuli, then instances of aggression in the real world can be causally explained by reference to antecedent exposure to violent stimuli. Such closed experiments do not license predictions about individual actions or regularities in open systems, because of interference (and the difficulties of anticipating generative and interference conditions). Instances of violent stimuli may not be regularly followed by aggressive actions in open systems, given social inhibition.

There are two essential conditions that must be satisfied if experiments in social psychological science are to support causal explanatory inferences to the real world. The causal dimension(s) under analysis must be effectively isolated from other causal conditions and interference. The causal dimension(s) and actions under analysis must be successfully reproduced and reidentified in experimental systems.

INTERNAL AND EXTERNAL VALIDITY

Social psychologists do recognize the importance of isolation and control in the evaluation of causal explanations. They often make distinctions between different research methods in terms of the degree of isolation and control that can be achieved. Tajfel and Fraser (1978) suggest a continuum of methods running from laboratory experiments (high isolation and control) through field experiments and controlled observation to participant observation (low on isolation and control). They also usually distinguish as a separate question the issue about the generalizability of research results in social psychology. Nevertheless, the two issues are held to be intimately related. It is often suggested that generalizations are more reliable the closer the research situation approximates the real-life situation, and that increases in laboratory control tend to create excessively unrealistic (or "unnatural" or "limited") social situations.

This peculiar point of view is regularly expressed in articulations of the standard distinction between *internal validity* and *external validity* (Campbell & Stanley, 1966). Laboratory experiments are held to maximize on internal validity: the isolation and control of the laboratory experiment enables us to make accurate judgments about causality in laboratory experiments. However, laboratory experiments are held to be low on external validity: the increasing artificiality of the experimental situation casts serious doubt about any causal inferences drawn about actions in the real world. Laboratory experiments are often contrasted with field studies, such as participant observation without intervention, which are held to be high on external validity since they deal with real-life situations, but low on internal validity because of the absence of isolation and control.

It is generally agreed that there is an important respect in which internal and external validity may be said to be inversely proportional: success in one area tends to be inversely related to success in the other (Miller, 1975; Tajfel & Fraser, 1978). Techniques that facilitate isolation and control tend to delimit the generalizability of results, and techniques that ensure generalizability tend to leave causal questions ambiguous: "The research decisions that increase internal validity often do so at the expense of external validity" (Conrad & Maul, 1981, p. 17).

These issues are certainly related, but they are *not* related in this fashion. On the contrary, the adequacy of any explanatory inference from the laboratory or field experiment to the real world is *directly* related to and dependent upon successful isolation and control. The external validity of an experiment is *directly* related to its internal validity. In any causal science, the adequacy of explanatory inferences to real-world open systems is directly proportional to the adequacy of closed experiments that provide evidential support for such inferences.[1]

It may be immediately noted that this sense of external validity is quite different from the sense that is normally employed by social psychologists in discussions of the relevance of experimental studies. Given his empiricist commitments, the practicing social psychologist almost invariably represents external validity in terms of predictive inferences about degrees of regular conjunction in real-world open systems.[2] This is, however, quite unjustified, and is a direct manifestation of the practitioner's failure to clearly distinguish between causal explanatory and descriptive correlative enquiries, and the special techniques and strategies appropriate to each.

The aim of an experimental analysis of human action is the identification of the enabling, stimulus, and interference conditions for human powers and liabilities. The successful discrimination of these conditions by ontological and control isolation enables the experimenter to provide causal explanations of actions in real-world open systems. Successful closure is a condition of explanatory but not predictive inference in real-world open systems.

Thus, if Milgram was successful in isolating a "wisdom-command" authority in his experiments on "destructive obedience," and if the experiments did in fact demonstrate the power of some authorities to generate destructive obedience in some persons (the liabilities of some persons to obey such an authority when commanded to harm another), then references to "wisdom-command" authorities can be employed to provide a causal explanation of real-world instances of destructive obedience when preceded by commands from such authorities (such as the Hofling et al. [1966] study and the Mai Lay massacre). The adequacy of such explanations entirely depends upon the adequacy of the Milgram experiment. If Milgram failed to isolate instances of authority and destructive obedience, then such causal explanatory inferences are quite unsupported by his studies.

It is simply beside the point to complain that Milgram's experiment is inadequate because it does not support any predictive inference about real-world regularities (even given antecedent instances of authoritarian commands), and it is to miscontrue the logic of experiment to make this sort of complaint about any experimental study. The closed experiment (laboratory or field) is not designed to estimate degrees of open-system regularity, nor can it be reasonably employed to do so, since it is quite unrepresentative of open systems (special steps are taken to eliminate and control interference conditions and alternative generative conditions that may be more or less frequently instantiated in the real world).

The artificiality of isolation is not an inadequacy of experiments. It is an intrinsic feature of the logic of experimentation and causal explanatory inference. Yet although the logic of closed experimentation and causal explanatory inference is common to all causal and experimental sciences, it is an entirely different question as to whether an experimental social psychology is in general capable of creating situations that satisfy these basic logical requirements. The real problems about laboratory experimentation in social psychology are problems of internal validity. They are problems asscociated with the attempt to create closed experiments in a social psychological science. The special problems of laboratory experimentation in social psychology are created by the difficulties of reproducing social psychological phenomena in isolation from their normal relational context.

Experimental Contamination

Social psychologists do recognize some real problems of internal validity with respect to laboratory experiments, although because of the empiricist conflation of causal explanatory and descriptive correlative enquiries, these are commonly misrepresented as problems about obtaining an uncontaminated sample. The creation of closed experiments in a social psychological science is especially problematic because of the "interaction paradoxes" of social psychological research.

In natural science the activity of the experimenter is often in large part responsible for the creation of the closed system under analysis, such as a sample of Uranium 239. But the activity of the experimenter plays no part in the causal generation of the observed effect. Uranium 239 would emit beta particles and transmute to Neptunium whether the experimenter was there or not. However, this is not obviously the case in experimental social psychology, where the activity of the experimenter, and especially the interaction between experimenter and subjects, often does appear to influence the outcome of the experiment. The relation between the experimental observer and the observed appears to be of a different order from the standard relation of natural science (with the possible exception of quantum mechanics). The very fact that subjects represent the experimental situation *as* an experiment, and that such representations may play a role in the production of actions, marks a critical difference between laboratory experiments and real-world social situations, and between experiments in natural and social psychological sciences: "A necessary precondition of the experimental method is that the phenomena being investigated should not be materially affected by the procedure used to investigate it. . . . No such assumption is possible, unfortunately, with human subjects" (Beloff, 1973, p. 11).

Now this is not strictly true. The activity of the experimenter in natural science does often influence the outcome of the experiment, although this effect is usually minimal, readily identifiable, and easily compensated for. For example, the measurement of an experimentally produced decrease in temperature or pressure may itself contribute to the decrease in temperature or pressure of the investigated system. Indeed, it is unfortunately the case that many experimentalists in social psychology treat the special problems of experimental social psychology as minor technical problems of more or less the same order (Barber, 1978). Experimenter-subject interactions are treated as introducing additional and contaminating variables into the experimentally created situation. They introduce the *artificiality of contamination.*

Rosenthal (1976) has documented a variety of forms of "experimenter bias": various experimenter variables such as the age, sex, race, and sociability of the experimenter appear to influence the actions of at least some experimental subjects. One special variant of experimenter bias is what Rosenthal calls the "experimenter expectancy" effect: the experimenter appears to unconsciously influence the actions of at least some subjects by covertly suggesting (via multifarious verbal and nonverbal cues) his expectation of the outcome of the experiment. Another type of problem is what Orne (1962) has termed the "demand characteristics" of social psychological experiments. The structure and format of the experiment itself suggests the experimental hypothesis to subjects who may act in conformity with their representation of what is expected of them in the experiment. The problem is compounded, if Rosenthal is correct, by the experimenter herself providing some of the cues.

It is true that this only generates objectionable confirmation of experimental hypotheses if subjects both recognize the experimental hypothesis and act in accord with it. Yet subjects can and do attempt to discern the experimental hypothesis, and the problem is compounded by subjects' low confession rates and their ability to act as if naive (Golding & Lichtenstein, 1970). Subjects are often docile (Fillenbaum & Fry, 1970) and cooperative (Orne, 1962), manifesting a desire to please the experimenter. They are concerned with appearing normal and preserving their self-esteem (Crano & Brewer, 1973), a common characteristic that Rosenberg (1969) has classified as "evaluation apprehension." Subjects are generally volunteers (Rosenthal & Rosnow, 1975), who are more likely, inter alia, to cooperate with the experimenter and seek social approval.

Certainly, such subject variables do not always influence action in the same direction, and indeed they are often in conflict (Sigall, Aronson, & Hoose, 1970). Nor is it suggested that subjects are invariably suspicious, that they invariably recognize the experimental hypothesis, or that they invariably act in accord with it. However, this is no advantage for the experimenter, since levels of subject suspicion, admission of suspicion, and reactions to suspicion appear to depend upon individual differences, which are rarely controlled variables in laboratory research (Stricker, Messick, & Jackson, 1967). The fact that some subjects may act in accord with incorrect representations of the experimental hypothesis, and others may resentfully act in direct opposition to the correctly represented experimental hypothesis, only compounds the problem.

It is also true that the operation and extent of the operation of these influences is itself a contentious question in experimental social psychology. Some experimenters have claimed success in replications of experimenter expectancy effects (Minor, 1970), but others have reported failed replications (Barber et al., 1969). Again such failures to replicate and the possible nonuniversal nature of such influences can be of little comfort for the experimental social psychologist. In natural science, the failure to replicate experimental results only establishes that such results do not constitute significant evidence instances, since clearly there is some failure of isolation and control. The central difficulty created by such contaminating influences is the creation of ambiguous experimental results: it is not clear to what extent the actions of experimental subjects are the product of experimenter-subject interactions. The failure to replicate and the possible nonuniversal nature of such influences only exacerbate the ambiguity of traditional experiments originally noted by Rosenthal and Orne.

However, this is not the major problem created by such contaminants. The most fundamental problem can be illustrated by considering one of Rosenthal's "technical solutions" to the problem of experimenter bias. Rosenthal's recommended strategy is to eliminate the human experimenter in favor of purely mechanical instruction and recording devices. But it may be objected that such a strategy merely serves to introduce another (albeit different) species of experimenter bias:

We are reminded of an experiment in which participants played a game with two kinds of opponents. One half of the participants were told they were playing a game with a computer, and the other half that they were playing with a person stationed in the next room. In both groups the moves made by the opponents were exactly the same. Yet the participants in the two groups used very different strategies and modes of play, depending upon whether they thought they were playing with a person or a computer. So a totally computerized experiment would itself provide a kind of experimenter bias that would prevent generalization to interaction situations outside the laboratory. (Harré & Secord, 1972, p. 61)

Such experiments would appear to tell us little or nothing about human powers and liabilities in ordinary social interactions, although they might very well illustrate some human powers and liabilities in man-machine interactions that have some explanatory relevance to human actions in relation to the new computer technology, or on manned space missions.

This last point suggests the real problem about laboratory experiments in social psychology. It is not so much a general problem about whether such experiments relate to real-life situations, but a question of *how* particular experiments are so related. For the presence of the experimenter, or a machine substitute, does not merely involve the introduction of additional and contaminating variables, while other variables remain constant. Rather, the activity of the experimenter in creating the experimental situation may so alter the nature of the investigated system that the social psychological phenomena generated in the laboratory may be quite *differ-*

ent from the social psychological phenomenon under investigation. These ambiguous experiments then become the object of various post hoc interpretations (of the social meaning of the experimental situation) and explanations (of the production of the action sequence). This has led at least one writer (Crowle, 1976) to recommend a procedure for the selection of "communal interpretations" based upon the descriptions of professional ethnographers rather than the experimenters themselves. This indicates the seriousness of the ambiguity created by experimental alteration, but does nothing to resolve it.

Experimental Alteration

The ambiguity of experiments created by artifactual contaminants is but an aspect of the much more fundamental problem of the experimental *alteration* of social psychological phenomena. The activity of the experimenter in isolating as aspect of a real-life social situation (although it is unfortunately often conceived as the creation of a representative sample), may not only influence the outcome of the experiment, but may *alter* or *transform* the nature of the phenomenon that is the putative object of analysis: "The very act of bringing a variable into the laboratory usually changes its nature" (Chapanis, 1967, p. 558).

In this respect, many experiments are unrepresentative in a radical sense that does undermine explanatory inference. Laboratory experiments may not reproduce even an isolated instance of a particular social psychological phenomenon, but a quite different phenomenon altogether. This poses the most serious threat to both the internal and external validity of laboratory experiments. The radical ambiguity created by alteration precludes causal explanatory inference about the laboratory situation and the real world, since it is not clear what kind of phenomenon is created in the laboratory experiment.

Furthermore, this problem arises because of the essential nature of social psychological phenomena. We have noted in some detail that human actions and social practices are relational in nature. Their identity is determined by their relation to other social psychological phenomena, including the critical relations of social and agent representation. Social psychological phenomena, such as trials, interviews, committees, trade union negotiations, family conflicts, and therapy sessions, are constituted by their social relational and representational dimensions. A jury trial is constituted as a jury trial by its relation to legal, judicial, and penal systems (and their legislative, bureaucratic, and executive agencies), and by participants' representations of the point and purpose of this form of activity. An employment interview is constituted by relations of authorization within an institutional setting, and at least the interviewer's representation that the point and purpose of the activity is to select personnel.

But consider then the difficulties of reproducing the influences affecting the judgments of jurors in a murder trial in isolation from all the social psychological relations that constitute real trials as trials, including the representation by participants that such relational criteria are satisfied. It is a critical assumption of the logic of closed experimentation and causal explanatory inference (to real-world open systems) that the phenomenon isolated in the closed laboratory experiment retains its *identity* under such isolation. *This assumption cannot be presumed to hold for social psychological phenomena.* For unlike (most) natural scientific phenomena (such as sulfur, plasmodium, increase in temperature, and uranium isotopes), which can be reidentified in both open and closed systems, social psychological phenomena may not retain their identity when isolated from their real-world relational contexts, *because their identity is determined by their real-world relational contexts.* A sample of tin retains its identity *as a sample of tin* when it is isolated in experiments from other factors (such as a local magnetic field) that may confound our causal judgments. But behaviors constituted as actions such as aggression and dishonesty do not retain their identity *as actions* when stripped of their constitutive social relational and representational dimensions.

The *artificiality of alteration* represents the most fundamental problem for experimental social psychology. We need to isolate social psychological phenomena in order to evaluate causal explanations of human action, but our activity of isolation may alter the very phenomena we are trying to investigate. The removal of constitutive relations (isolation) or introduction of novel constitutive relations (contamination) may alter the very nature of the phenomenon investigated. In consequence, laboratory experiments may fail to reproduce the phenomenon that is the object of investigation. Often this is the case because the laboratory experiment will fail to reproduce the agent representations that are partially constitutive of human actions, and often this will be the case because the experiment does not or cannot reproduce the normal relational social context. If a laboratory experiment does not reproduce the normal social relations and representations of an employment interview, or introduces novel relations and representations, it cannot be presumed to reproduce a laboratory analogue of employment interviews, and accordingly cannot provide support for any theoretical explanation of the social dynamics of employment interviews.

Recent defenders of the laboratory experiment in social psychology (Berkowitz & Donnerstein, 1982; Kruglanski, 1976) are correct to stress that the successful laboratory reproduction of social psychological phenomena depends upon the establishment of experimental rather than mundane realism. The reproduction of many social psychological phenomena depends upon the successful reproduction of agent representations that are partially constitutive of the phenomenon under study. For if such agent representations are not uniformly recreated in laboratory experiments, it will often be the case that the investigated independent (enabling or stimulus conditions) or dependent (consequent action) variables are not success-fully reproduced. It is this potential failure of internal validity that poses the greatest threat to the external validity of experiments by precluding causal explanatory inferences to the real world.[3] If the laboratory experi-ment does not successfully reproduce a phenomenon such as human aggression, it cannot be employed to support causal explanations of human aggression in the real world.

Yet such commentators rather too readily presume that the standardiza-tion of subject representations is regularly and unproblematically achieved in laboratory experiments. Specifically, they fail to recognize that the re-moval of normal concomitances and dislocation from the normal social context may alter the relational nature of the phenomenon isolated in the laboratory, generating subject representations that are quite different from those that the experiment was designed to reproduce. Berkowitz and Donnerstein (1982) define human aggression as "the deliberate injury of another," and this seems to be a fair representation of the social meaning of human aggression. Yet it is far from obvious that this is how subjects represent their behavior in "aggression" experiments. The absence of sig-nificant others (friends, colleagues, family, etc.) who might represent the action as aggressive and accordingly change their attitudes and relations toward the subject, may not simply imply the removal of a possible in-terference condition in the form of social inhibition, but may in fact pre-vent the agent from representing his action as injurious to another. This is especially likely when the experimenter provides a theoretical rationale and justification for behaviors such as the infliction of electric shocks on another. Indeed, and this is especially true when a learning rationale is provided, subjects may represent their actions as *beneficial* to the "victim" (Baron & Eggleston, 1972). Kane, Joseph, and Tedeschi (1976) have argued that the employment of the "Berkowitz paradigm" in the investiga-tion of "retaliatory aggression" may activate the salient norm of "negative reciprocity" ("an eye for an eye"), generating a quite different form of action from "implusive, retaliatory aggression." Subjects in such experi-ments often represent their actions as morally beneficial to the "offender."

Precisely analogously, Milgram moves rather too quickly from the reasonable assumption that his subjects were convinced that they were in-flicting *painful* electric shocks to the assumption that they represented their actions as *harmful*, and to the causal explanatory conclusion that most peo-ple in the real world would engage in actions harmful to others upon the command of authorities (in the absence of interference). The Milgram ex-periment is particularly illuminating since its partial success in reproduc-tion is an accidental effect of the phenomenon studied. There seems little doubt that the Milgram experiment was successful in isolating a "wisdom-authoritarian" command structure. The experimenter was represented as a genuinely competent authority by subjects. It is important to note, how-ever, that successful reproduction was achieved in this respect because of a special feature of the Milgram experiment. The laboratory experiment in social psychology is itself an instance of the phenomenon under investigation. The laboratory experiment in social psychology constitutes precisely such a "wisdom-authoritarian" structure: subjects adopt an attitude of subordinating trust in the experimenter, assuming that, despite appearances, such competent authorities would not allow anything really dangerous to happen in a laboratory (Aronson & Carlsmith, 1968; Baumrind, 1964; Orne & Holland, 1968). Furthermore, it is precisely for this reason that it is doubtful if Milgram's subjects represented their actions as really harmful to their "victims." Milgram's experimenter constantly emphasized that although the shocks were painful, they were not harmful, and it may very well be the case that representations of genuine harm play a causal role in the production of disobedience in such situations (Mixon, 1972).

Indeed, the fact that most laboratory attempts to investigate social psychological phenomena take place within such a wisdom-authoritarian structure casts doubt about many experimental investigations of phenomena such as destructive obedience, aggression, risk taking, and anxiety. Analogously, special features of the laboratory experiment such as "evaluation apprehension," the absence of familiar and significant others, and the general dislocation from the normal social relational context, may lead subjects to represent situations and actions in ways that are peculiar (if not unique) to the laboratory experiment (Harré & Secord, 1972).

THE AMBIGUITY OF EXPERIMENTS

The ambiguity of experiments in social psychology is not simply a matter of evaluating alternative and competing causal explanations of the production of human action advanced by experimental and scientific observers. Ambiguity also arises because subjects themselves may find the experimental situation ambiguous and represent the experiment in ways that are quite different from the experimenter's intention (Forward, Canter, & Kirsch, 1976; Ginsberg, 1979; Harré & Secord, 1972; Weber & Cook, 1972). Indeed, the explanatory ambiguity for the scientific observer may be largely a function of the ambiguity of the experimental situation for subjects themselves. In isolation from the normal social relational context and given the peculiar features of the experimental situation, the social meaning of the experimental situation may be indeterminate for subjects. This will produce variable rather than standardized representations of the experimental situation, none of which can be presumed to be in accord with the representation that is partially constitutive of the phenomenon investigated.

It is no answer to this problem to make a distinction between the theoretical definitions of the experimenter and the folk definitions of the subjects themselves, since the definitions of actor and observer are nonconstitutive, and since the actor's representation of her behavior is often partially constitutive of human action. Neither the actor's not scientific observer's classification of a laboratory behavior as an act of aggression or dishonesty constitutes it as an act of aggression or dishonesty. But actors' representations of their behavior as directed to the injury of another or the receipt of property rightly belonging to another must be reproduced in experiments if such experiments are to provide evidential support for causal explanations of aggression and dishonesty.

Nor is it any answer to claim that variable subject representations are controlled variables in laboratory experiments, since such variance is "canceled out" or diluted by the random assignment of subjects to control and experimental groups. This strategy simply avoids the issue of variable representations but does nothing to address it. It provides no resolution at all to the problems of experimental reproduction and explanatory inference. For if some subjects do not represent their behavior as directed to the injury of another or the removal of another's property, then the experimental conditions cannot provide any causal account of their aggressive and dishonest actions, because their behaviors are *neither acts of aggression or dishonesty*. This is like allowing the inclusion of an indeterminate number of other elements (iodine, sulfur, lead) to be included in the controlled experimental analysis of the powers of a particular element (chlorine). It makes nonsense of the experiment.

This is not to deny that variable subject representations of situations and actions are of causal explanatory interest in their own right. But if explanations of different actions in terms of different agent representations are to be evaluated in experiments, then such representations must be standardized in different experimental groups, or discriminated within the same experimental group via agent accounts. It may well be the case that some aggressive and dishonest acts can be explained in terms of violent stimuli and social pressure from teenage peers, but that other aggressive and dishonest acts may be best explained in terms of the agent's failure to represent his action as aggressive and dishonest. Such explanations in terms of social perception can only be evaluated via experimental isolation if variable representations are discriminated in experiments.

It is important to stress again that there are two types of experimental ambiguity for the scientific observer. Experimental situations may be ambiguous for the scientific observer both in terms of the causal explanation of the actions of experimental subjects, and the social meaning of the actions of experimental subjects. However, it should be obvious that the two forms of ambiguity are closely related: the experimenter cannot even begin to draw causal conclusions from experiments until he has determined the social relations and representations reproduced or created in the experiment. He may be faced with an impossible situation if the experimental situation is itself ambiguous for the subjects, who may in consequence represent the situation and their consequent behavior in a variety of ways and act for the sake of a variety of reasons. At the furthest extreme, it may be the case that the actions of some experimental subjects can only be explained in terms of creative personal meanings developed from the indeterminacies of the laboratory context. Such explanations may have relevance only to the peculiar social world of the laboratory experiment.

The reason why an analysis of agent accounts of their representation of situation and behavior is required should also be stressed. This is not required because of a misguided belief about the general accuracy of agents' causal explanations of their own actions. A realist philosophy of experimental social psychological science does not treat agents' causal accounts as sacrosanct or even privileged.[4] The adequacy of any causal explanation is an empirical matter to be determined by experimental isolation. But we must exploit subjects' accounting skills in traditional laboratory experiments if we are to discriminate agent representations that are often partially constitutive of human actions and that *may* function as agents' reasons for action.[5]

The behavior of experimental subjects cannot be taken as the criterion for the presence or absence of agent representations, since the behavior of subjects may be constituted as a variety of different actions according to different representations (some examples of identical behaviors may be instances of aggression if they are represented as directed to the injury of another, others may not be if they are not represented in this way), and the same form of action may be produced by agents for the sake of a wide variety of reasons and influenced by a wide variety of causes. Nor can we in this case appeal to the social context to delineate agent representations (as we can often do in the real world), for it is precisely the social context of the laboratory experiment that is itself ambiguous, for subjects and consequently for scientific observers.

The requirement that agent representations must be discriminated in laboratory experiments should be uncontentious. It simply amounts to the requirement that the constitutive and potentially explanatory dimensions created in laboratory experiments should be identified. For otherwise classificatory and causal judgments about the phenomena created in laboratory experiments can only be pure conjecture, supplying grist to the mill of the hermeneutical psychologist. The scientific psychologist's exclusive concentration on "observable" behavior precludes rather than promotes objectivity in the experimental evaluation of causal explanations of human action. It increases rather than decreases the ambiguity of experiments.

Artificiality and Reality

It is frequently objected that since ambiguity is a common enough feature of social life, there is nothing wrong with the creation of ambiguous experiments. This riposte is usually advanced as part of a more general complaint about the viability of the distinction between the "artificial" laboratory experiment and the "real" world. After all, it is frequently protested, the social psychological laboratory is part of the real world (subjects and experimenters are real people), and many situations outside the laboratory are artificial (some dinner parties and retirement speeches praising a universally despised colleague) and ambiguous (it may not be clear whether a situation is an emergency, or whether the boss's questioning at a dinner party is polite conversion or informal interview for a promoted position).

However, this is to miss the point about the distinction between the laboratory experiment and the real world outside the laboratory, and the point about the problem of experimental alteration and ambiguity. The distinction between the (real world of the) laboratory experiment and the real world (outside of the laboratory) is essentially a distinction between a (at least partially) closed system and an open system. The point of the closed experiment is to identify causal generative processes via the isolation of hypothetical causal variables and the control of alternative possible mechanisms of generation and interference. Of course, the laboratory experiment in any science always remains ambiguous in the sense that we can never be certain that all the relevant variables have been isolated and controlled,[6] but the closed experiment is a great improvement over the ambiguity of observations in open systems in which alternative mechanisms of generation and interference may be present, and vary according to contingencies of circumstance. The central rationale of the closed experiment in any science is that the isolation and control of experimental intervention *reduces* the ambiguity of causal interpretation that is characteristic of open-system observations. The real problem with laboratory experiments in social psychology is that the isolation and control of the laboratory may increase the ambiguity of causal interpretation by increasing the ambiguity about the phenomena created in laboratory experiments.

The actions of subjects in laboratory experiments are, of course, real actions in the real world. The point to be stressed, however, is that real-world laboratory phenomena can only provide support for causal explanations of phenomena in the real world outside the laboratory if the constitutive and potentially explanatory dimensions of the real world are reproduced and discriminated in laboratory experiments. Laboratory experiments can only support explanations of instances of aggression outside the laboratory experiment if laboratory experiments are successful in reproducing instances of aggression. Laboratory experiments can only support explanations of attitude change in terms of cognitive dissonance if cognitive dissonance and attitude change are reproduced in laboratory experiments.

The critical doubts about laboratory experimentation are not doubts about the reality or statistical frequency of the causal systems created. They are doubts about the *identity* of the phenomena created in laboratory experiments. As Secord (1982) notes, the fact that young children are not invariably aggressive when exposed to adult aggression does not itself undermine causal accounts of child aggression in terms of modeling, based upon the behavior of children in laboratory experiments who view adults hitting a Bobo doll (Bandura, Ross, & Ross, 1961). What does undermine such causal accounts are our reasonable doubts about whether a child hitting a Bobo doll is acting aggressively (rather than simply playing). Furthermore, our general doubts about the identity of laboratory phenomena are based upon a recognition of the fact that traditional laboratory techniques may not preserve the social relational and representational dimensions of human action. For this reason, laboratory experiments may not be able to reproduce artificial social psychological phenomena that occur outside of the laboratory, such as the artificialities of dinner parties and retirement speeches.

Of course, some real-world situations and actions are ambiguous. When these are the object of causal investigation in a scientific social psychology, then it is entirely right and proper to reproduce this characteristic in laboratory reproductions that investigate the causal production of actions in precisely these situations. But this does nothing to justify the ambiguities of laboratory experiments designed to investigate the causal production of actions in situations that are not ambiguous. Nor can explanations based on experimental reproductions of ambiguous situations be uncritically extended to cover situations that are unambiguous. It may be the case, for example, that Milgram's experiment does demonstrate that some agents are liable to act in a potentially harmful way upon the commands of authorities, if it is not clear to agents that their actions are really harmful. Milgram's experiment may support such an explanation of the actions of nurses in the Hofling et al. (1966) study who obeyed the orders of doctors to administer doses of a drug beyond the maximum recommended dosages. This cannot be presumed to provide an adequate explanation of the actions of persons who obey the orders of authorities when their actions are clearly harmful to others, as in the case of concentration camp attendants and the soldiers in the My Lai massacre. Ambiguity is a special feature of some real-life situations outside the laboratory. It is not an intrinsic virtue of the laboratory experiment.

EXPERIMENTAL ARTIFACTS

It is true that experimenters sometimes legitimately create laboratory phenomena that are not intended to be reproductions of real-world phenomena. Experimenters often intentionally create genuinely novel phenomena and regularities in laboratory experiments (Henschel, 1980). This is quite common in natural science. The experimenter will often create isolated and controlled systems that are known not to occur naturally outside of the artificial laboratory situation. When the experimenter has determined the causal principles of the artificially created system, she often goes on the recreate novel instances of the system in the real world outside of the laboratory. For example, she may create electrical systems that obey

Ohm's law, or create transuranic elements or synthetic compounds for use in nuclear reactors or the petrochemical industry. In this sense, technology is often the experiment in reverse. The isolation and control of the laboratory is extended to the world outside the laboratory to create new phenomena (or to create or eliminate regularities).

In an analogous way the social psychologist may artificially create genuinely novel phenomena in laboratory experiments. Henschel (1980) gives the examples of biofeedback techniques for self-control of autonomic responses and chimpanzees employing the sign language of the deaf. Other examples would be sleep or sensory deprivation, new psychoactive drugs, novel work practices or employment interview techniques, or hypothetical trials in which the jury determines both the guilt or innocence of the accused and the sentence. This is, of course, an entirely legitimate enterprise, yet it is palpably not the purpose of most experiments in social psychology, which aim to reproduce isolated and controlled examples of naturally occurring social psychological phenomena, such as aggression, dishonesty, and attitude change, in order to evaluate causal explanations of them. The fact that some experiments in social psychology are explicitly designed to create artifacts is no justification for the failure of other experiments designed to reproduce the relations and representations that are constitutive of naturally occurring social psychological phenomena. Furthermore, experiments that create novel systems will only have explanatory relevance to the possibilities of action in the world outside the laboratory if experiments designed to create novel forms of work practices, employment interviews, and trials by jury are successful in reproducing the constitutive relations and representations of the workplace, the employment interview, and trial by jury.

It is also true, as Mook (1983, p. 380) argues, that frequently in experimental evaluations of causal explanations ". . . we are not making generalizations, but testing them." Often the point of the experiment is to investigate what *can* happen in the laboratory, rather than what does or will happen in the real world, or what *ought* to happen in the restricted laboratory setting given a particular causal or theoretical explanation. But, of course, this is always the point of the closed experiment in social psychological science. It is never legitimately employed to support accounts of what does or will happen in open systems. However, this defense of artifactuality simply ignores the identity question.

Thus, for example, the Higgens and Marlatt (1973) study that aimed to manipulate different levels of subject anxiety via the threat of electric shocks, and provided subjects with access to alcohol if they so desired, was designed to test the "tension-reduction" theory of alcoholism. According to Mook, the point of this experiment was not to generalize from the restricted and artificial laboratory setting to the real world, in the sense of making open-system predictions that individuals who are tense or anxious will drink alcohol if available. The point of this experimental artifact was to assess a theoretical causal explanatory account of alcoholism by reference to a specific prediction about what ought to happen in precisely this socially novel laboratory situation. If laboratory-manipulated anxiety does not lead to alcohol consumption, then the tension-reduction explanation has been shown to be false or in need of qualification. Mook claims that this is a clear example of the hypothetico-deductive method (and the "method of falsification") as applied to the experimental evaluation of causal and theoretical explanations.

But it remains of critical importance to distinguish between the artifactuality of experimental isolation, which is central to the logic of experimentation, and the artifactuality of alteration, which is anathema to it. Mook is, of course, quite correct to distinguish between the "generality of findings" in the sense of possibilities of predictive inference, and the "generality of theoretical conclusions" in the sense of possibilities of explanatory inference. The unrepresentative nature of subjects and setting precludes predictive inferences to open systems, nevertheless we intend it to be the case that "the processes we dissect in the laboratory also operate in the real world " (Mook, 1983, p. 385). Yet this is precisely the doubt that arises with respect to putative laboratory "dissections" because of the problem of experimental alteration. Laboratory studies of alcohol consumption will only support or refute (or qualify) theoretical causal accounts of alcohol consumption in the world outside the laboratory in terms of "tension reduction," if laboratory experiments are successful in reproducing real anxiety, and the real anxieties of potential drinkers.

Mook notes (1983, p. 383) that "the nagging fear and self doubts of the everyday may have a quite different status from the acute fear of electric shock." Indeed they might. For reasons already mentioned, the laboratory experiment may not be successful in reproducing an "acute fear of electric shock." Because of the subordinating trust of experimental subjects, such experiments may not be successful in reproducing real anxiety. Yet even if the experiment is successful in creating the acute anxiety of anticipatory fear of electric shocks, it is extremely doubtful if this is characteristic of the common and everyday anxieties of potential drinkers, and thus grossly implausible as the basis of a potential explanation of the human liability to consume alcohol to avoid personal or social problems.

For the man faced with painful electric shocks, the acceptance of offered alcohol may very well be a rational exercise of a personal power, since alcohol may usefully serve to deaden the pain. For the same reason, a patient may accept an anesthetic to deaden the pain of surgery. This is quite different from the conflicts, dilemmas, and disappointments of a social and personal nature (troubles at work or home) that may drive a man to seek temporary relief but not resolution of his anxieties by drowning them in alcoholic euphoria or stupor. A man's drinking to avoid externally induced physical pain is a rational way of coping with such pain. A man's drinking to avoid the anxieties intrinsic to many personal and social commitments and conflicts represents a failure to cope with such anxieties, commitments, and conflicts (or contrast the actions of a soldier who drinks to avoid the pain of a field amputation without anesthetic with the actions of a soldier who drinks to eliminate or reduce the fear of being wounded in battle).

Although there are occasions when experimenters intentionally create pure experimental artifacts, few experiments are constructed with only the laboratory in mind. The tension-reduction account is normally advanced as a causal explanation of at least some instances of real-world alcohol consumption and alcoholism. Most experiments only aim to be artifactual in the sense that the isolation they achieve is rarely to be found in everyday social life. If laboratory experiments do not in fact reproduce *any* of the present dimensions of the social psychological world, they have no explanatory relevance with respect to it.

ECOLOGICAL VALIDITY AND EXPERIMENTAL REALISM

One methodological consequence of the above arguments is that experimenters should be more sensitive to the issue of the *ecological validity* of experiments (Brunswick, 1955), defined in this context as the reidentifiability of everyday social and psychological phenomena in laboratory experiments.[7] Recent defenders of the laboratory experiment are quite correct to stress the importance of *experimental realism*. The demonstration of the successful reproduction of partially constitutive subject representations should be recognized as the critical criterion of the adequacy of laboratory experiments. The present analysis reveals that ecological validity and experimental realism are in fact articulations of the same basic requirement: the successful reproduction of the everyday social psychological phenomena that are the object of experimental analysis. This is a simple consequence of the previous point that the external validity of experiments (their ability to support causal explanatory inferences) is a function of their internal validity (their ability to isolate causal explanatory factors).

Once again it should be stressed that the present emphasis on the discrimination of the social relational and representational dimensions of actions in experimental studies does not vouchsafe causal explanations of action in terms of these dimensions. It is simply to insist that without the discrimination of these dimensions we cannot make any judgments about the identity of the forms of action created in laboratory experiments. Nor does the emphasis on agent accounts in the discrimination of agents' representations vouchsafe any causal explanations in terms of their avowed reasons. It is simply to insist that without such a discrimination we cannot even begin to experimentally assess competing causal explanations, which include those that make reference to social perception and agents' avowed reasons.

However, sensitivity to the issues of ecological validity and experimental realism is not enough. The recognition of the problem of experimental alteration does not itself ensure its resolution, far less its resolution via traditional experimental techniques. It does not itself resolve the difficulties of reproducing social relational phenomena under conditions of experimental isolation. One may be perfectly aware of the social relational and representational dimensions of employment interviews and jury trials, but at a complete loss as to how to reproduce the relations and representations constitutive of these phenomena in isolative laboratory experiments, short of the total reproduction of real interviews and jury trials.

THE FIELD EXPERIMENT

However, it should not be too hastily concluded that the laboratory experiment in social psychology should be abandoned in favor of the field experiment. The field experiment has the advantage over the traditional laboratory experiment in terms of the identification of actions and causal explanatory dimensions. It is, of course, much easier to ensure the satisfaction of many constitutive social relations and representations in field experiments, since the field experimenter may choose to conduct his experiment in preestablished contexts. Given the cooperation of the appropriate authorities, he may conduct special employment interviews or investigations of dishonesty in real business organizations or supermarkets.

But the field experiment achieves this gain in identification at the cost of causal ambiguity. In the field experiment, it is much more difficult to eliminate or control additional causal and interference conditions. Investigations of dishonesty in supermarkets are easily disrupted by meddling aunts and children, not to mention store detectives and off-duty policemen. Investigations of bystander apathy are easily disrupted by policemen on duty and muggers. It is usually easy enough to determine in field experiments and real life that persons have been aggressive and changed their attitudes. It is much more difficult to determine why they have done so.

In the end, field experimentation may prove to be the most effective means of empirically evaluating causal explanations of human action. Whether or not this will prove to be the case depends upon the effectiveness of alternative strategies designed to overcome the problems of experimental contamination and alteration. Two such strategies are the deception experiment and experimental simulation.

12
Intensional Simulation

In Chapter 11 it is argued that the central problem for an experimental social psychological science is the alteration of social psychological phenomena in isolative experiments. In particular, it is stressed that the dislocation of behavior from its normal social relational context makes it enormously difficult to reproduce and standardize the participant agent representations that are partially constitutive of actions such as honesty and aggression.

Nevertheless, the fact that most social psychological phenomena are partially constituted by participant agent representations creates a potential advantage for the experimental social psychologist, if she can make a virtue out of this necessity. For it is sufficient for the purposes of experimental isolation and explanatory inference that laboratory experiments are successful in reproducing participant agent representations, since the partially constitutive nature of these representations will ensure the reidentifiability of social psychological phenomena in isolative experiments, and ensure the explanatory relevance of such experiments to real-life situations. Thus, it is not necessary in laboratory experiments to reproduce actual instances of aggression and dishonesty, or employment interviews or jury trials. It is sufficient to reproduce the participant agent representations that are partially constitutive of these phenomena.

The experimenter cannot achieve isolation without alteration by traditional laboratory techniques, given the social relational nature of social psychological phenomena. The field experiment avoids the problem of alteration at the cost of causal ambiguity. To achieve isolation without alteration in experimental studies, the experimenter must aim to create an *intensional simulation*. He must reproduce the intensional contents of participant agent representations of behavior and context that are partially constitutive of actions and social practices.

There are two present strategies for intensional simulation. One is the *deception experiment*, which attempts to deceive subjects into representing context and action according to constitutive dimensions. The other is the *simulation experiment*, in which participants are instructed to represent context and behavior according to constitutive dimensions. The simulation experiment is more frequently classified as a "role-playing" experiment, although this classification is seriously misleading in a variety of ways.

Of course, all experiments involve the simulation of actual and possible dimensions of real-world systems. And both the deception experiment and simulation experiment involve intensional simulation. The difference between the two strategies is that simulation experiments aim for an *intentional* intensional simulation of agent representations, by instructing subjects to act as if they represented context and behavior in the experimentally desired fashion. The deception experiment aims to achieve intensional simulation without the intentional cooperation of subjects, by deceiving subjects into representing context and behavior in the experimentally desired way. The term *simulation experiment* or *experimental simulation* is used in this chapter to refer to studies employing intentional intensional simulation, to avoid the cumbersome nature of this expression. It is also used to avoid the misleading connotations of the term *role-playing experiment*, although it is employed to refer to many of the studies conventionally classified as role-playing experiments. It is at the same time clearly recognized that deception experiments also aim for simulation via intensional simulation.

The Deception Experiment

The standard reaction to the "interaction paradoxes" of experimental social psychology is the deception experiment. The aim of the deception strategy is to eliminate or alleviate contaminating variables by deceiving the subject that the object of the experiment is different from the real object of the experiment. The deception experiment, like the social psychology experiment in general, has been the object of vigorous and sustained criticism for the past two decades (Forward, Canter, & Kirsch, 1976; Ginsburg, 1978; Harré & Secord, 1972; Kelman, 1967). Again this appears to have had little effect upon practice. Laboratory studies employing deception continue to represent an increasing proportion of social psychological research. No doubt, part of the reason for this is the apparent lack of a viable alternative. Practitioners remain sceptical about field experiments and observations (with some justification) and dismissive of simulation experiments (with little justification). However, it is also likely due to the fact that the sound methodological objections are regularly obscured by or subordinated to moral objections.

It is worth noting that there are no moral objections to experimentation that are unique to the deception experiment. Many commentators object to deception per se, holding that it is always morally unjustifiable to deceive subjects. Yet this is not an intrinsic feature of the deception experiment, and can be avoided by "forewarning" subjects about the possibility of deception in particular experiments (Horowitz & Rothschild, 1970), or experiments in general (Holmes & Bennett, 1974). Furthermore, standard moral objections to the anxiety and distress suffered by subjects in deception experiments simulating aggression, danger, and dishonesty apply equally to any form of experimentation, including simulation experiments. Significantly, apologists for experimental simulation often make reference to the very real suffering and anxiety experienced by subjects in some simulation experiments as the basis of claims about the experimental realism of this method (for example, Mixon's [1972] and O'Leary, Willis, and Tomich's [1970] simulation of Milgram's experiment, or Hanay, Banks, and Zimbardo's [1973] simulation of prison dynamics). It is tautologically true that any experimental strategy that achieves experimental realism will be traumatic for subjects in successful reproductions of traumatic social psychological phenomena. Although the very real moral problems of any form of human experimentation should not be underestimated, the intrinsic problems of the deception experiment are not moral but methodological.

DECEPTION AND AMBIGUITY

It must be recognized that the primary aim of the deception experiment is to deal with the problem of contaminating variables, and in particular the "experimenter expectancy" effect and the "demand characteristics" of the experiment. The idea of the deceptive "cover story" is to disguise the real point and purpose of the experiment, which may be discerned by subjects and which may influence their laboratory actions if such a cover story is not provided. The critical problem of experimental alteration is simply ignored. In consequence, the deception strategy tends to exacerbate rather than resolve or alleviate the problem of alteration. For this problem of laboratory experimentation is more akin to the "uncertainty principle" in quantum mechanics than the minor problems of measurement interference in the natural sciences. The manipulation of experimental subjects beyond a certain degree becomes counterproductive.

This can perhaps best be illustrated by considering Milgram's response to Orne's (Orne & Holland, 1968) doubts about the plausibility of the deception involved in his experiments on destructive obedience. Orne complains that:

The experiment is presented as a study of the effect of punishment on learning. The investigator presumably is interested in determining how the victim's rate of learning is affected by punishment, yet there is nothing that he requires of the S (teacher) that he could not as easily do himself. (Orne & Holland, 1968, p. 289)

Milgram is quite caustic and dismissive in his reply (Milgram, 1972) to Orne on this point, claiming that if Orne had taken the trouble to read his original research report, he would have noted that a sufficient rationale was presented to subjects for their participation as "teachers." Subjects were told (Milgram, 1963, p. 373):

We don't know how much punishment is best for learning, and we don't know how much difference it makes as to who is giving the punishment, whether the adult learns best from a younger or older person than himself, or many things of that sort. So in this study we are bringing together a number of adults of different occupations and ages. And we're asking some to be teachers and some to be learners. We want to find out just what effect different people have on each other as teachers and learners, and also what effect punishment will have on learning in this situation.

Now this rationale documents two objectives of the "learning experiment": the influence of punishment or degree of punishment on learning, and the influence of different types of teachers. But with respect to the first objective, the presence of subject "teachers" is redundant. Punishment could equally well be administered in varied measures by the experimenter, or indeed (and perhaps more systematically) by a machine. More significantly, the rigidity of the experimental setup effectively precluded the influence of personality variables such as the age, sex, or social class of the subject teachers (except perhaps in the "touch proximity" condition). The timing, nature, and graduation of shocks were predetermined by the experimenter's instructions. At the stage in the experiment at which the "learner" refuses to continue and fails to respond, continuation of punishment becomes pointless.

It is probably just as extreme for Orne to claim that most subjects saw through the deception as it is for Milgram to claim that most did not. What this disagreement does illustrate, however, is that the experiment was probably as ambiguous for the subjects as it has proved to be for later commentators. The most plausible interpretation is simply that the subjects found the experience unreal, absurd, and highly ambiguous: "No, I don't want to go on. This is crazy. I don't see any sense to this, to knocking him out or something." (Subject transcripts quoted in Milgram, 1974)

The important point to note about this ambiguity, documented by many critics, is that it is not an accidental feature of Milgram's experiment, or indeed of any deception experiment. Rather, the delimitation of cues that generated the ambiguity is almost a logical consequence of the deception rationale. As Miller (1972) and J. Cooper (1976) have stressed, the main point of the deception strategy is to eliminate or alleviate contaminating artifactual variables. However, this means that the experiment as described to subjects (the cover story) cannot be a real experiment at all. For this would be to introduce new, albeit different, contaminating variables. It is, therefore, hardly surprising that subjects regularly represent the "experiment" as pointless, unreal, and highly ambiguous (Forward et al.,

1976; Harré & Secord, 1972; Jourard, 1968; Mixon, 1972; Orne & Holland, 1968). The meaning of the experimental situation is underdetermined by the information available, and this tends to generate variable rather than standardized representations of the laboratory situation. The deception experiment is indeed closely analogous to the ambiguous figures that are regularly presented as analogues of scientific observation in the discussions of relativist philosophers of science and hermeneutical psychologists. The difference is that in this case the ambiguity for the scientific observer is not a function (or not a sole function) of the limited information available to the scientific observer. It is rather a function of the limited information available to the subjects themselves, which may result in quite diverse representations of the experimental situation. Indeed, it may very well be the case that many deception experiments do not reveal the subtle stimulus influences on human action, but are rather examples of creative human agency. The laboratory subject may often not know how to represent the situation in conventional ways. He may literally have to make sense of it by himself.

The deception strategy has the right idea. It attempts to achieve an intensional simulation. It aims to reproduce and standardize subject representations that are partially constitutive of social psychological phenomena, without attempting to reproduce the normal relational context. Yet because it simply ignores the fact that such representations are normally based upon or influenced by the relational nature of the normal social context, it is bound to fail with respect to the problem of alteration. Trying to generate representations that are plainly inappropriate (for the subjects) in the context of the laboratory experiment only exacerbates the ambiguity of the experimental situation for subjects.

The fundamental methodological problem may be illustrated by considering the "forewarning" strategy designed to avoid the moral objections to deception per se. In an Asch-type experiment on conformity, Horowitz and Rothschild (1970) used a group of deceived subjects, a group of subjects fully briefed about the real point of the experiment, and a group forewarned that the real purpose of the experiment was being withheld from them. The deceived and forewarned groups behaved in a closely similar fashion, exhibiting a higher degree of conformity than the prebriefed group. The authors claim that their work resolves the moral issue without loss of experimental realism. This may resolve the moral problem, but it does *nothing* to resolve the problem of alteration. The Horowitz and Rothschild study demonstrates that subjects who were explicitly informed that the experiment was ambiguous behaved in the same fashion as those subjects who were supposed to be deceived. This hardly provides grounds for supposing that experimental realism was successfully achieved. Indeed, it suggests precisely the opposite. It suggests that the experimental situation was as ambiguous for the subjects in the deceived group as it was for subjects in the forewarned group.

Experimental Simulation

The idea of employing simulation as an experimental strategy has received considerable attention in the past two decades. Although simulation has been used as an assessment, experimental, and therapeutic technique for many years (Ginsburg, 1978), controversy arose when it was recommended as an alternative to deception, because of the moral and methodological doubts about deceptive techniques (Argyris, 1975; Brown, 1965; Forward et al., 1976; Ginsburg, 1978; Harré & Secord, 1972; Jourard, 1968; Kelman, 1967; Ring, 1967; Schultz, 1969).

Mainstream methodologists remain unconvinced and generally dismissive of simulation as an experimental strategy (Aronson & Carlsmith, 1968; J. Cooper, 1976; Freedman, 1969; Miller, 1972). Empirical evaluations of simulation as an experimental strategy remain ambiguous. Greenberg (1967), Horowitz and Rothschild (1970), and Willis and Willis (1970) report qualified success. Darroch and Steiner (1970), Simons and Pilliavin (1972), and Holmes and Bennett (1974) report qualified failure. Naturally enough, commentators differ in their interpretation of the significance of such studies. Defenders of simulation suggest that the qualified success indicates that simulation is a potentially useful experimental strategy (Alexander & Scriven, 1977). Critics claim that the qualified failure demonstrates the inherent inadequacy of experimental simulations.

ACTIVE SIMULATION

Most of the straightforwardly dismissive complaints (Aronson & Carlsmith, 1968; Freedman, 1969) about the "inevitable" lack of realism and involvement in experimental simulations are quite unjustified. Various studies have attested to the degree of realism and involvement that can be achieved in experimental simulations (Janis & Man, 1965; Mixon, 1972). The simulated attack and defense of Grindstone Island (Olson & Christiansen, 1966) and the Stanford prison study (Hanay et al., 1973) had to be prematurely terminated because the participants became too involved. Analogously, Mixon (1972) notes that subjects who participated in his simulation of Milgram's experiment exhibited the same "spontaneous nervous and emotional behaviour" as Milgram's subjects.

It should be stressed that the type of simulation considered as an experimental strategy is what may be termed *active* or *participative* simulation. In this type of experiment, participants are asked to act in accord with scripted representations that are possible representations of real-world social contexts (Smith, 1975). For example, they are asked to represent the situation as if they were a candidate in an employment interview; as if they were a person who has to make a counter-attitudinal speech; as if they were a policeman who has to arrest a black offender in a ghetto area; as if they represented a situation as a threat or an emergency; as if they were requested by an authority to harm another; as if they were a juror deciding the guilt or innocence of a defendant with a psychiatric history; or as if they represented their wife as being unfaithful, and so on. The essential feature of this form of simulation is that participants act as if they represented social reality according to the constitutive dimensions requested by the experimenter.

The term *role playing* is something of a misnomer for this form of experimental strategy. It is true that in some experimental simulations the subjects are asked to represent the situation as if they occupied the social roles of juror, policeman, or interviewee, but these are special examples of experimental simulation, rather than the general form of all experimental simulations. The aim of such experimental simulations is to reproduce the participant agent representations that are partially constitutive of actions in social contexts, in order to discriminate the enabling, stimulus, and interference conditions for actions that are exercises and manifestations of human powers and liabilities.

For this reason, the spontaneous emotion and anxiety manifested in experimental simulations are no guarantee of *experimental* realism and ecological validity. As Yardley (1982) notes, the emotion exhibited in the Stanford prison study only illustrates that involvement can be achieved in experimental simulations. She argues that it is extremely doubtful if subjects in this experiment represented their situation and action in ways that are characteristic of real warders and real prisoners. One might very well seriously question why such a study employed student "guards" and "prisoners" rather than volunteer warders and prisoners themselves. After all, if the experiment is designed to discriminate the enabling and stimulus conditions of human powers and liabilities by reproducing the constitutive representational dimensions of prison life, then persons who occupy (or have occupied) the social role of warders and prisoners are obviously best able to simulate the forms of representation characteristic of such contexts. Precisely the same point, of course, applies to deception experiments. The fact that subjects were involved and exhibited "spontaneous nervous and emotional behavior" in the original Milgram experiment and simulations of it does not demonstrate that participants in these experiments represented their behavior as harmful to the "victim." Precisely the same involvement and "spontaneous nervous and emotional behavior" can be observed in theater audiences who watch the final poker scene of Marlow's *Edward II*, or in students who view videorecordings of the Milgram experiment (although both are fully aware that no one is really being harmed).

Nevertheless, it is important to stress the active and participative nature of experimental simulations. This is because many critics of experimental simulation focus on nonactive and nonparticipative studies in which subjects describe what they think they would do in particular situations, including deception experiments. A classic example of this type of common complaint is Freedman's (1969, p. 114) dismissive rejection of simulation experiments:

> . . . The data from role playing are people's guesses as to how they would behave if they were in a particular situation . . . Role playing tells us what men think they would do. It does not tell us what men would actually do in the real situation.

Freedman is clearly thinking here of essentially *passive* investigations in which subjects faced with a described situation or videotape of an interaction describe how they would act in such a situation. Yet although this type of enquiry is sometimes recommended by hermeneutical psychologists as an interpretative alternative to causal experimentation, it is clearly incorrect to characterize it as the general form of experimental simulation.

EXPERIMENTAL CONSTRUCTION

The primary advantage of (active) experimental simulation is that it has the potential to achieve *isolation without alteration*. The participant in an experimental simulation can represent the situation as if all the normal social relations of a social context are satisfied, without representing them in a determinate and thus causally confounding form. For example, experimental simulations may be employed to isolate the conditions that promote and impede the human liability to disclose negative information about a colleague in the course of an employment or promotion interview. The participants can represent the situation as if all the normal relations of authorization, employment, and work association are satisfied, without representing them in any specific form. By progressively constructing more specific forms of the basic context, by producing more detailed scripts for the simulation (the colleague is a relation or fellow trade unionist or of a different religion or race; assurances of confidentiality or promotion; represented demands rather than requests; represented obligations to interviewer or colleague for past favors; self-disclosure by the interviewer, etc.), conditions that underlie such a liability, and conditions that enable the agent to surmount such a liability, may be identified. Furthermore, the same technique of construction can be employed to discriminate conditions that may alter the relational nature of the original social context. An analysis of the accounts of participants in such simulations can determine the conditions under which a promotion interview comes to be represented by the interviewee as a hostile interrogation.

Analogously, the same technique of construction may be employed to identify the conditions underlying the liabilities of policemen to become aggressive in the context of an arrest; of social workers to ignore real indicators of child abuse; of ordinary agents to be apathetic, dishonest, and aggressive; or the conditions that enable lawyers and psychiatrists to be convincing, teachers to be effective communicators and moral exemplars, and citizens to surmount pressures to conform. The same technique of construction can be employed to discriminate conditions that may transform participants' representations of social contexts: from representation of possible danger to representations of a personal threat; from representations of strong discipline in a family to representations of possible danger to a child; from representations of harmless humor to representations of personal insult; from representations of innocence to representations of guilt, and so forth.

Experimental simulation represents the closest analogue to closed and controlled experimentation in natural science. The practice of constructing social contexts by scripted simulation represents the closest parametric equivalent of experimental studies designed to discriminate generative and interference conditions. It is the only experimental strategy that can accommodate both the logic of experimental isolation and causal explanatory inference and the legitimate hermeneutical concerns about the priority (but not the exclusivity) of social meaning in a science of action.

Certainly much empirical work remains to be done on the technology of effective simulation, on how to make the simulation as lifelike as possible for participants (Alexander & Scriven, 1977; Ginsburg, 1979; Hendrick, 1977). Common sense suggests that experimental simulations are more likely to be effective either when the normal physical props are recreated in the laboratory (a mock interview room, court, prison, workshop, or classroom), or when the simulation is created in a real-world physical context (a real interview room, court, prison, workshop, or classroom). The latter type of situation may make such forms of experimental simulation seem indistinguishable from field experimentation. However, experimental simulations have the advantages both of discrimination and superior control of the simulated dimensions.

Some have argued[1] that experimental simulation will only constitute an adequate experimental strategy when it is recognized that role playing is a variable human skill. This has led to the suggestion that participants in experimental simulations should be selected from a population of (perhaps specially trained) subjects with demonstrated role-playing skills (Forward et al., 1976; Greenberg, 1967; Kelman, 1967; Sarbin & Allen, 1968), and that techniques for assessing role-playing skills should be developed for the selection of effective role players. No doubt there is some truth in this. It would be generally preferable to employ those who have some experience of a social role in simulations involving social roles. Thus, it would be desirable to employ real teachers and past jurors in simulations of the classroom and trial by jury. Subjects simulating emergencies, opportunities for dishonesty, or threats to one's self-esteem may, however, be drawn from the general population.

In this respect, the term *role-playing experiment* is highly misleading as a description of experimental simulation, since it suggests that effective simulation requires the special abilities of the skilled theatrical actor, who (through empathy or careful research) can convincingly reproduce the actions and emotions of others. This special skill is quite alien to experimental simulations. It ought to be stressed again that experimental simulations, like any other form of experimental enquiry, are not designed to predict what self or other would actually do in real-world open systems. They are designed to discriminate the conditions that promote and impede human powers and liabilities. If a participant in an experimental simulation role plays anyone at all, she role plays herself, or herself in a social role (teacher, doctor, lawyer, social worker, etc.) with which she is familiar. This just means that in an experimental simulation she acts as if she represents a potentially real-life situation in a specific way.

EVALUATION OF EXPERIMENTAL SIMULATION

There have been many empirical and experimental studies of the efficacy of experimental simulation. Most of these have only served to confound the issue. Most of the experimental comparisons of simulation and deception strategies are inadequate for the simple reason that the simulation studies lacked realism, involvement, and active participation. The studies by Greenberg (1967), Darroch and Steiner (1970), and Holmes and Bennett (1974) involved essentially passive and nonparticipative forms of simulation: the dependent variables were subjects' fallible predictions about the actions or feelings of subjects in the original deception experiments. As this type of simulation cannot be seriously recommended as an experimental strategy, its limited success (in predicting the outcome of deception experiments) has little bearing on the question of the efficacy of active experimental simulation. It is true that Horowitz and Rothschild (1970), Willis and Willis (1970), Simons and Pilliaven (1972), and Kopel and Arkowitz (1974) did use approximations of active experimental simulation and achieved a mixed measure of success. However, simply instructing subjects to behave spontaneously hardly ensures subject involvement and effective simulation.

Such "evaluations" of experimental simulation are inadequate because the simulations employed are scarcely representative of the real potential of experimental simulation. Yet the issue goes deeper than this. Miller (1972) correctly notes that even if experimental simulations can reproduce the behavioral outcomes of deception studies, this is insufficient "proof" of their equivalence in terms of the causal generation of behavior. Miller with some justification argues that the behavior of subjects in the Horowitz and Rothschild (1970) "forewarned" simulation could be due to either group influence, or "faithful subject" role playing, or cooperation by suspicious subjects who saw through the deception (or a combination of these factors). What he fails to note is that precisely the same point can be made about the original deception experiment which is simulated by this study. When one remembers that laboratory deceptions employing potentially suspicious and cooperative subjects are often held to be validated via their reproduction of the behavioral outcomes of field experiments (Berkowitz & Donnerstein, 1982), this suggests a double standard with respect to simulation and deception strategies.

The attempt to evaluate simulation as an experimental strategy by reference to deception experiments is of questionable value because of the serious doubts about the experimental realism and ecological validity of deception experiments. Comparisons of simulations and deception experiments would only provide adequate evaluations of simulation as an experimental strategy if the desired subject representations were regularly reproduced and standardized in deception experiments. But it is precisely this claim that is seriously disputed by contemporary critics, and these current doubts about the adequacy of deception experiments provide the main motivation for the recommendation of simulation as an alternative experimental strategy.

Most "experimental comparisons" of simulation and deception experiments are not genuine evaluations at all. The relative success of simulation experiments and deception experiments in reproducing constitutive representational dimensions is not measured at all, only the ability of simulation to reproduce the results of deception experiments, which are quite uncritically taken as the standard of experimental realism and ecological validity. Within this conceptual and practical framework it is inevitable that, *whatever* the outcome of such comparisons, simulation experiments will be represented as secondary, derivative, and thus ultimately redundant (Freedman, 1969; Miller, 1972).

There is in any case an inherent ambiguity about talk concerning the repetition, replication, or reproduction of deception experiments. This may mean simulating the social psychological phenomenon putatively investigated in the original deception experiment: the reproduction of the desired representations in closed experiments. Or it may mean the simulation of the social psychological phenomenon created in the original deception experiment: the reproduction of the representations of subjects in the original deception experiment. For reasons that have already been discussed in some detail, it cannot be assumed that these social psychological phenomena will be regularly equivalent. And in *neither* case can congruence of results be anticipated.

In the former case, congruence of experimental actions cannot be anticipated because the experimental simulation may reproduce the representations that are partially constitutive of the phenomenon investigated, but that were *not* reproduced in the original or contemporaneous deception experiment. (They may reproduce the independent or dependent variables investigated but not reproduced in the deception experiment.) Thus, for example, one would not expect participants in a simulation of the Milgram experiment to reproduce the actions of the original subjects, if participants in a simulation act as if they represented their actions as harmful, and if it is doubtful if Milgram's original subjects represented their actions in this way.

In the latter case, the simulation of deception experiments themselves, it is hardly surprising that simulations fail to replicate the results of the original experiments, in which subjects were presented with highly ambiguous situations. Since the actual representations of the original subjects in the deception experiment are (usually) unknown, the simulation cannot be effectively scripted. It is indeed no more surprising than the fact that attempts to replicate the outcomes of ambiguous (for the subjects) deception experiments by other deception experiments meet with similar mixed success. A good example of this is the controversy in the 1980–1981 issues of the *Bulletin of the British Psychological Society* following the gross failure by Perrin and Spencer (1980) to replicate in a recent deception experiment the results of the original conformity experiments of Asch (1951). Many commentators on the issue report successes and failures over the years. If it is true that the delimited cues of many deception experiments underdetermine subject representations and create serious ambiguity, it is hardly surprising, if attempted replications of deception experiments by either simulations or other deception experiments generate variable subject representations and, thus, variable outcomes, especially as such experiments will be particularly sensitive to minor variations in cues. While it may be legitimate to evaluate simulation as an experimental strategy via attempts to simulate the actions of agents who represent situation and actions in a specifically meaningful way, it is not legitimate to evaluate simulations via attempts to simulate the actions of subjects in situations lacking in meaning. While it is possible to assess equivalence of represented meaning, it hardly makes sense to talk about equivalence of ambiguity.

This does not mean that deception experiments cannot be used as a standard against which experimental simulations can be assessed. It does mean that deception experiments cannot be taken uncritically as the standard and the criterion for experimental adequacy. Claims that simulations are inadequate because they fail to duplicate the "subtler" interactions of deception experiments simply beg two important questions: that more effective (in terms of subject involvement and lifelike settings) simulations cannot reproduce such effects, and that such effects are not themselves pure artifacts of ambiguous experimental situations.

Experimental simulation can only be evaluated by reference to the production of actions for which the relational and representational dimensions have been empirically discriminated. Yet this is also misleading, since it suggests both that experimental simulations are employed to anticipate actions in open systems, which is false, and that they require some *independent* empirical justification, which is also false. Notice that no one ever asks for an independent empirical justification of the deception experiment or the field experiment.

Empirical evaluations of experimental simulations are evaluations of *how* simulations can be most effectively created, not of *whether* they can be. For there can be little doubt that human actions *can* be reproduced in such experiments. This is because the ability to produce some actions and the inability to produce others is part of *what it means* to attribute a human power or liability to an agent. Actions in experimental simulations are genuine exercises and manifestations of human powers and liabilities. Part of what it means to attribute a persuasive power to another is that she can persuade others in lifelike simulations. Part of what it means to attribute aggressive or dishonest liabilities to agents is that they will be aggressive and dishonest in lifelike simulations. A teacher who has the power to communicate effectively can manifest this power in a simulated context if she really has this power. The simulated context may be reconstructed in various ways to discriminate enabling and interference conditions. Analogously, someone who is liable to become aggressive in the presence of violent stimuli or a social worker who is liable to ignore indicators of child abuse will manifest this liability in experimental simulations if they are really subject to it. The simulated context may be reconstructed in various ways to discriminate means of surmounting this liability. There can be little serious doubt that powers and liabilities can be exercised and manifested in experimental simulations, *since it is only the constitutive social relations and representations that are simulated, not the powers and liabilities themselves.* The real empirical work required for the development of simulation as an experimental strategy is the discrimination of conditions that encourage subject involvement or *intensional engagement* in experimental simulations (for a useful beginning, see Yardley [1982]).

EXPERIMENTAL ARTIFACTS

Experimental simulations are primarily designed to avoid the problems of experimental alteration. They aim to achieve isolation without alteration. It is also worth noting that they are largely immune from the standard artifactual problems of laboratory experiments, since many of the standard criticisms assume that they are especially prone to artifactual influences such as "evaluation apprehension" and "demand characteristics."

The evaluation apprehension generated by the presence of other participants in a simulation (or any other form of experimental enquiry) is itself an intrinsic feature of most social interactions outside or inside the laboratory, and as such constitutes a legitimate object of experimental investigation by the progressive construction of simulated contexts. The evaluation apprehension generated by the presence of the experimenter is a different matter. Potential evaluation by an external authority is not an intrinsic feature of social interaction, although it is common to many forms of it (the practice of teaching, science, law, medicine, etc.). However, it presents no problem for experimental simulations. The participant who cannot perform in an effective simulation either lacks the power or the experimenter's presence acts as an interference condition. The latter possibility can simply be determined by the participant's ability to perform in real-life situations.

For the teacher who can communicate effectively in the normal classroom situation, but cannot in an experimental simulation, the experimenter's presence clearly acts as an interference condition. Furthermore, it can be confidently presumed that the latter type of case will be quite rare. Most persons who cannot be persuasive and communicate effectively under conditions of evaluation simply lack the power. Politicians and teachers who are hopelessly flustered by the presence of influencial bureaucrats or supervisors usually make poor politicians and teachers. For others, such evaluation apprehension may function as an enabling or promoting condition. Some persons may perform best under conditions of evaluation. Such empirical matters are a proper object of evaluation by experimental simulation.

Evaluation apprehension is even less of a problem with human liabilities, despite the fact that this is regularly presented as the most serious weakness of experimental simulations. It is frequently objected that participants in simulations will "feign good." As they are essentially "play-acting" they will present themselves in the best possible light. There may be some justification in directing this criticism against passive simulations. Agents' claims about how they would behave in described scenarios no doubt involve a strong presentational element. Few may be inclined to admit that they would be dishonest, aggressive, ignore signs of real danger to children, or obey an order to harm another in described scenarios, even if they knew that they would.

But there is no justification in applying this criticism to active experimental simulations. In real life, many agents would dearly love to be able to surmount their liabilities under conditions of evaluation by significant others and external authorities. Unfortunately, they cannot, and betray their liabilities to be aggressive and dishonest to wives and store detectives. Precisely the same is true of experimental simulations. If the simulation is effective, the agent will manifest a liability if she is prone to it. It is just false to claim that participants in simulations under conditions of evaluation do not manifest genuine human liabilities; the whole rationale of personnel evaluation is based upon the established empirical fact that they do. Mixon (1980, p. 177) cites Mill's (1972) description of a test designed to screen applicants for employment as a police officer. The candidate is asked:

. . . to role play an officer making an arrest of a drunk in an alley. Upon returning to his cruiser, he finds himself in the midst of a hooting, jeering crowd yelling for the release of the prisoner, and blocking his access to his vehicle.

Although in this direct evaluation most subjects want to present themselves in the best light, the simulation is demonstrably effective in reproducing human liabilities: "Some candidates have collapsed into complete immobility under such stress, while others have simulated gunfire on the hapless 'crowd'."

Analogously, novice and experienced pilots make potentially lethal errors in flight simulators, despite the fact that their promotion depends upon effective performance. In actual fact it is often *more difficult* to surmount liabilities in these forms of simulation employed as personnel evaluations. These situations are in an important respect *more* lifelike than real life. For the characters simulated by other police officers and social workers in such evaluations are composites of the worst sorts of characters they have come across in their years of experience. The crowds and families simulated by experienced policemen and social workers are the worst of all possible worlds. If trainee policemen and social workers can retain their patience and objectivity under these conditions, they can deal with anything in real life.

In this sense, of course, experimental simulations are artificial. However, it is exactly the right sort of artificiality (of isolation). Factors that may enable agents to surmount liabilities are absent, so the simulation is a poor basis for prediting the actions of agents in the real world. But this form of simulation does enable the experimenter to identify conditions that enable agents to surmount liabilities, such as the moral support of an experienced colleague. For the same reason it does not matter if some agents can surmount their liabilities in some simulations, or that some simulations are ineffective, since it is not the aim of the simulation experiment to license predictions about individual actions in real life. *Any* simulation is effective if agents manifest powers and liabilities in simulated contexts. The simulated context can then be reconstructed to discriminate enabling, stimulus, and interference conditions. Any participant who cannot refrain from aggressive actions in one simulation can be employed in other simulations to discriminate further conditions that promote or impede such actions, or that enable the agent to surmount the liability.

The second form of objection to experimental simulations is that the simulated context will embody "demand characteristics." This is not, however, a legitimate objection to experimental simulations. *It is part of the point of the experimental simulation.* For part of the rationale of the simulation of real-life social contexts is to determine precisely what demands of the context promote and impede various forms of action. The experimenter wishes to identify, for example, the implicit rules and social expectations of the social contexts of jury trials, interviews, marital disputes, wage negotiations, and so on. Indeed, this is the whole point and purpose of the recent research tradition directed to the discrimination of the logic of "situated action" (Brenner, 1980; Ginsburg, 1979; Ginsburg, Brenner, & von Cranach, 1985). Demand characteristics are methodologically problematic only when they are the *wrong* demand characteristics, when the laboratory experiment does not reproduce the demand characteristics of the social context studied, because it does not reproduce the constitutive representational dimensions of it.[2] The central argument of the past two chapters is that traditional laboratory experiments and deception experiments fail in precisely this way, and that the simulation strategy can effectively reproduce the very real demands of everyday life (rather than the peculiar demands of ambiguous experimental contexts).

Experimental simulation provides the closest analogue of experimentation in the natural sciences. Its full potential has not even begun to be exploited, or at least not by practitioners of social psychological science. Experimental simulation is a strategy regularly exploited by large legal firms in their preparation for major cases.[3] A whole variety of prosecution and defense strategies are tried on participants in trial simulations to identify those that are most likely to be successful. Despite the enormous expense of these simulations, lawyers and clients have no doubt about their ecological validity. It works for them. Only the dogmas of scientific empiricism blind the scientific psychologist to the power of experimental simulations. Experimenters in social psychological science are correct to base their work on the logic of experimentation in natural science. But there is simply no reason why experimenters should base their work upon the *social practice* of natural scientific experimentation. The development of social psychological science might be better served if they based their work upon some of the social practices of law firms and police departments.

13
The Evaluation of Psychological Therapy

The Interminable Debate

Hans Eysenck's landmark study (1952) poses an intellectual challenge to any clinician who provides a theoretical explanation of the efficacy of any form of psychological treatment of psychological disorders. According to Eysenck, any theoretical account of the therapeutic efficacy of any form of psychological therapy is only supported by successful therapeutic outcomes if these treatments produce improvement (or cure) rates superior (and significantly superior) to those rates achieved by clients who receive no form of psychological therapy. Any positive evaluation of any form of psychological therapy must demonstrate improvement rates superior to "spontaneous remission." Eysenck's own conclusions about the uselessness of psychoanalytic therapies (and usefulness of behavior therapies [1960, 1965]) have been the object of vigorous and sustained criticism, largely based upon the questionable nature of the criteria that Eysenck employed to make judgments of therapeutic success and failure (Bergin, 1971; Lambert, 1976; Miles, Barrabee, & Finesinger, 1951; Rozenzweig, 1954). This "interminable debate" (Skelton-Robinson, 1980) rages on.

Nevertheless, Eysenck's basic methodological point is itself unobjectionable. He merely stressed the need for the isolation of the theoretically therapeutic factors in any form of psychotherapy. However, despite the fact that later "meta-analyses" of evaluation studies have suggested that practically any form of psychological therapy produces recovery rates superior to spontaneous remission rates (Luborsky, Singer, & Luborsky, 1975; Smith & Glass, 1977), many researchers remain dissatisfied with the experimental and quasi-experimental techniques employed in individual studies to isolate the theoretically efficacious elements of psychological therapy. Many of these critics have continued to focus on the perceived inadequacy of control groups employed in evaluation studies (Kazdin & Wilcoxon, 1976; Kazdin & Wilson, 1978; Rachman & Wilson, 1980; Wilson & Rachman, 1983). In this chapter it is argued that control groups employed in therapy evaluations continue to be inadequately conceived, for reasons that derive from a fundamental misunderstanding of the nature of the problems of experimental isolation in evaluation studies.

There has undoubtably been some change from the original conception of a control for spontaneous remission. There was never any real suggestion that the improvement of persons suffering from psychological disorder who receive no treatment is spontaneous in the sense of "uncaused." The sense of "spontaneous" employed by Eysenck simply referred to causal factors that are not included in conventional theoretical accounts of the efficacy of standard forms of psychotherapy. Furthermore, it was quickly realized that the concept of a "no-treatment" group is a distorting fiction, since evidence suggests that initial interviews and assessment by professional therapists or general medical practitioners, or indeed sympathy and succor received from colleagues, spouses, friends, and priests, can have a powerful therapeutic effect (Karlsruher, 1974; Malan, 1975). There has been a significant shift from early attempts to demonstrate the superiority of conventional psychological treatments over spontaneous remission, to putative demonstrations of the *independence* of psychological treatment effects from so-called "nonspecific" effects. Since the 1960s, evaluation studies have regularly employed "placebo" or "pseudotherapy" control treatment groups to control for those elements of psychological therapies that are not included in theoretical accounts of their efficacy. There has also been increasing recognition of the *social psychological* nature of these nonspecific elements of psychological therapy. Unfortunately, these control treatment groups are generally misconceived because of a failure to appreciate the methodological implications of the social psychological dimensions of therapy.

The Social Psychology of Therapy

Frank (1961; 1974) has consistently argued that psychological therapy is necessarily a social psychological phenomenon best approached from the standpoint of an applied social psychologist. There have, of course, been many explanations and applications of social psychological factors in psychological therapy (for a comprehensive review, see Strong, 1978). Frank's essential point is, however, more fundamental, and does not vouchsafe any particular social psychological theory of psychological therapy. It reminds us that psychological therapy is intrinsically a social psychological *phenomenon*, since it is intentionally sought and practiced by individuals in meaningful social contexts.

One of the immediate and most significant implications of this point is that evaluation studies of psychological therapy inherit the problems of experimentation in social psychology. To a limited degree this has been recognized by researchers, insofar as nonspecific factors have come to be conceptualized and operationalized in terms of "experimental contaminants," which contribute to "experimental error" in evaluation studies. The traditional problems of experimental social psychology are thought to be simply transferred to evaluation studies. Evaluations are held to be methodologically problematic because of the presence of "demand characteristics" and "experimenter effects" (Bernstein & Nietzel, 1977; McGlynn, 1972; Shapiro & Morris, 1978). Yet this conception reveals a failure to recognize the most fundamental problem of *alteration* in experimental social psychology, and the special and peculiar manner in which this problem is manifested in evaluation studies.

Will (1980, p. 204) correctly identifies the critical question for the methodology of evaluation studies as: "What constitutes the empirical analogue of the closed system of the experiment?" The methodological problems of experimental evaluations of psychological therapy are largely the problems of achieving the *isolation* of the theoretical factors that are the object of experimental or quasi-experimental evaluation. According to most traditional accounts, the main problems of achieving experimental isolation in social psychology or therapy evaluation arise from the presence of experimental contaminants such as "experimenter bias," "experimenter expectancy," "demand characteristics," "evaluation apprehension," and so forth. These unfortunate experimental "artifacts" are traditionally conceived as relatively unproblematic technical difficulties that are defined as the addition of alien and contaminating variables (Barber, 1978). The methodological ideal of experimental social psychology is the elimination or attenuation of such confounding variables. Yet it has been noted that this methodological ideal simply exacerbates the most fundamental problem of alteration in traditional experiments. The elimination as much as the addition of such "contaminating" variables may alter or transform the very nature of the system studied.

We have also noted that experimental social psychologists do not always or even regularly attempt to achieve the *ontological* isolation of social psychological phenomena. As in natural science, the discrimination of the causal powers of a system or feature of a system may be achieved by *logical* or *control* isolation, by the creation of a control system that (ideally) reproduces everything but those features of the system whose causal powers are the object of experimental investigation. The same is true with respect to evaluations of psychological therapy, in which it is impossible to ontologically dislocate the active components of psychological therapy from the social and personal contexts in which they occur. This means that if the theoretically active components of psychological therapies are to be isolated in evaluation studies, then control treatments must (ideally) reproduce everything but the theoretically efficacious components of the psychological therapy which is the object of evaluation.

Control treatments regularly fail to approximate this ideal not simply because of the practical problems of achieving control isolation (which are real enough), but also because the nature of control treatments is misconceived. Psychological therapy evaluations inherit the problems of experimental alteration and transformation in social psychology because of the constitutive social and representational dimensions of the therapy session. But they also inherit them in a fashion that reverses the standard laboratory problem. For whereas alteration occurs in experimental social psychology in part because of the *presence* of "contaminating" factors such as demand characteristics and experimenter expectancy, alteration in evaluation studies occurs precisely because of the *absence* or *attenuation* of such factors in control treatment groups.

Frank (1974) has suggested that the feature common to all successful psychological therapies is the opportunity to interact with a trusted or respected person in the course of activities that both believe may produce a therapeutic change. This is not itself a causal explanatory hypothesis (although a causal account based upon this claim is in fact avowed by Frank). Rather it is a description of the social constitution of the therapy session: diverse behaviors as constituted as forms of psychological therapy by being represented by clients and therapists as potentially therapeutic.

The important consequence of this point is that with respect to the evaluation of psychological therapy, experimenter expectancies and demand characteristics function *not as experimental contaminants but as constitutive dimensions of the therapy session.*[1] The therapist's commitment to the efficacy of the therapy, the client's perception of the treatment as credible, and his expectancy of improvement or cure, are not additional and alien variables that confound the evaluation, but are constitutive dimensions of any psychological therapy that may be an object of experimental evaluation. Since these elements are constitutive dimensions of the therapy session, and thus common to any therapy session whatever the particular form of psychological therapy employed (be it psychoanalytic, behaviorist, personal construct, or some combinatory package, etc.), these elements should be effectively reproduced in any control treatment that aims to reproduce everything but the theoretically efficacious elements of diverse forms of psychotherapy.

In this fundamental respect, therapy evaluations are in fact disanalogous to experiments in social psychology. For the therapist aims to directly produce specific psychological change in his clients in a manner in which the experimental social psychologist does not. The experimental social psychologist aims to produce a social psychological system whose operation is the object of his experimental analysis. The therapist's goals and activities are an *intrinsic* feature of the psychological therapy which is the object of experimental evaluation. The experimental psychologist's goals and activities are an *extrinsic* feature of the system investigated by the experimental social psychologist (just as the activities of natural scientific investigators are extrinsic features of the physical and biological systems studied by them—with the possible exception of quantum mechanical phenomena).

Of course, the therapist conducting the investigated form of therapy in an evaluation study may or may not be identical to the experimenter who conducts the evaluation study, and the experimental social psychologist may or may not include himself within the investigated system. But these are contingent facts about individual evaluation studies and experiments, which are quite independent of the conceptual fact that the therapist's activity *must always be a component of the system investigated in evaluation studies*.

The experimenter's expectancy is a potential contaminant of the investigated system in experimental social psychology. The therapist's expectancy is an integral feature of the investigated system in therapy evaluations. The treatment of experimenter-subject and therapist-client interactions as methodologically equivalent is both unjustified and seriously distorts the logic of control isolation in evaluation studies. While it is entirely appropriate to devise strategies for eliminating or attenuating experimenter-subject interactions in experimental social psychology, it is utterly inappropriate to attempt the same with respect to therapist-client interactions that are partially constitutive of any form of psychological therapy, and should thus be fully reproduced in any experimental or control treatment.

The same basic point may be alternatively expressed by noting that the evaluation of psychological therapy is more closely analogous to a field experiment than a laboratory experiment. The particular psychological therapy that is the object of isolation and evaluation is just a particular instance of the common and socially meaningful phenomenon that is the therapy session. The constitutive conditions of therapy are present in those instances of therapy that are the object of experimental evaluation just because no attempt at ontological isolation is made. As in any other therapy session, both therapists and clients engage in activities with more or less optimistic expectations, and the contexts of therapies that are the object of experimental evaluation are as natural as any other context (indeed they are often conducted in whatever is the natural context for the therapist, be it a psychoanalytic couch or specially designated treatment area). The isolation of the theoretically powerful elements of any particular psychological therapy can only be achieved by the creation of a parallel control treatment system that attempts to reproduce everything but the theoretically efficacious elements of the treatment that is the object of evaluation.

Psychological therapy is not *itself* an attempt to achieve ontological or control isolation of the activities that produce therapeutic change. It is a clinical intervention designed to promote specific therapeutic change. Since social psychological factors such as credibility of treatment, expectancy, and therapist commitment are integral dimensions of any form of psychological therapy, they must be effectively reproduced in control treatments if evaluation studies are to produce critical observations supporting theoretical causal explanations of therapeutic change in terms of the special forms of psychological therapy that are the object of evaluation.

Essentially the same point can also be made via a denial of Eysenck's criticism of clinical studies of psychoanalytic or any other form of therapy (although the general argument can also be seen as essentially a development of Eysenck's demand for adequate controls in evaluation studies). Eysenck's argument about the superiority of experimental studies of therapy is neatly stated in the following passage (1959, p. 228):

> What then is the evidence on which psychoanalysis is based? Essentially it is clinical rather than experimental. . . . Suffice it is to remember that clinical work is often very productive of theories and hypotheses, but weak on proof and verification; that in fact the clinical method by itself cannot produce such proof because investigations are carried out with the avowed purpose of aiding the patient, not of putting searching questions to nature.

It is simply false to claim that psychological therapies that have the "avowed purpose of aiding the patient" cannot themselves be the object of experimental isolation. All that is true is that they cannot be the object of ontological isolation. The fact that psychological therapies have the "avowed purpose of aiding the patient" does not mean that they cannot be the object of control isolation in evaluation studies that put "searching questions to nature." The two purposes are not mutually exclusive, and the latter purpose cannot be adequately served in evaluations employing control treatments unless the former purpose is also engaged in both experimental and control treatments.

Natural Negotiation Hypothesis

A number of researchers have noted that many control treatments do embody rather dubious assumptions about levels of credibility and expectancy (Kazdin & Wilcoxon, 1976; McGlynn & McDonell, 1974). Such doubts led Borkovec and Nau (1972) to conclude that the mixed results of evaluation studies may be due to the differential levels of credibility and expectancy generated in different experimental and control treatments. But although such theorists are rather more sensitive to the problems of control treatments, they continue to represent such factors as experimental contaminants, or, at best, as necessary enabling conditions for effective psychological therapy.

Yet if control treatment groups are to function as adequate controls for credibility, expectancy, and commitment, such constitutive dimensions of the therapy session must be treated as potentially *sufficient* for therapeutic change. What may be termed the *natural negotiation* hypothesis can serve as a formal alternative hypothesis for any control treatment with respect to any investigated experimental treatment. In accord with Frank's (1974) constitutive definition of psychological therapy, the *natural negotiation* hypothesis makes the *additional causal claim* that therapeutic change is the *result* of an interaction with a trusted or respected person in activities that both believe may produce therapeutic change. There is a degree of empirical support for this hypothesis (Bergin & Lambert, 1978; Gurin, Veroff, & Feld, 1960; Malan, 1975). Karlsruher (1974) has reviewed the beneficial effects of various forms of nonprofessional natural negotiation, and at least one study has suggested that some forms of nonprofessional negotiation can be as effective as professional therapies (Strupp & Hadley, 1979).

In the long run, this explanation of therapeutic change may receive more or less empirical support. But its methodological significance will always remain the same. Control treatments will only function effectively to isolate the theoretically efficacious elements of experimental therapies if they are designed as credible alternative treatments and administered by practitioners committed to their efficacy.

This hypothesis is simply not taken seriously in traditional research strategies for evaluation studies, which treat such factors as forms of experimental contamination. In consequence, such factors are attenuated in control treatments, whose primary logic of design is to *exclude* the theoretically efficacious elements of the experimental therapy under investigation. This purely negative rationale can hardly be expected in practice to produce control treatments that are perceived by clients as *at least as* credible as the experimental treatment (although there is no reason in principle why this cannot be achieved). Furthermore, since control treatments are generally administered by therapists committed to the efficacy of the experimental but not the control treatment, there is serious risk of a kind of negative "experimenter effect." Certainly there is little reason to suppose that therapists administering control treatments are *at least as* committed to their efficacy as those therapists who administer the experimental treatments (and good reasons to suppose otherwise given the general scepticism about the natural negotiation hypotheses).

Wilkins (1979, p. 323) has noted that the term *nonspecific effects* is defined negatively in relation to usually quite different theoretical-experimental treatments. Control treatments are designed to exclude quite different theoretically efficacious elements in different evaluation studies. Given the present research rationale, there is unlikely to be any feature or cluster of features common to all treatments that purport to control for nonspecific effects. This feature alone may explain the mixed results of many evaluation studies.

The present complaint goes deeper than this, however. The negative rationale for control treatments tends to produce a serious attenuation of the constitutive dimensions of psychological therapy in control treatments. This contributes to an almost inevitable but entirely spurious "accumulation of support" for conventional psychological therapies that are the object of experimental evauluation. It also has another insidious effect. It creates an equally spurious impression of parsimony with respect to traditional theoretical explanations of therapeutic change. Given the negative rationale and, thus, the heterogeneous constitution of control treatments, "nonspecific" explanations of change invariably appear ad hoc.

Another factor that contributes to the negative conception and construction of control treatments is their conception by practitioners as somehow analogous to placebo treatments in medicine. Indeed, control treatments are frequently designated as "placebo treatments." There has been some recent doubt expressed about the adequacy of such a conceptualization (Critelli & Neuman, 1984; Kirsch, 1978), and it is in fact doubtful if there are any good grounds for maintaining this analogy.

The *placebo effect* is primarily a medical term that refers to some physiological change produced by nonmedical means, usually with the implicit or explicit recognition that the change is produced (directly or indirectly) by psychological means. The effect in medicine is real enough. Placebos can mimic the influence of pharmacologically active drugs and have direct effects on bodily organs and organic disease (Shapiro & Morris, 1978). The distinction between "medical" and "placebo" effects is made in terms of the causal conditions and mechanisms held to be responsible for therapeutic physiological change, between medical treatments that produce physiological change by physiological means such as surgery and pharmacologically active drugs, and placebo treatments that produce therapeutic physiological change by psychological or psychophysiological means (such as the patient's expectation of improvement consequent to "drug" therapies employing substances that are pharmacologically inert). The placebo effect acquired negative connotations in medicine partly because the effect was unreliable and little understood, but mainly because developed medical techniques demonstrated therapeutic effects greatly superior to placebos.

With respect to the evaluation of psychological therapy, this contrast is vitiated because both experimental and control treatments *aim to produce therapeutic change by psychological means*. There can be little present doubt (given the evidence) that natural negotiation can produce real therapeutic change (and not merely artifactual and inaccurate commentaries by clients and therapists). And if the argument of this chapter is sound, there is no present reason to suppose that conventional professional treatments that are the object of experimental evaluations are any more effective, efficient, or reliable than the most effective forms of natural negotiation.

The natural negotiation hypothesis provides a more positive rationale for control treatments. It reminds us that psychological therapy is intrinsically a social psychological phenomenon derived from natural negotiation in the social world. It can be developed but not divorced from this context. The natural negotiation hypotheses reminds us that professional and nonprofessional therapies are grounded in relations and representations that are part of the natural social order, such as representations of the possibilities of therapeutic change (which regularly provide the motivation for seeking help and succor from a friend, colleague, priest, family member, or professional therapist).

The natural negotiation hypothesis provides a rationale common to all effectively constructed control treatments. Control treatments constructed according to the natural negotiation hypothesis control for the possibility, common to all forms of professional therapies, that professional interactions are simply represented as potentially more effective than negotiation with nonprofessionals, or maximize many of the social psychological elements that may be relatively deficient in some forms of natural negotiation (e.g., professional therapists as a group may be more committed to the efficacy of their treatments than friends or colleagues, or may adopt a more positive attitude to problems of a sexual or criminal nature than priests or family members).

This common rationale for the construction of natural negotiation control treatments also has the significant methodological consequence that there is simply no need to employ a different control treatment for every experimental treatment. This is only necessary if control treatments are designed to exclude the heterogeneous theoretical elements of a range of different experimental treatments. A single natural negotiation control treatment in which the constitutive dimensions of any form of therapy are maximized can serve as a control treatment in relation to any experimental treatment, so long as variables such as the nature and severity of the psychological disorder are matched. A fairly small number of such studies could serve as adequate control treatments in relation to all other forms of psychological therapy. Indeed, given the special practical problem of finding therapists genuinely committed to the efficacy of natural negotiation, it may be better if researchers concentrated on the quality of a limited number of control treatments.

Control treatments constructed according to the natural negotiation hypothesis assess the efficacy of the constitutive social psychological relations and representations of all forms of therapy. Such common factors should be effectively reproduced rather than attenuated in control treatment groups. This rationale would also support the inclusion in control treatments of any other nonconstitutive factors that evidence suggests contribute to the improved efficacy of any form of therapy, such as "anticipatory socialization" (Sloane, Cristol, Pepernik, & Staples, 1970).

Indeed, the above arguments suggest a stronger thesis, which is justifiable independently on moral grounds (since the evidence suggests that such factors do play some positive role in therapeutic change), but advanced on primarily methodological grounds. Since a natural negotiation control treatment controls for the possibility that the constitutive dimensions of all therapies are simply more potent in professional therapies, it should not simply reproduce but aim to *maximize* credibility, expectancy, and commitment.[2]

Theory and Efficacy

The claim that adequate control treatments should aim to maximize credibility, expectancy, and commitment does not involve any confusion of issues of theory and efficacy. For it might be objected that the above analysis has simply confused questions about the overall efficacy of psychological therapy with theoretical questions about the explanation of more or less efficacious psychological therapies. Two versions of this general complaint may be distinguished.

First, it may be objected that the maximization of these factors in control treatment groups simply confounds the outcome in studies designed to evaluate a theoretical account of the efficacy of a particular form of therapy. In these studies such factors do function as experimental contaminants. This is because the employment of natural negotiation treatments may obscure the operation of the specific factors isolated in the experimental treatment, via the more potent exploitation of the social psychological factors common to experimental and control treatments. If the experimentally isolated elements of a novel or conventional form of therapy fail to achieve improvement rates significally superior to the control treatment, then this may be because the constitutive features of any form of therapy, such as credibility, expectancy, and commitment, are more effectively exploited in the control treatment.

But if this does prove to be the case, then so much the worse for the experimental treatment. For then we have no reason to suppose that such a treatment represents an advance in efficacy over natural negotiation, nor any reason to suppose that its limited efficacy cannot simply be explained in terms of natural negotiation. It is true that an experimental treatment may achieve superior improvement rates simply because it exploits such constitutive features more effectively than the control treatment. It is also true that although such a result does represent a real gain in efficacy, it does not provide unambiguous support for the standard theoretical account of the efficacy of the experimental therapy, for this can also be explained in terms of the natural negotiation hypothesis. But this is precisely the complaint of the present chapter.

Second, it may be objected that the above arguments at most apply to evaluations of the overall effectiveness of particular therapies in relation to control treatments, in which it may be appropriate to maximize credibility, expectancy, and commitment. But it might be arued that modern therapy outcome research more commonly involves the comparison of two alternative experimental treatments, or components of a single form of treatment, or parametric variations of a single form of treatment.

The first answer to this is that the argument of this chapter is precisely to the effect that the natural negotiation hypotheses should be treated as an alternative hypotheses that purports to provide a sufficient explanation[3] of therapeutic change, and that so-called "control" or "placebo" or "pseudotherapy" treatments should be conceived as alternative treatments constructed on the basis of this hypothesis. According to the rationale of this hypothesis, factors such as credibility, expectancy, and commitment should be maximized.

The second answer is that with respect to the comparison of two alternative treatments, components of a single treatment, or parametric variations of a single treatment, the natural negotiation hypothesis will always provide a potential explanation of any differences in experimental outcome. The only alternatives to the maximization of natural negotiation factors are attenuation or equalization. But it is far from obvious that differential attenuation produces any epistemic advantage, and may in fact be counterproductive. For if factors such as credibility, expectancy, and commitment play at least an enabling role in effective therapy, then the joint efficacy of the compared therapies is also likely to be attenuated, making it difficult to discriminate significant differences in outcome. It is extremely difficult to produce equality of credibility, expectancy, and commitment, since any change in form of treatment, component of treatment, or parametric variation of components, may produce a parametric variation in credibility, expectancy, and commitment.

It is, however, quite wrong to suppose that comparative outcomes are theoretically ambiguous when such factors are differentially maximized, and this is true irrespective of whether any treatment is formally designated as a natural negotiation control treatment. For any treatment in which such factors are maximized can serve as a control for any other form of treatment (or compositional or parametric variant), so long as these factors are maximized to *at least the same degree* as those in the other treatment. If one treatment, A, produces outcomes that are significantly superior to another form of treatment, B, while B is *at least as* credible as A and involves *at least as much* client and therapist expectancy and therapist commitment as A, then the superior success of treatment A cannot be (at least wholly) accounted for in terms of the natural negotiation hypothesis, and provides clear-cut support for the theoretical account of the efficacy of treatment A. The equality of credibility, expectancy, and commitment is just a limiting case of this requirement. But it is not an ideal example of it. The independence of therapeutic effects from natural negotiation factors is in fact more clearly demonstrated when these components are maximized to a greater degree in the treatment that serves as a control for natural negotiation.

This critical point may be illustrated by considering Smith's (1976) evaluation of the theoretical account of the efficacy of transcendental meditation. Smith used an experimental group that involved two daily sessions of sitting plus standard transcendental meditation (TM) procedures. The control treatment, called "periodic somatic activity," was designed to reproduce the "form, complexity and expectation fostering aspects of transcendental meditation" (Smith, p. 630), and involved a daily exercise routine that involved sitting twice daily, but none of the standard TM procedures. From the absence of statistically significant differences in outcome after 6 months ($p > .6$), Smith concluded that the efficacy of TM is not due to factors described in standard TM theory, and has nothing to do with the specific TM procedures employed.

Consider now the epistemic situation if steps had been taken to attenuate factors such as expectancy, credibility, and commitment. This may well have obscured the real potential of TM therapy (or the control treatment for that matter) by reducing the effects of both TM and natural negotiation, and precluding the demonstration of statistically significant differences in outcome. Consider next the situation in which such factors are maximized but equalized: any significant difference in therapeutic outcome counts unambiguously for either TM or natural negotiation. Consider finally the situation in which these factors are maximized to a greater degree in the control treatment: then a statistically significant difference in favor of TM provides even greater support for theoretical accounts of the efficacy of TM; a statistically significant difference in outcome in favor of the control treatment under this condition provides even greater support for the natural negotiation hypothesis. (The other possible combinations are either ambiguous or provide support only for the natural negotiation hypothesis.)

In these situations it does remain ambiguous as to whether the limited efficacy of the alternative treatment B (relative to treatment A), which serves as the natural negotiation control treatment, is itself to be explained in terms of the standard theoretical account or in terms of natural negotiation. But this question can be answered by repeating the procedure with the inclusion of a specially created natural negotiation control treatment that has no theoretical justification other than the natural negotiation hypothesis.

Finally, it is probably worth remarking that the distinction between issues of theory and efficacy is not worth pressing too far. While not providing the only form of evidential support for theoretical accounts of psychological disorders and the efficacy of treatments of such disorders, the efficacy (and differential efficacy) of forms of psychological treatment still remains a critical test of such theoretical accounts in the same way that the efficacy (and differential efficacy) of treatments of physical diseases such as smallpox and tuberculosis provided a critical test (although not the only test) of the adequacy of theories about such diseases and their treatment.

It must be stressed again that the recognition that the constitutive dimensions of psychological therapy are social psychological in nature does not itself vouchsafe any social psychological *theory* of psychological disorders and their treatment. An experimental evaluation of a form of therapy based upon personal construct theory, for example, just as much as any therapy based upon psychoanalytic or behavior theory, requires the employment of an effective natural negotiation control treatment. Of course, the natural negotiation hypothesis itself provides a social psychological account of therapeutic change, but the present argument *does not accord this account any privileged status*.

Nevertheless, it is worth noting that there is some support for the natural negotiation account. Meta-analyses of psychological therapy outcomes (Luborsky et al., 1975; Smith & Glass, 1977) suggest that practically any form of psychological therapy is effective and that all forms of psychological therapy are more or less equally effective. Only the constitutive dimensions of any form of therapy are likely to be common elements in all forms of equally effective therapy. It is, however, doubtful that natural negotiation will prove to be a panacea for all forms of psychological disorder and distress. One reason for doubting this is the inadequacy of the individual evaluation studies upon which such meta-analyses are based. It is much more likely that evaluations employing maximized natural negotiation will demonstrate that some psychological therapics are superior to maximized natural negotiation, and that others are not.

Nevertheless, the possibility is worth mentioning for the following reason. If experimental evaluations did provide strong support for the natural negotiation hypothesis for even some disorders, it would present professional practitioners with a unique dilemma. Deception on the part of the therapist with respect to his account of the theoretical rationale would seem to be a necessary requirement if such therapies are to be maximally effective. For it seems highly unlikely that clients would find the natural negotiation rationale as credible as conventional rationales in terms of psychoanalytic, personal construct, and behaviorist theories.

This final point is worth making to completely dissociate the present argument from a common moral drawn by critical commentators from the perceived inadequacy of experimental evaluations of psychological therapy. Scriven (1974), giving evidence to the APA Ethics Committee, suggested that all practitioners of psychological treatment should be required to notify their clients that the treatments they were about to receive had never been demonstrated to be superior to a placebo. While recognizing the inadequacy of many experimental evaluations of psychological therapy, the present argument shows that such a conclusion is based upon an inappropriately negative conception of control treatments, and would in fact be counterproductive with respect to the evaluation and development of effective psychological therapy.

Epilogue

This book articulates and integrates a realist philosophy of social psychological science and a social constitutionist philosophy of human action. It does not pretend to have resolved all the conceptual problems of social psychological science, although it does hope to have gone some way to dissolve some of the traditional confusions that have vitiated much contemporary debate. There are a host of remaining implications that could be drawn from the present analysis, and a host of qualifications that could be made. I hope to discuss some of these implications and qualifications in future volumes and on the pages of the appropriate academic journals. There are also a number of recognized inadequacies and weaknesses that I hope to resolve by the same means.

Two residual inadequacies perhaps deserve special mention in conclusion. The first concerns the development of explanatory and exploratory theories in social psychological science. More could (and perhaps should) have been said on these matters, and I hope to remedy this deficiency in future volumes on social and psychological forms of explanation. Yet it should be recognized that there is a limit to philosophical contributions on these matters. Many recent critics have complained about the conceptual poverty of explanatory theory in social psychological science. In this volume the source of this poverty has been diagnosed as fundamentally mistaken empiricist conceptions of the nature of scientific theory and its relation to its evidential grounds. But there are no easy philosophical or theoretical resolutions of this problem. The only route to theoretical improvement and achievement is via the creative efforts of theoretical scientists. Analogously, the greatest impediment to progress in social psychological science may be the present impoverishment of exploratory theories (cf. Meehl, 1978). This impoverishment also has its roots in mistaken empiricist assumptions about the evidential grounding of explanatory theories. But again there are no easy answers, only the creative potential of individual scientists. Nevertheless, the following point ought to be stressed. If the general argument of this volume is sound, then without the development of adequate exploratory theories, the prospects for a science of action are grim. We can look forward to nothing more than a historical succession of incommensurable theories and ambiguous experiments.

The second inadequacy concerns the occasional references to social context, biography, and agent accounting as the basis for exploratory theories in social psychological science. These are not intended as a priori desiderata, but as suggestions of plausible theoretical resources that have been underexploited. One of these suggestions requires special comment. The idea that social psychological science should be grounded in agent accounts will be treated by many practitioners as anathemic to the notion of scientific analysis. Yet I believe that nothing more than empiricist dogma supports this reaction.

I do not pretend that many practitioners will be convinced by the limited discussion of this issue in the present volume. I plan to devote a whole future volume to it. In conclusion I can only indicate the source of my own optimism concerning the potential of agent accounts. This lies in the recognition that much of human psychology, like most of human action, is also socially constituted. If this is the case, then one would antipate a much more intimate connection between mind, discourse, and action than is found in most theories, but which our folk intuitions would lead us to expect. Ultimately, this might lead not only to a theoretical grounding of the exploratory potential of agent accounts, but also to a developed form of social psychological science in which we might hope to discriminate some of the intimate links between explanatory and exploratory theories that are characteristic of developed theoretical spirals in the advanced physical sciences. This is perhaps a long—and perhaps a very long—way off. This volume is part of an attempt to demonstrate that there are no in-principle impediments to the approximation of this ideal.

Notes

Chapter 1

1. Although the arguments of the present volume are primarily directed toward social psychologists, much of the discussion has relevance for psychology in general and other social sciences such as sociology, anthropology, economics, and so forth. This is because the notion of social psychological science is defined by reference to its subject matter, that is, as any form of scientific discipline concerned with furnishing explanations of those human behaviors that have social and psychological dimensions.

2. For a survey of these paradoxes, see Schlesinger (1974).

3. Indeed, it may be argued that the significance of novel predictions can only be accommodated by a realist interpretation of theory (Leplin, 1988; Musgrave, 1987).

4. See Craig (1956).

Chapter 4

1. *Enabling conditions* are defined as conditions that are necessary conditions for the manifestation of a causal power. *Stimulus conditions* are defined as conditions that, in conjunction with enabling conditions, are sufficient for the manifestation of a causal power. Although it is somewhat arbitrary to assign some conditions as enabling and others as stimulus conditions, the distinction is not itself arbitrary. For it may be the case that some causal powers have no stimulus conditions. See Chapter 9.

2. The reason of this qualification is because human power ascriptions only license predictions about what the agent *can* do, not what she *will* do. See Chapter 9.

3. Although some modification of the analysis of causal powers is required when one considers human powers. See Chapter 9.

4. To be fair to Harré and Secord, this is not a very clear statement of their own argument, which is mainly concerned with the *identity* of behaviors produced in traditional laboratory experiments. This important issue is discussed in Chapter 11.

5. This claim, however, requires some qualifications. See Chapter 10.

6. See Chapter 13.

Chapter 5

1. It should be noted that the term *intentional object* is employed in this volume in a sense quite different from the sense in which this term is employed by phenomenological philosophers such as Brentano and Husserl. According to the present usage, intentional objects are the real-world (natural, social, and psychological) particulars to which our thoughts and perceptions are directed.

2. It is not suggested that it is easy to construct transformation rules in social psychological science. The articulation of such rules is at the heart of the theoretical enterprise, and requires the theorist to explain *how* the dimensions described by the theory are instantiated in the system to be explained: for example, how the dimensions of ritual are instantiated in trade union negotiations. This is no easy task.

3. Again it is not suggested that this is an easy enterprise, only that there are no in-principle impediments to its achievement.

4. For a more detailed discussion of these issues, see Greenwood (1987).

5. It would be naive to pretend that this limited discussion of self-knowledge will convince many practicing psychologists. It is included merely as an attempt to defuse some of the traditional sceptical doubts about the accuracy of agents' accounts of their psychology, held by most psychologists in the scientific psychological tradition. I plan to devote a future volume to the consideration of this particular (and perhaps the most damaging) dogma of empiricism.

6. This is not to suggest that correspondence rules should be identified with auxiliary hypotheses, although they are not clearly distinguished in the literature, and Popper (1959, p. 51) at least appears to make the identification.

7. However, it is worth remembering that the position of Hanson and Kuhn is not really fundamentally different from the original empiricism of Carnap and Schlick. In the early versions of logical positivism, physical object concepts were treated as "logical constructions," differing only in degree from the "logical constructions" of scientific theory. See Chapter 1.

8. This looks like Hanson and Kuhn are committed to an unusually strong version of what is sometimes termed the Sapir-Whorf thesis (Whorf, 1956), according to which our perceptual abilities are held to be relative to our linguistic resources. A common illustration is the claim that since Eskimos have a number of different words for snow and English speakers only one, Eskimos can perceive differences in snow that English speakers cannot.

Yet a limited vocubulary seems to impose no more intrinsic limitations on the perceptual capacities of English speakers than it does for huskies or polar bears. The empirical evidence relating to this thesis looks increasingly doubtful. For example, the wide cultural variance in the language of color does not seem to correspond to any variance in the abilities of persons to perceive the different ranges of the color spectrum (Berlin & Kay, 1969; Rosch, 1974). Mary Hesse (1974) argues that the perceptual discrimination of objective similarities and differences is a necessary enabling condition for the learning of socially constructed concepts and language. Recent empirical work in the area simply serves to illustrate this essentially philosophical point (Clark and Clark, 1977; Slobin, 1971).

9. See Note 1.

10. In 1903, 8 years after Röntgen discovered X rays, the French physicist Blondlot

announced his "discovery" of the existence and properties of a new type of radiation, which he called N rays. His observations were "confirmed" by another distinguished researcher at the University of Nancy, Augustin Charpentier. Both published reports on the properties of N rays the same year in *Comptes rendus*, the *Annals of the French Academy of Sciences*. By 1904, there were 54 scientific reports of N rays in the *Comptes rendus*, and in the same year Blondlot received the prestigious Prix Leconte (partly for his work on N rays). In 1905, the American Professor of Optics and Spectroscopy, R.W. Woods, visited Blondlot's laboratory, and demonstrated that the "observations" of the various documented experimental manifestations of N rays were simply a product of delusion and wishful thinking on the part of the individual scientists concered. (For a detailed account of the N-ray affair, see Klotz, 1980).

In this particular example, there is a clear sense in which the "observations" made were constructed according to a presupposed theory, analogous to the role of motivational factors in some psychological theories of perceptual error. But this form of theory informity of observations has no useful role to play in the scientific enterprise, and there is no reason to suppose that it is an intrinsic and ineliminable feature of scientific observation. The perceptual errors of Blondlot and his colleagues were after all demonstrated to be perceptual errors, and were recognized as such by the international scientific community.

11. The distinction between *explanatory* and *exploratory* theories is introduced for expository convenience, to distinguish between (respectively) theories that are (at any particular time) the object of observational evaluation and theories that are employed in making critical observations. Of course, an explanatory theory may be employed sometimes as an exploratory theory, and any exploratory theory may itself be explanatory.

12. For a detailed account of this episode, see Watson (1978).

13. See, for example, Brown (1977), p.179: "Thus *seeing as* is a special case of *seeing that*; to see an object as a galvenometer is to see that it is a galvenometer."

14. This is not to deny that our analysis of the historical acceptance and rejection of scientific theories must take into account the intensional contents of what contemporary scientists *believed* they were observing (Brown, 1977). We are perhaps obliged to explain Brahe's rejection of the Copernican theory partly in terms of what Brahe believed he observed when viewing a sunrise. However, we are not therefore obliged to accept that Brahe observed a moving sun or that the sun moved. On the contrary, since our current beliefs are informed by our best current explanatory theories based upon observations informed by our best exploratory theories, we are obliged to deny this.

15. There is a sense in which it may be said that observations do presuppose the theory that is the object of evaluation, as Feyerabend often suggests. But the argument of this section demonstrates that even the most extreme version of this claim poses no threat to objectivity.

In the first place, our earlier point ought to be stressed again. It is frequently the case that the exploratory theory, which informs the critical observations in favor of an explanatory theory, does *not* presuppose the explanatory theory (as in the DNA and Copernican examples cited). That is, it is always a contingent question whether the theory informing the critical observation is to be identified with the explanatory theory, which is the object of observational evaluation.

Second, we should not confuse this rare situation with the common fact that the putative domains of explanatory and exploratory theories necessarily overlap. In this quite innocent sense, it is always true to say that theory-informed observations of entity X presuppose that there are Xs. An exploratory theory employed to evaluate the claims of an explanatory theory will necessarily specify *how* the structures, charges, wavelengths, lifetimes, and so forth of the entities postulated by the explanatory theory will manifest themselves in the apparatus. But there is no guarantee that the structures, charges, wavelengths, lifetimes, and so forth predicted by the explanatory theory will be manifested in the apparatus. Although observations of X informed by the exploratory theory presuppose that there are Xs, the employment of the exploratory theory does not presuppose this. It only specifies how Xs will manifest themselves in the apparatus, *if* they exist or have the properties attributed to them by the explanatory theory.

Third, even in the limiting case where the exploratory theory can be identified in whole or part with the explanatory theory, any attempt to abandon or modify the exploratory theory to accommodate recalcitrant data will not only eliminate the prior support for the explanatory theory based upon the exploratory theory, but also the support for other explanatory theories based upon it (assuming, as is often the case, that the domain of exploratory theories (e.g., of microscopes) is often greater than the domain of explanatory theories (e.g., about proteins).

16. See Harré (1981), p. 176.

17. Consideration of space has largely precluded discussion of the scientific empiricist claim about the historically cumulative nature of scientific knowledge, and the relativist denial of this claim. Nevertheless, the arguments of this section do suggest that our intuitions about the theoretical progress of science can be rationally justified.

18. Yet again, it is not suggested that it is easy to develop exploratory theories in social psychological science, or indeed that it easy to develop these particular ones. It is only to suggest that these currently underdeveloped and devalued resources should be more rigorously exploited. Nevertheless, it is worth stressing that most empirical enquiries in social psychological science are characterized by an almost complete lack of systematically exploited exploratory theories (cf. Meehl, 1978). Exploratory theories are usually only brought in when something goes wrong (as it often does), which explains why they usually appear ad hoc.

19. For a brief but excellent discussion of some of the most serious shortcomings of the surrealist position, see Leplin (1987).

Chapter 7

1. In this section, it is assumed for the sake of argument that there are conceptual truths relating social psychological phenomena and their consequences, in order to show that this does not preclude the possibility of causal explanations. Nevertheless, according to the arguments of Chapters 5, 8, and 9 and the latter half of this chapter, it is in fact denied that the conceptual truths of social psychology science describe causal relationships.

2. This distinction was first introduced by Kant (1787), and developed by Black

(1962), Schwayder (1965), and Searle (1970). Harré, Clarke, and De Carlo (1985) make an analogous distinction between "situational definitions" and "action rules."

3. This is not to deny that a reference to an agent's representation of constitutive rules may figure in a causal account of their actions. See this chapter and Chapter 9.

4. The same point might be alternatively expressed by stating that human actions and practices are constituted by intrinsic (internal) relations to entities that are extrinsic (external) to them.

5. Cf. the discussion of social and psychological theories in Chapter 5.

Chapter 8

1. See Chapter 5.

2. This is not to deny that the social worlds of some animals have representational dimensions, only that they lack the dimensions partially constitutive of slavery and trials by jury.

3. Precisely the same point applies to majority classifications of actions constituted by participant agent representations. The collective consensus about the definition of aggression, for example, in terms of the intention to injure another, is no guarantee that the majority will be consistent or accurate when it comes to the discrimination of instances of aggression (behaviors directed to the injury of others). The majority will be inaccurate in their classification of individual actions as aggressive if the behaviors concerned are not directed to the injury of others. The majority will be inconsistent if they regularly characterize the actions of one group (e.g., black youths) as aggressive but not the actions of another group (e.g., white policemen), and if the behaviors of individuals in both groups are directed toward the injury of others.

4. It is in the development of such theories that the important role of tranformation rules is perhaps most apparent (see Chapter 5). The employment of such theories requires the articulation of tranformation rules specifying how the dimensions described in the theoretical explanation are instantiated in the social psychological phenomenon explained. To characterize the actions of husbands and wives as instances of power negotiation or reputation management is not enough. An adequate theoretical explanation needs to demonstrate how the dimensions of power negotiation and reputation management are instantiated in the actions of husbands and wives.

5. It is worth stressing that it is an entirely contingent fact that this presumption has proven to be empirically warranted in the natural sciences. See Chapter 9.

6. This is not to deny that there is an important and interesting question about the demarcation of distinctly social and psychological forms of causal explanation, although it is not considered in this volume.

7. This is the intuition behind the familiar philosophical claim that no purely behavioral taxonomy could provide an adequate classification of human action (Peters, 1958). Any purely behavioral analysis of signaling, for example, would include too much and too little, since any specified form of behavior will not count as

an act of signaling without the appropriate representations and relations, and any behavior (or lack of behavior) can count as an instance of signaling given the appropriate representations and relations (that is, if it is represented by the agent as directed to the communication of a message and exploits a conventionally agreed symbolization of a behavior). Thus, waving an arm in the air constitutes an act of signaling in some contexts but not in others; keeping one's arm stationary represents a signal in some contexts but not in others.

8. It is assumed, of course, that many human behaviors do have social psychological dimensions. It is also assumed that no reasonable person would deny this. Nevertheless, the hard-nosed empiricist might object that although the reality of these dimensions is not denied, there is no a priori reason why our scientific classifications should be based upon these dimensions rather than others, for example, in terms of physical movements or their effects.

In one respect this is undeniable. The scientific psychologist is free to adopt any classification system she chooses. Yet two points are worth making in response to this. In the first place, the scientific psychologist does not as a matter of fact restrict her explanations to behaviors defined in terms of movements or physical effects. Most of the explanations avowed by scientific psychologists purport to be explanations of *socially meaningful* actions such as aggression, dishonesty, attitude change and so forth, which are intentionally directed and socially located. In consequence, she must be concerned with the reproduction of these dimensions in empirical enquiries, if such enquiries are to have explanatory relevance.

Second, although one could classify human behavior in terms of movements and effects, it may be questioned whether this is likely to promote the purposes of theoretical and experimental science. This is most doubtful. It is most unlikely that one would find systematic connections between descriptions and explanations of behavior if behaviors are defined in these terms, far less any interesting ones. While recognizing that the social and psychological dimensions of integrated and coordinated human behaviors do not vouchsafe any particular social or psychological explanations of them, it is not remotely plausible to suppose that the structure and order of the social world is in general *causally independent* of agents' representations of these dimensions.

9. In consequence, nothing much hangs upon the consensual adequacy of the particular definitions of aggression, dishonesty, and so forth that are advanced in this volume. No doubt they could be improved upon, but they are not intended as the last word. Rather, they aim to provide reasonable approximations of the consensual social meaning of these forms of action. It is also perhaps worth mentioning in this context that some of the illustrative examples employed in this volume are recognized to be more or less contentious. It is hoped that the distinctions that they are designed to illustrate (e.g., the distinction between actions constituted by participant agent versus collective representations) remain defensible despite some doubts about their precise boundaries. Finally, it should also be noted that the employment of natural or social psychological theories as illustrative examples does not embody any commitment to their accuracy (thus Milgram's account of obedience is employed without inconsistency in some illustrative contexts that suggest its accuracy, in other contexts that suggest the opposite).

10. The important implications of these limits are discussed in Chapter 9.

11. See, for example, Simons and Pilliavin (1972).

12. See, for example, Farrington and Kidd (1977).

Chapter 9

1. Although strictly speaking it is historically inaccurate to attribute this doctrine to Hume (see this chapter and Chapter 1), this is how the Humean account of causality is generally interpreted.

2. Stimulus conditions or variables are defined as conditions that are part of a set of conditions that are ontologically sufficient for the production of an effect (as conditions, which in conjunction with other enabling conditions, are ontologically sufficient to produce an effect).

3. This must be stressed to distinguish the present account of agency as self-determination from many contemporary accounts that also treat agency explanations as a form of causal explanation. Many philosophers and psychologists have attempted to define agency in terms of actions that are produced by a privileged set of internal psychological variables. According to this account, many actions are produced by the agent's reasons, in the sense that some want-belief matrix is held to be sufficient for the production of action (Alston, 1977; Atkinson & Birch, 1970; Davidson, 1980; Fodor, 1975). Thus the distinction between agency explanations and other forms of causal explanation is made in terms of a distinction between different kinds of stimulus variables sufficient to produce action (Kruglanski, 1979; Locke & Pennington, 1982).

But this version of "psychological determinism" or "soft determinism" (Stace, 1952) is in fact a denial of agency as ordinarily understood, since it entails that the agent could not have done otherwise given her psychological state (Taylor, 1974). (This is not to deny that agent reasons *can* sometimes function as stimulus conditions, or as enabling conditions in a stimulus variable account. See this chapter.)

4. It is perhaps worth acknowledging that the concept of agency discussed and defended in this chapter is more or less identical to traditional libertarian analyses of freedom, and in particular to Kant's conception of human freedom as "determining, but not determinable" (1787, A556/B584).

5. However, there are limits to the predictability of actions based upon conventional rules and reasons. See this chapter.

6. See Chapter 1.

7. For a more detailed presentation of the arguments of this section, see Greenwood (1989).

8. Notwithstanding Kant's own idiosyncratic definition of possibility in terms of *epistemic possibility* (1787, B266).

9. In this respect, it is quite wrong to claim that contemporary physical scientists working on the subatomic level have abandoned the classical conception of causality, by treating such phenomena as spontaneously produced. Quantum theorists, for example, still strive to relate systematically the states of subatomic systems to their antecedent states (and with a high degree of success), and provide theoretical explanations of the powers and liabilities of such systems in terms of their antecedent states. These accounts describe conditions that *enable* subatomic phenomena to be "spontaneously" produced (in the sense that they are not causally determined by any empirical conditions).

10. In the light of these remarks, a number of other points are worth noting. It is not a condition of agency that an action be self-determined for the sake of *conscious* reasons. The actions of a person who acts from an unconscious motive of revenge or a Freudian wish-sublimation may still be self-determined for the sake of

these reasons, for her actions may not be determined by any stimulus conditions. Indeed, one would expect to find instances or representational indeterminacy on the unconscious level. For example, there are an indeterminate number of ways in which a wish may be sublimated or a feeling displaced. A man with an anal fixation may chose a career in chemistry or become a painter. This is precisely analogous to indeterminacy on the conscious level. A man who aims to gratify his pornographic interests may trade in pornographic literature or join the vice squad. This no doubt explains much of the empiricist antagonism to depth psychology (Eysenck, 1959; Popper, 1963), but does not justify it. Rather than an inadequacy of Freudian and other theories that take agent reasons seriously, representational indeterminacy should be recognized as an ontological fact about our psychological life that is in need of theoretical explanation.

The significance of this point is not restricted to depth psychology. The rules that govern our everyday interactions and linguistic discourse may be only dimly perceived by agents, who may be poor articulators of them. But this does not mean that our actions are ontologically determined by these rules. Most of us retain the power to utter meaningless and ungrammatical nonsense, and to violate the rules of interaction (in the ways suggested by Garfinkel (1967), for example).

Agency should not be confused with *autonomy*. Our actions may be influenced by a host of factors beyond our knowledge and control, and some may properly be said to be externally manipulated exercises of agency. As Secord notes (personal communication), the sophisticated con man may swindle the agent by persuading him of the merits of a prima facie attractive project. The swindled agent has been manipulated by the con man, but he may only have himself to blame, if he could have resisted the temptation.

The discussion of agency in this chapter should not be taken to imply an atomistic conception of social interaction as a complex aggregate of individual actions, despite its individualistic and existential emphasis. The point of this chapter is to defend agency accounts against the presupposition of stimulus variable determination, not to vouchsafe such a theoretical perspective. Indeed, as should be obvious to the reader, the general argument of this volume favors an embedded relational conception of human interaction, as indeed does the latter part of the argument of this chapter. The indeterminacy of agent representations is theoretically located in the indeterminacy of socially embedded rules and reasons. Analogously, the particular illustrative examples of individual moral dilemmas is not meant to suggest that moral dilemmas are intrinsically individual dilemmas. On the contrary, it is probably true that most moral dilemmas are necessarily socially negotiated.

Finally, it ought to be mentioned that a commitment to the possibility and plausibility of human agency does not entail an unrealistically optimistic conception of human nature. Nothing guarantees that agents with the power of self-determination will act for good reasons or for morally good reasons. The actions of many agents may be self-determined for the sake of malice, greed, and wanton destruction. They may be self-determined exercises of pure evil or stupidity. Sartre's student could have left for Tangiers with the family savings and the local fille légère.

Chapter 11

1. It is not denied that *present* attempts to improve the internal validity of experiments do decrease their external validity. As noted later in this chapter, this is because attempts to achieve experimental isolation tend to *alter* the phenomena under investigation. What is denied is that this inverse relation is an *intrinsic* feature of experimentation in any science, including social psychological science.

2. Thus, *external validity* was originally defined by Campbell and Stanley (1966) in terms of the generalizability of experimental correlations to different populations, situations, and so forth.

3. It is in this sense that conventional strategies for achieving experimental isolation do cast doubt upon the external validity of experiments.

4. See Chapter 5.

5. Cf. Secord (1987).

6. In this sense, all experiments are *epistemically* open. See Chapter 4.

7. However, this is not the way "ecological validity" was originally defined by Brunswick (1955), who used the term to refer to the reliability of experimental correlations as open-system predictors.

Chapter 12

1. Including myself. See Greenwood (1983).

2. Experimental evaluations of psychological therapy present an extreme example of this. For in this case the "demand characteristics" of the therapy session are an intrinsic feature of the therapy session: they are constitutive dimensions of the therapy session. See Chapter 13.

3. I owe this piece of information to a former graduate student, who wishes to remain anonymous.

Chapter 13

1. Cf, Chapter 12, Note 2.

2. One strategy for maximizing client expectancy would be to allow clients to choose between experimental and control treatments presented to them as alternative forms of treatment (Devine & Fernald, 1973; Gordon, 1976; Purser, 1982). This would not ensure equality of expectancy, but this presents no methodological problem, as will be noted presently.

Purser's (1982) study is a particularly good illustration of the natural negotiation strategy. Purser maximized credibility in his control treatment by presenting a form of treatment in which subjects played a series of interactive games with a computer. Clients were informed that speech dysfluency (the disorder studied) was associated with a brainform called "the contingent negative variation." Clients were linked to the computer via "recording electrodes" attached to their foreheads and "neurophysiological processors," and informed that the difficulties of the game were adjusted according to the level of their brain activity. Thus, adopting a frame of mind that would lead to success in the games would lead to control of the wave-form, and thus speech production. Although this rationale was entirely fictitious, the procedure was very convincing for the clients who chose this form of treatment, according to post experimental questionnaires and structured interviews. Purser also maximized therapist commitment by presenting the same rationale to the therapists who were specially trained in this procedure, and who were senior undergraduate speech therapists who denied any doubts about its credibility, according to their accounts upon debriefing. In comparison with a standard form of cognitive-behavioral treatment for speech dysfluency (based upon E.B. Cooper's [1976] *Personalized Fluency Control*), although both experimental and control treatments led to statistically significant improvement rates with respect to frequency and rate of dysfluency, there were no statistically significant differences between treatment outcomes.

3. To say that natural negotiation is potentially sufficient for therapeutic change, or to say that the natural negotiation hypothesis provides a sufficient explanation of therapeutic change, is not to say that a reference to natural negotiation provides a *theoretically* sufficient explanation: that is, an explanation that is sufficient as an adequate theoretical explanation of the *mechanism* of therapeutic change. Certain factors may be determined as causally sufficient to generate a certain effect, without any real knowledge of the mechanism responsible. Thus it can be determined that female Anopheles mosquito bites are causally sufficient to generate malaria in some persons, but only a reference to the action of plasmodium on blood cells provides a theoretical explanation of the generation of malaria. The natural negotiation hypothesis, like any other hypothesis, does of course require further theoretical development and empirical evaluation of its account of the mechanism of therapeutic change. However the recognition of its (present) theoretical inadequacy does nothing to undermine its methodological significance.

References

Achinstein, P. (1968). *Concepts of science*. Baltimore: John Hopkins University Press.

Adair, J.G. (1973). *The human subject: The social psychology of the psychology experiment*. Boston: Little, Brown.

Alexander, C.N., & Scriven, G.D. (1977). Role-playing: an essential component of experimentation. *Personality and Social Psychology Bulletin*, *3*, 455–466.

Alston, W.P. (1977). Self-intervention and the structure of motivation. In T. Mischel (Ed.), *The self: Psychological and philosophical issues*. Oxford: Basil Blackwell.

Anderson, B.F. (1971). *The psychology experiment*. Belmont: Brooks-Cole.

Anderson, J.R. (1978). Arguments concerning representations for mental imagery. *Psychological Review*, *85*, 249–277.

Anderson, J.R. (1981). Concepts, propositions, and schemata: What are the cognitive units? In J.H. Flowers (Ed.), *Nebraska Symposium on Motivation (1980): Cognitive Processes* (Vol. 28) Lincoln : University of Nebraska Press.

Anscombe, G.E.M. (1957). *Intention*. Oxford: Basil Blackwell.

Anscombe, G.E.M. (1971). *Causality and determination*. Cambridge: Cambridge University Press.

Arendt, H. (1964). *Eichmann in Jerusalem: A report on the banality of evil*. New York: Viking.

Argyle, M. (1978). An appraisal of the new approach to the study of social behaviour. In M. Brenner, P. Marsh, & M. Brenner (Eds.), *The social contexts of method*. London: Croom Helm.

Argyris, C. (1975). Dangers in applying results from experimental social psychology. *American Psychologist*, *30*, 469–485.

Armstrong, D.M. (1968). *A materialist theory of the mind*. London: Routledge and Kegan Paul.

Aronson, E., & Carlsmith, J.M. (1968). Experimentation in social psychology. In G. Lindsey & E. Aronson (Eds.), *Handbook of social psychology* (Vol. II). Reading, MA: Addison-Wesley.

Asch, S.E. (1951). Effects of group pressure upon the modification and distortion of judgements. In H. Guetzkow, H. (Ed.), *Group, leadership, and men*. Pittsburgh: Carnegie Press.

Atkinson, J.W., & Birch, D. (1970). *The dynamics of action*. New York: Wiley.

Austin, J.L. (1962). *How to do things with words.* Oxford: Oxford University Press.

Ayers, M.R. (1968). *The refutation of determinism.* London: Methuen.

Babbie, E.R. (1975). *The practice of social research.* Belmont, CA: Wadsworth.

Bacon, F. (1620). *Novum organum.*

Bakan, D. (1966). The test of significance in psychological research. *Psychological Bulletin, 66,* 423–437.

Bandura, A., Ross, D., & Ross, S.A. (1961). Transmission of aggression through imitation of aggressive models. *Journal of Abnormal and Social Psychology, 63,* 575–582.

Barber, X.T. (1978). *Pitfalls in human research: Ten pivotal points.* New York: Pergamon.

Barber, X.T., Calverly, D.S., Forgione, A., McPeake, J.D., Chaves, J.F., & Brown, B. (1969). Five attempts to replicate the experimenter bias effect. *Journal of Consulting and Clinical Psychology, 33,* 1–10.

Barnes, B. (1977). *Interests and the growth of knowledge.* London: Routledge and Kegan Paul.

Baron, R.A., & Eggleston, R.J. (1972). Performance on the "aggression machine": Motivation to help or harm? *Psychonomic Science, 26,* 321–322.

Barrett, W. (1962). Positivism. In W. Barrett & H.D. Aiken (Eds.) *Philosophy in the twentieth century.* Vol. 2 New York: Harper & Row.

Baumrind, D. (1964). Some thoughts on ethics of research: After reading Milgram's "Behavioral study of obedience." *American Psychologist, 19,* 421–423.

Beaman, K.L., Klentz, P.J., & McQuirk, B. (1978). Increasing helping rates through information dissemination: Teaching pays. *Personality and Social Psychology Bulletin, 4,* 406–411.

Bell, P.B., & Staines, P.J. (1981). *Reasoning and argument in psychology.* London: Routledge and Kegan Paul.

Beloff, J. (1973). *Psychological sciences.* London: Crosby Lockwood Staples.

Bem, D.J. (1967). Self-perception: An alternative interpretation of cognitive dissonance phenomena. *Psychological Review, 74,* 183–200.

Bem, D.J. (1972). Self-perception theory. In L. Berkowitz (Ed.), *Advances in experimental social psychology,* (Vol. 6). New York: Academic Press.

Bennett, J. (1971). *Locke, Berkeley, Hume.* Oxford: Oxford University Press.

Berger, P., & Luckmann, T. (1966). *The social construction of reality.* New York: Doubleday.

Bergin, A.E. (1971). The evaluation of therapeutic outcomes. In A.E. Bergin & S.L. Garfield (Eds.), *Handbook of psychotherapy and behavior change.* New York: Wiley.

Bergin, S.L., & Lambert, M.J. (1978). The evaluation of therapeutic outcomes. In S.L. Garfield & A.E. Bergin (Eds.), *Handbook of psychotherapy and behavior change* (2nd ed.). New York: Wiley.

Berkeley, G. (1710). *Treatise concerning the principles of human knowledge.*

Berkeley, G. (1721). *De motu.*

Berkowitz, L., & Donnerstein, E. (1982). External validity is more than skin deep: Some answers to criticisms of laboratory experiments. *American Psychologist, 37,* 245–257.

Berkowitz, L., & LePage, A. (1967). Weapons as aggression-eliciting stimuli. *Journal of Personality and Social Psychology, 7,* 202–207.

Berlin, B., & Kay, P. (1969). *Basic color terms: Their universality and evolution.* Chicago: University of Chicago Press.

Berne, E. (1970). *Games people play.* London: Penguin.

Bernstein, D.A., & Nietzel, M.T. (1977). Demand characteristics in behavior modification: The natural history of a "nuisance". In M. Hersen, R.M. Eisler, & P.M. Miller (Eds.), *Progress in behavior modification* (Vol. 4). New York: Academic Press.

Bhaskar, R. (1975). *A realist theory of science.*Leeds: Leeds Books.

Bhaskar, R. (1979). *The possibility of naturalism.* Sussex: Harvester Press.

Black, M. (1962). *Models and metaphors.* Ithaca: Cornell University Press.

Bloor, D. (1976). *Knowledge and social imagery.* London: Routledge and Kegan Paul.

Boden, M. (1977). *Artifical intellignce and natural man.* Sussex: Harvester Press.

Bohannan, L. (1966). Shakespeare in the bush. *Natural History.* August/September.

Borgatta, E.E., & Bohrnstedt, G. (1974). Some limits on generalizability from social psychological experiments. *Social methods and research, 3,* 111–120.

Borkovec, T.D., & Nau, S.D. (1972). Credibility of analogue therapy rationales. *Journal of Behavior Therapy and Experimental Psychiatry, 3,* 257–260.

Boyd, R.N. (1985). *Realism and scientific epistemology.* Cambridge: Cambridge University Press.

Braithwaite, R.B. (1953). *Scientific explanation.* Cambridge: Cambridge University Press.

Brehm, S.S. (1976). *The application of social psychology to clinical practice.* New York: Wiley.

Brenner, M. (1980). The structure of action. In M. Brenner (Ed.), *The structure of action.* Oxford: Basil Blackwell.

Brenner, M. (1982). Actor's powers. In M. von Cranach & R. Harré (Ed.), *The analysis of action.* Cambridge: Cambridge University Press.

Bridgeman, P.W. (1927). *The logic of modern physics.* New York: Macmillan.

Bridgeman, P.W. (1936). *The nature of physical theory.* Princeton: Princeton University Press.

Broad, C.D. (1925). *The mind and its place in nature.* London: Kegan Paul.

Brown, H.I. (1977). *Perception, theory and commitment.* Chicago: Chicago University Press.

Brown, R. (1965). *Social psychology.* New York: Free Press.

Bruner, J.S. (1975). From communication to language: A psychological perspective. *Cognition, 3,* 255–287.

Bruner, J.S. (1979). Psychology and the image of man. In H. Harris (Ed.), *Herbert Spencer Lectures, 1976.* Oxford: Oxford University Press.

Brunswick, E. (1955). Representative design and probabilistic theory in a functional psychology. *Psychological Reivew, 62,* 193–217.

Campbell, D.T. (1969). Prospective: Artifact and control. In R. Rosenthal & R.L. Rosnow (Eds.), *Artifact in behavioral research.* New York: Academic Press.

Campbell, D.T., & Stanley, J.C. (1966). *Experimental and quasi-experimental designs for research.* Chicago: Rand McNally.

Campbell, N. (1921). *What is science?* New York: Dover Publications.

Carnap, R. (1928). *Der Logische Aufbau der Welt.* Berlin.

Carnap, R. (1937). Testability and meaning. *Philosophy of Science, 4,* 1–40.

Carnap, R. (1966). *Philosophical foundations of physics.* (M. Gardner, Ed.) New York: Basic Books.

Cartwright, D. (1965). Influence, leadership and control. In J. March (Ed.), *Handbook of organizations.* Chicago: Rand McNally.

Cartwright, N. (1983). *How the laws of physics lie.* Oxford: Oxford University Press.

Chalmers, A.F. (1976). *What is this thing called science?* Queensland: University of Queensland Press.

Chapanis, A. (1967). The relevance of laboratory studies to practical situations. *Ergonomics, 10,* 557–577.

Chapman, A.J., & Jones, D.M. (Eds.). (1980). *Models of man.* Leicester: British Psychological Society.

Churchland, P.M. (1979). *Realism and the plasticity of mind.* Cambridge: Cambridge University Press.

Churchland, P.M. (1985). The ontological status of observables. In P.M. Churchland & C.A. Hooker (Eds.), *Images of science.* Chicago: University of Chicago Press.

Clark, H.H., & Clark, E.V. (1977). *Psychology and language.* New York: Harcourt Brace Jovanovich.

Clarke, D.D., & Crossland, J. (1985). *Action systems.* London: Methuen.

Cochrane, R., & Duffy, J. (1974). Psychology and scientific method. *Bulletin of the British Psychological Society, 27,* 117–121.

Collett, P. (1977). *Social rules and social behaviour.* Oxford: Basil Blackwell.

Collingwood, R.G. (1946). *The idea of history.* Oxford: Oxford University Press.

Compte, A. (1830). *Cours de philosophie positive.*

Conrad, E. & Maul, T. (1981). *Introduction to experimental psychology.* New York: Wiley.

Cooper, E.B. (1976). *Personalized fluency control: An integrated behavior and relationship therapy for stutterers.* Alabama: Teaching Resources Corporation.

Cooper, J. (1976). Deception and role-playing: On telling the good guys from the bad guys. *American Pshchologist, 31,* 605–610.

Coulter, J. (1979). *The social construction of mind.* London: MacMillan.

Craig, W. (1956). The replacement of auxiliary expressions. *Philosophical Review, 65,* 35–55.

Crano, W.D., & Brewer, M.B. (1973). *Principles of research in social psychology.* New York: McGraw-Hill.

Critelli, J.W., & Neuman, K.F. (1984). The placebo: Conceptual analysis of a concept in transition. *American Psychologist, 39,* 32–39.

Crowle, A.J. (1976). The deceptive language of the laboratory. In R. Harré (Ed.), *Life sentences.* Chichester: Wiley.

Darroch, R.K., & Steiner, I.D. (1970). Role-playing: An alternative to laboratory research? *Journal of Personality, 38,* 302–311.

Davidson, D. (1980). *Essays on actions and events.* Oxford: Oxford University Press.

Davidson, D. (1984). First person authority. *Dialectica, 38,* 101–111.

Deese, J. (1972). *Psychology as science and art.* New York: Harcourt Brace Jovanovich.

Dennett, D.C. (1981). True believers: The intentional strategy and why it works. In A.F. Heath (Ed.), *Scientific explanation.* Oxford: Clarendon Press.

Devine, D.A., & Fernald, P.S. (1973). Outcome effects of receiving a preferred, randomly assigned, or non-preferred strategy. *Journal of Consulting and Clinical Psychology, 41,* 104–107.

De Waele, J-P. (1971). *La methode des cas programmes.* Bruxelles: Dessart.

Dilthey, W. (1937). *Gesammelte Schriften.* Munich.

Dipboye, R.L., & Flanagan, M.F. (1979). Research settings in industrial and organizational psychology: Are findings in the field more generalizable than in the laboratory? *American Psychologist, 34,* 141–150.

Dray, W. (1957). *Laws and explanation in history.* Oxford: Oxford University Press.

Duhem, P. (1906). *La theorie physique: Son objet et sa structure.* Paris.

Durkheim, E. (1895). *The rules of sociological method.* Paris.

Eiser, J.R. (1980). *Cognitive social psychology: A guidebook to theory and research.* London: McGraw-Hill.

Ellis, B. (1985). What science aims to do. In P.M. Churchland & C.A. Hooker (Eds.), *Images of science.* Chicago: University of Chicago Press.

Elms, A.C. (1975). The crisis of confidence in social pshchology. *American Psychologist, 30,* 967–976.

Enç, B. (1976). Spiral dependence between theories and taxonomy. *Inquiry, 19,* 41–71.

Eysenck, H.J. (1952). The effects of psychotherapy: An evaluation. *Journal of Consulting Psychology, 16,* 319–324.

Eysenck, H.J. (1959). *Uses and abuses of psychology.* Harmondsworth: Penguin.

Eysenck, H.J. (1960). The effects of psychotherapy. In H.J. Eysenck (Ed.), *Handbook of abnormal psychology.* London: Pitman.

Eysenck, H.J. (1965). The effects of psychotherapy. *International Journal of Psychiatry, 1,* 99–142.

Farrington, D.P., & Kidd, R.F. (1977). Is financial dishonesty a rational decision? *British Journal of Social and Clinical Psychology, 16,* 139–146.

Feigl, H. (1970). Beyond peaceful coexistence. In R.H. Stuewer (Ed.), *Minnesota studies in the philosophy of science: V.* Minneapolis: University of Minnesota Press.

Feigl, H. (1974). Empiricism at bay? In R. Cohen & M. Wartofsky (Eds.), *Boston studies in the philosophy of science* (Vol. XIV). Dordrecht: Reidel.

Festinger, L.A. (1957). *A theory of cognitive dissonance.* Evanston, IL: Row, Peterson.

Festinger, L. & Carlsmith, J.M. (1959). Cognitive consequences of forced compliance. *Journal of Abnormal and Social Psychology, 58,* 203–210.

Feyerabend, P.K. (1963). Materialism and the mind-body problem. *Review of Metaphysics, 17,* 49–66.

Feyerabend, P.K. (1970) Consolations for the specialist. In I. Lakatos & A. Musgrave (Eds.), *Criticism and the growth of knowledge.* Cambridge: Cambridge University Press.

Feyerabend, P.K. (1975). *Against method.* London: New Left Books.

Fillenbaum, S., & Fry, R. (1970). More on the "faithful" behavior of suspicious suspects. *Journal of Personality, 38,* 43–51.

Fine, A. (1984). The natural ontological attitude. In J. Leplin (Ed.), *Scientific realism.* Chicago: Chicago University Press.

Fodor, J.A. (1975). *The language of thought.* Harvard: Harvard University Press.

Forsyth, D.R. (1976). Crucial experiments and social psychological enquiry. *Perso-*

nality and Social Psychology Bulletin, 2, 454–459.

Forward, J., Canter, R., & Kirsch, N. (1976). Role enactment and deception methodologies. Alternative paradigms? *American Psychologist, 31*, 595–604.

Frank, J.D. (1961). *Persuasion and healing.* Baltimore: Johns Hopkins University Press.

Frank, J.D. (1974). Psychotherapy: the restoration of morale. *American Journal of Psychotherapy, 131*, 271–274.

Freedman, J.L. (1969). Role-playing: Psychology by consensus. *Journal of Personality and Social Psychology, 13*, 107–114.

Freid, S.B., Gumper, D.C., & Allan, J.C. (1973). Ten years of social psychology: Is there a growing commitment to field research? *American Psychologist, 28*, 155–156.

Gadamer, H.G. (1975). *Truth and method* (G. Barden & J. Cumming, Trs.) New York: Seabury.

Garfinkel, H. (1967). *Studies in ethnomethodology.* Englewood Cliffs, NJ: Prentice-Hall.

Gauld, A., & Shotter, J. (1977). *Human action and its psychological investigation.* London: Routledge and Kegan Paul.

Geach, P. (1975). Teleological explanation. In S. Körner (Ed.), *Explanation.* Oxford: Basil Blackwell.

Gergen, K.J. (1973). Social psychology as history. *Journal of Personality and Social Psychology, 26*, 309–320.

Gergen, K.J. (1977). The social construction of self-knowledge. In T.S. Mischel (Ed.), *The self: psychological and philosophical issues.* Oxford: Basil Blackwell.

Gergen, K.J. (1978). Experimentation in social psychology: A reappraisal. *European Journal of Social Psychology, 8*, 507–527.

Gergen, K.J. (1982). *Toward transformation in social knowledge.* New York: Springer-Verlag.

Gergen, K.J. (1985). The social construction movement in modern psychology. *American Psychologist, 40*, 266–275.

Gergen, K.J., & Davis, K.E. (1985). *The social construction of the person.* New York: Springer-Verlag.

Gholson, B., & Barker, P. (1985). Kuhn, Lakatos, and Laudan: Applications in the history of physics and psychology. *American Psychologist, 40*, 755–769.

Gibson, J.J. (1979). *The ecological approach to visual perception.* Boston: Houghton-Mifflin.

Giddens, A. (1974). *Positivism and sociology.* London: Heinemann.

Giddens, A. (1976). *New rules of sociological method.* London: Hutchinson.

Giere, R.N. (1985). Constructive realism. In P.M. Churchland & C.A. Hooker (Eds.), *Images of science.* Chicago: Chicago University Press.

Ginsburg, G.P. (1978). Role-playing and role performance in social psychological research. In M. Brenner, P. Marsh, & M. Brenner (Eds.), *The social contexts of method.* London: Croom Helm.

Ginsburg, G.P. (1979). The effective use of role playing in social psychological research. In G.P. Ginsburg (Ed.), *Emerging strategies in social psychological research.* New York: Wiley.

Ginsburg, G.P., Brenner, M., & von Cranach, M. (1985). *Discovery strategies in the psychology of action.* London: Academic Press.

Goffman, E. (1959). *The presentation of self in everyday life.* New York: Doubleday.

Golding, S.L., & Lichtenstein, E. (1970). Confession of awareness and prior knowledge of deception as a function of interview set and approval motivation. *Journal of Personality and Social Psychology, 14,* 213–223.

Goldman, A.I. (1970). *A theory of human action.* Princeton: Princeton University Press.

Goodman, N. (1947). The problem of counterfactual conditionals. *Journal of Philosophy, 44,* 113–128.

Gordon, R.M. (1976). Effects of volunteering and responsibility on the perceived value and effectiveness of a clinical treatment. *Journal of Consulting and Clinical Psychology, 44,* 799–801.

Greenberg, M.S. (1967). Role-playing: An alternative to deception? *Journal of Personality and Social Psychology, 7,* 152–157.

Greenwald, A.G. (1975). On the inconclusiveness of "crucial" cognitive tests of dissonance versus self-perception theories. *Journal of Experimental Social Psychology, 11,* 490–499.

Greenwood, J.D. (1983). Role playing as an experimental strategy in social psychology. *European Journal of Social Psychology, 13,* 235–254.

Greenwood, J.D. (1987). Emotion and error. *Philosophy of the Social Sciences, 17,* 487–499.

Greenwood, J.D. (1989). Kant's third antinomy: Agency and causal explanation. *International Philosophical Quarterly.* In press.

Gumb, R.D. (1972). *Rule-governed linguistic behaviour.* The Hague: Mouton.

Gurin, G., Veroff, J., & Feld, S. (1960). *Americans view their mental health.* New York: Basic Books.

Habermas, J. (1970). *Zur Logic der Sozialwissenschaften.* Frankfurt: Suhrkamp.

Hacking, I. (1983). *Representing and intervening.* Cambridge: Cambridge University Press.

Hamlyn, D.W. (1982). The concept of social reality. In P.F. Secord (Ed.), *Explaining human behavior: Consciousness, human action and social structure.* Beverly Hills: Sage.

Hanay, C., Banks, W.C., & Zimbardo, P.G. (1973). Interpersonal dynamics in a simulated prison. *International Journal of Criminology and Penology, 1,* 69–97.

Hanson, N.R. (1958). *Patterns of discovery.* Cambridge: Cambridge University Press.

Harré, R. (1970). *The principles of scientific thinking.* Chicago: Chicago University Press.

Harré, R. (1972). *The philosophies of science.* Oxford: Oxford University Press.

Harré, R. (1979). *Social being.* Oxford: Basil Blackwell.

Harré, R. (1981). *Great scientific experiments.* Oxford: Phaidon.

Harré, R., Clarke, D., & De Carlo, N. (1985). *Motives and mechanisms: An introduction to the psychology of action.* London: Methuen.

Harré, R., & Madden, E.H. (1975). *Causal powers.* Oxford: Basil Blackwell.

Harré, R., & Secord, P.F. (1972). *The explanation of social behaviour.* Oxford: Basil Blackwell.

Heft, H. (1982). Incommensurability and the "omission" in Gibson's theory: A second reply to Heil. *Journal for the Theory of Social Behaviour, 12,* 345–347.

Heidegger, M. (1962). *Being and time.* (J. Macquarrie & E. Robinson, Trans.). New York: Harper & Row.

Heil, J. (1979). What Gibson's missing. *Journal for the Theory of Social Behaviour, 9,* 265–269.

Hekman, S. (1984). Action as a text: Gadamer's hermeneutics and the social scientific analysis of action. *Journal for the Theory of Social Behavior, 14,* 333–354.

Hekman, S. (1986). *Hermeneutics and the sociology of knowledge.* Notre Dame: University of Notre Dame Press.

Hempel, C.G. (1958). The theoretician's dilemma. A study in the logic of theory construction. In H. Feigl, M. Scriven, & G. Maxwell (Eds.), *Minnesota studies in the philosophy of science.* (Vol. 2). Minneapolis: University of Minnesota Press.

Hempel, C.G. (1962). Explanation in science and history. In R.G. Colodny (Ed.), *Frontiers of science and philosophy.* Pittsburgh: University of Pittsburgh Press.

Hempel, C.G. (1965). *Aspects of scientific explanation.* New York: Free Press.

Hempel, C.G. (1966). *Philosophy of natural science.* Englewood Cliffs, NJ: Prentice-Hall.

Hempel, C.G., & Oppenheim, P. (1948). Studies in the logic of explanation. *Philosophy of Science, 15,* 137–175.

Hendrick, C. (1977). Role-taking, role-playing, and the laboratory experiment. *Personality and Social Psychology Bulletin, 3,* 467–478.

Henriques, J., Hollway, W., Urwin, C., Venn, C, & Walkerdine, V. (1984). *Changing the subject: Psychology, social regulation and subjectivity.* London: Methuen.

Henschel, R.L. (1980). The purposes of laboratory experimentation and the virtues of deliberate artificiality. *Journal of Experimental Social Psychology, 16,* 466–478.

Heron, J. (1981). Philosophical basis for a new paradigm. In P. Reason & R. Rowan (Eds.), *Human enquiry: A sourcebook of new paradigm research.* New York: Wiley.

Hesse, M.B. (1970). Is there an independent observation language? In R. Colodny (Ed.), *The nature and function of scientific theories.* Pittsburgh: University of Pittsburgh Press.

Hesse, M.B. (1974). *The structure of scientific inference.* London: Macmillan.

Hesse, M.B. (1976). Models versus paradigms in the natural sciences. In L. Collins (Ed.), *The use of models in the social sciences.* London: Tavistock Press.

Higbee, K.L., Millard, R.J., & Folkman, J.R. (1982). Social psychology research during the 1970s: Predominance of experimentation and college students. *Personality & Social Psychology Bulletin, 8,* 180–183.

Higgens, R.L., & Marlatt, G.A. (1973). Effects of anxiety arousal on the consumption of alcohol by alcoholics and social drinkers. *Journal of Consulting and Clinical Psychology, 41,* 426–433.

Hofling, C.K., Brotzman, E., Dalrymple, S., Graves, N., & Pierce, C.M. (1966). An experimental study in nurse-physician relationships. *The Journal of Mental and Nervous Disease, 143,* 171–180.

Holmes, D.S., & Bennett, D.H. (1974). Experiments to answer questions raised by the use of deception in psychological research: I. Role-playing as an alternative to deception; II. Effectiveness of debriefing after deception; III. Effect of informed consent upon deception. *Journal of Personality and Social Psychology, 29,* 358–367.

Holton, G. (1981). Thematic presuppositions and the direction of scientific advance. In A.F. Heath (Ed.), *Scientific explanation*. Oxford: Clarendon Press.

Horowitz, I.A., & Rothschild, B.H. (1970). Conformity as a function of deception and role-playing. *Journal of Personality and Social Psychology, 14*, 224–226.

Hudson, L. (1970). The choice of hercules. *Bulletin of the British Psychology Society, 23*, 287–292.

Hull, C.L. (1937). Mind, mechanism, and adaptive behavior. *Psychological Review, 44*, 1–32.

Hull, C.L. (1943). *Principles of behavior*. New York: Appleton-Century-Crofts.

Hume, D. (1739). *A treatise on human nature.*

Hume, D. (1748). *An enquiry concerning human understanding.*

Janis, I.L., & Mann, L. (1965). Effectiveness of emotional role-playing in modifying smoking habits and attitudes. *Journal of Experimental Research in Personality, 1*, 84–90.

Jourard, S.M. (1968). *Disclosing man to himself*. New York: Litton.

Kane, T.R., Joseph, J.P., & Tedeschi, J.T. (1976). Person perception and the Berkowitz paradigm for the study of aggression. *Journal of Personality and Social Psychology, 6*, 663–673.

Kant, I. (1787). *Critique of pure reason.*

Karlsruher, A.E. (1974). The nonprofessional as a psychotherapeutic agent. *American Journal of Community Psychology, 2*, 61–77.

Kazdin, A.E., & Wilcoxon, L.A. (1976). Systematic desensitization and nonspecific treatment effects: A methodological evaluation. *Psychological Bulletin, 5*, 729–758.

Kazdin, A.E., & Wilson, G.T. (1978). *Evaluation of behavior therapy: Issues, evidence and research strategies*. Cambridge, MA: Ballinger.

Kelman, H. (1967). Human use of human subjects: The problem of deception in social psychological experiments. *Psychological Bulletin, 67*, 1–11.

Kelman, H. (1972). The rights of the subject in social research: an analysis in terms of relative power and legitimacy. *American Psychologist, 27*, 987–1016.

Kirsch, I. (1978). The placebo effect and the cognitive-behavioural revolution. *Cognitive Therapy and Research, 2*, 255–264.

Klotz, I.M. (1980). The N-ray affair. *Scientific American, 242*, 122–131.

Kneale, W. (1949). *Probability and induction*. Oxford: Clarendon Press.

Koch, S. (1962). Behaviorism. *Encyclopedia Britannica.*

Koch, S. (1964). Psychology and emerging conceptions of knowledge as unitary. In T.W. Wann (Ed.), *Behaviorism and phenomenology: Contrasting bases for modern psychology*. Chicago: University of Chicago Press.

Koertge, N. (1972). For and against method. *British Journal for the Philosophy of Science, 23*, 274–290.

Kopel, S.A., & Arkowitz, H.S. (1974). Role-playing as a source of self-observation and behavior change. *Journal of Personality and Social Psychology, 29*, 677–686.

Kruglanski, A.W. (1975). The human subject in the psychology experiment: Fact and artifact. In L. Berkowitz (Ed.), *Advances in experimental social psychology*, (Vol. 8). New York: Academic Press.

Kruglanski, A.W. (1976). On the paradigmatic objections to experimental psychology. *American Psychologist, 31*, 655–633.

Kruglanski, A.W. (1979). Causal explanation, teleological explanation: On radical particularism in attribution theory. *Journal of Personality and Social Psychology*, *37*, 1447–1457.

Kuhn, T. (1962). *The structure of scientific revolutions*. Chicago: University of Chicago Press.

Kuhn, T. (1970). *The structure of scientific revolutions* (2nd ed). Chicago: University of Chicago Press.

Lakatos, I. (1970). Falsification and the methodology of scientific research programmes. In L. Lakatos & A. Musgrave (Eds.), *Criticism and the growth of knowledge*. Cambridge: Cambridge University Press.

Lambert, M.J. (1976). Spontaneous remission in adult neurotic disorders: A revision and summary. *Psychological Bulletin*, *83*, 107–119.

Latané, B., & Darley, J.M. (1970). *The unresponsive bystander: Why doesn't he help?* New York: Appleton-Century-Crofts.

Ledwidge, B. (1978). Cognitive behavior modification: A step in the wrong direction? *Psychological Bulletin*, *85*, 353–375.

Leplin, J. (1984). Truth and scientific progress. In J. Leplin (Ed.), *Scientific realism*. Berkeley: University of California Press.

Leplin, J. (1987). Surrealism. *Mind*, *XCVI*, 519–524.

Leplin, J. (1988). Novel prediction. Unpublished manuscript.

Levin, M. (1984). What kind of explanation is truth? In J. Leplin (Ed.), *Scientific realism*. Berkeley: University of California Press.

Locke, D., & Pennington, D. (1982). Reasons and other causes: Their role in attribution processes. *Journal of Personality and Social Psychology*, *42*, 212–223.

Louch, A. (1966). *Explanation and human action*. Oxford: Basil Blackwell.

Luborsky, L., Singer, R., & Luborsky, L. (1975). Comparative studies of psychotherapies. *Archives of General Psychiatry*, *32*, 995–1008.

Lukes, S. (1968). Methodological individualism reconsidered. *British Journal of Sociology*, *19*, 119–129.

Lunzer, E.A. (1968). *The regulation of behaviour*. London: Staples.

MacCorquodale, K., & Meehl, P.E. (1948). On a distinction between hypothetical constructs and intervening variables. *Psychological Review*, *55*, 95–107.

Mach, E. (1894). *Popular scientific lectures*.

MacIntyre, A. (1958). *The unconscious*. London: Routledge and Kegan Paul.

MacIntyre, A. (1964). Is understanding religion compatible with believing? In J. Hick (Ed.), *Faith and the philosophers*. London: Macmillan.

MacIntyre, A. (1971). The idea of a social science. In A. MacIntyre (Ed.), *Against the self-images of the age*. London: Duckworth.

Mackie, J.L. (1974). *The cement of the universe*. Oxford: Clarendon Press.

Madden, E.H. (1971). Hume and the fiery furnace. *Philosophy of Science*, *38*, 64–78.

Malan, D.H. (1975). Psychodynamic changes in untreated neurotic patients. *Archives of General Psychiatry*, *32*, 110–126.

Manicas, P.T., & Secord, P.F. (1983). Implications for psychology of the new philosophy of science. *American Psychologist*, *38*, 399–413.

Margolis, J. (1983). *Culture and cultural entities: Towards a new unity of science*. Dordrecht, Holland: Reidel.

Margolis, J. (1984). *Philosophy of psychology*. Englewood Cliffs, NJ: Prentice-Hall.

Marsh, P., Rosser, E., & Harré, R. (1978). *The rules of disorder.* London: Routledge and Kegan Paul.

Masterson, M. (1970). The nature of a paradigm. In I. Lakatos & A. Musgrave (Eds.), *Criticism and the growth of knowledge.* Cambridge: Cambridge University Press.

Maxwell, G. (1963). The ontological status of theoretical entities. In H. Feigl & G. Maxwell (Eds.), *Scientific explanation, space and time.* Minneapolis: University of Minnesota Press.

McCall, R.B. (1980). *Fundamental statistics for psychology.* New York: Harcourt Brace Jovanovich.

McClintock, C.G. (Ed.). (1972). *Experimental social psychology.* New York: Holt.

McGinn, C. (1979). Action and its explanation. In N. Bolton (Ed.), *Philosophical problems of psychology.* London: Methuen.

McGlynn, F.D. (1972). Systematic desensitization under two conditions of induced expectancy. *Behaviour research and therapy, 10,* 229–234.

McGlynn, F.D., & McDonell, R.M. (1974). Subjective ratings of credibility following brief exposure to desensitization and pseudotherapy. *Behaviour Research and Therapy, 12,* 141–146.

McGuire, W.J. (1967). Some impending orientations in social psychology. *Journal of Experimental Social Psychology, 3,* 124–139

Meehl, P.E. (1978). Theoretical risks and tabular asterisks: Sir Karl, Sir Ronald and the slow progress of soft psychology. *Journal of Consulting and Clinical Psychology, 46,* 806–834.

Melden, A.I. (1961). *Free action.* London: Routledge and Kegan Paul.

Miles, H.W., Barrabee, E.L., & Finesinger, J.E. (1951). Evaluation of psychotherapy. *Psychosomatic Medicine, 13,* 83–105.

Milgram, S. (1963). Behavioral study of obedience. *Journal of Abnormal and Social Psychology, 67,* 371–378.

Milgram, S. (1972). Interpreting obedience: Error and evidence. In A.G. Miller (Ed.), *The social psychology of psychological research.* London: Collier-Macmillan.

Milgram, S. (1974). *Obedience to authority.* New York: Harper & Row.

Mill, J.S. (1843). *A system of logic.*

Mill, J.S. (1866). *Auguste Compte and positivism.*

Miller, A.G. (1972). Role-playing: An alternative to deception? A review of the evidence. *American Psychologist, 27,* 623–636.

Miller, S. (1975). *Experimental design and statistics.* London: Methuen.

Mills, R.R. (1972). *New directions in police selection.* Paper presented to American Psychological Association, Honolulu, HA. Quoted in Mixon (1980).

Minor, M.W. (1970). Experimenter-expectancy effect as a function of evaluation apprehension. *Journal of Personality and Social Psychology, 15,* 326–332.

Mixon, D. (1972). Instead of deception. *Journal for the Theory of Social Behaviour, 2,* 145–177.

Mixon, D. (1980). The place of habit in the control of action. *Journal for the Theory of Social Behaviour, 10,* 169–186.

Mook, D. (1983). In defence of external validity. *American Psychologist, 38,* 379–387.

Musgrave, A.E. (1973). Falsification and its critics. In P. Suppes et al. (Eds.),

Logic, methodology and philosophy of science (Vol. IV). Amsterdam: North-Holland.

Musgrave, A. (1985). Realism versus constructive empiricism. In P.M. Churchland & C.A. Hooker (Eds.), *Images of science*. Chicago: University of Chicago Press.

Musgrave, A. (1987). Deductive heuristics. Paper presented to Piedmont Philosophy of Science Association, Virginia Polytechnic, March, 1987.

Nagel, E. (1939). *Principles of the theory of probability*. Chicago: Chicago University Press.

Nagel, E. (1961). *The structure of science*. New York: Harcourt, Brace and World.

Neurath, O. (1932). Protokollsatze. *Erkenntnis, 3*.

Nicod, J. (1934). *Foundations of geometry and induction*. (P. Weiner, Trans.) London.

Nisbett, R.E., & Ross, L. (1980). *Strategies and shortcomings of social judgement*. Englewood Cliffs, NJ: Prentice-Hall.

Nisbett, R.E., & Wilson, T.D. (1977). Telling more than we can know: Verbal reports on mental processes. *Psychological Review, 84*, 231–259.

O'Leary, C.J., Willis, F.N., & Tomich, E. (1970). Conformity under deceptive and non-deceptive techniques. *Sociological Quarterly, 11*, 58–60.

Olson, T., & Christiansen, G. (1966). *The grindstone experiment: Thirty one hours*. Toronto: Canadian Friends Service Committee.

Orne, M.T. (1962). On the social psychology of the psychological experiment: With particular reference to demand characteristics and their implications. *American Psychologist, 17*, 776–783.

Orne, M.T., & Holland, C.T. (1968). On the ecological validity of laboratory deceptions. *International Journal of Psychiatry, 6*, 282–293.

Palermo, D.S. (1971). Is a scientific revolution taking place in psychology? *Science Studies, 1*, 135–155.

Perrin, S., & Spencer, C. (1980). The Asch effect—a child of its time? *Bulletin of the British Psychological Society, 32*, 405–406.

Peters, R.S. (1958). *The concept of motivation*. London: Routledge and Kegan Paul.

Peterson, G.L. (1981). Historical self-understanding in the social sciences: The use of Thomas Kuhn in psychology. *Journal for the Theory of Social Behaviour, 11*, 1–30.

Polanyi, M. (1958). *Personal knowledge*. London: Routledge and Kegan Paul.

Popper, K.R. (1959). *The logic of scientific discovery*. London: Hutchinson.

Popper, K.R. (1963). *Conjectures and refutations*. London: Routledge and Kegan Paul.

Popper, K.R. (1972). *Objective knowledge*. Oxford: Clarendon Press.

Potter, J. (1981). The development of social psychology: Consensus, theory and methodology in the *British Journal of Social and Clinical Psychology*. *British Journal of Social Psychology, 20*, 249–258.

Przibram, H. (1926). Paul Kammerer als biologe. *Monistische Monatshefte*.

Purser, H.W. (1982). *The psychology of treatment evaluation: Stuttering*. M. Phil. thesis, Institute of Psychiatry, London.

Putnam, H. (1975). The meaning of meaning. In *Philosophical papers II*. New York: Cambridge University Press.

Putnam, H. (1981). *Reason, truth and history*. Cambridge: Cambridge University Press.

Quine, W.V.O. (1953). Two dogmas of empiricism. In *From a logical point of view*. Cambridge, MA: Harvard University Press.

Quine, W.V.O., & Ullian, J.S. (1970). *The web of belief*. New York: Random House.

Rachman, S., & Wilson, G.T. (1980). *The effects of psychological therapy* (2nd ed). Oxford: Pergamon.

Reed, E.S., & Jones, R.K. (1981). Is perception blind? : A reply to Heil. *Journal for the Theory of Social Behaviour, 11*, 87–91.

Richer, J. (1975). Two types of agreement—two types of psychology. *Bulletin of the British Psychological Society, 28*, 342–345.

Ricoeur, P. (1977). The model of the text: Meaningful action considered as a text. In F. Dallmayr & T. McCarthy (Eds.), *Understanding and social inquiry*. Nortre Dame: Nortre Dame University Press.

Ring, K. (1967). Experimental social psychology: Some sober questions about some frivolous values. *Journal of Experimental Social Psychology, 3*, 113–123.

Rommetveit, R. (1978). On negative rationalism in scholarly studies of verbal communication and dynamic residuals in the construction of human intersubjectivity. In M. Brenner, P. Marsh, & M. Brenner (Eds.), *The social contexts of method*. London: Croom Helm.

Rorty, R. (1965). Mind-body identity, privacy, and categories. *The Review of Metaphysics, 19*, 24–54.

Rosch, E. (1974). Linguistic relativity. In A. Silverston (Ed.), *Human communication: Theoretical perspectives*. New York: Halstead Press.

Rosenberg, A. (1980). *Sociobiology and the preemption of social science*. Baltimore: John Hopkins University Press.

Rosenberg, M.J. (1969). The conditions and consequences of evaluation apprehension. In R. Rosenthal & R. Rosnow (Eds.), *Artifact in behavioral research*. New York: Academic Press.

Rosenthal, R. (1976). *Experimenter effects in behavioral research*. (2nd ed). New York: Appleton-Century-Crofts.

Rosenthal, R., & Rosnow, R.L. (1975). *The volunteer subject*. New York: Wiley.

Rosenzweig, S. (1954). A transvaluation of psychotherapy: A reply to Hans Eysenck. *Journal of Abnormal and Social Psychology, 49*, 298–304.

Rosnow, R.L., & Rosenthal, R. (1970). Volunteer effects in behavioral research. In *New directions in psychology*. New York: Holt, Rinehart & Winston.

Rosnow, R.L., & Rosenthal, R. (1976). The volunteer subject revisited. *Australian Journal of Psychology, 28*, 97–108.

Rosser, R.M. (1982). Life with artificial organs: Renal dialysis and transplantation. In E. Shepherd & J.P. Watson (Eds.), *Personal meanings: The First Guy's Hospital symposium on the individual frame of reference*. Chichester: Wiley.

Rozevoom, W.W. (1970). The fallacy of the null-hypothesis significance test. In P. Badia, A. Haber, & R.P. Runyon (Eds.), *Research problems in psychology*. Reading, MA: Addison-Wesley.

Russell, B. (1962). *Mysticism and logic*. London: Allen and Unwin.

Ryan, A. (1970). *The philosophy of the social sciences*. London: Macmillan.

Sade, D. (1965). Some aspects of parent-offspring and sibling relations in a group of rhesus monkeys, with a discussion of grooming. *American Journal of Physical Anthropology, 23*, 1–17.

Salmon, W.C. (1971). Statistical explanation. In W.C. Salmon et al. (Eds.), *Statis-*

tical explanation and statistical relevance. Pittsburgh: University of Pittsburgh Press.

Sarbin, T.R., & Allen, V.L. (1968). Role theory. In G. Lindzey & E. Aronson (Eds.), *Handbook of social psychology* (2nd ed., Vol. 1). Reading, MA: Addison-Wesley.

Sartre, J.P. (1948). *Existentialism and humanism.* (P. Mairet Trans.) London.

de Saussure, F. (1916). *Cours de linguistique generale.* Paris: Payot.

Schachter, S. (1965). The interaction of cognitive and physiological determinants of emotional state. In P.H. Leidermann & D. Shapiro (Eds.), *Psychobiological approaches to social behaviour.* London: Tavistock.

Schachter, S., & Singer, S. (1962). Cognitive, social and physiological determinants of emotional state. *Psychological Review, 69,* 379–399.

Schlesinger, G. (1974). *Confirmation and confirmability.* Oxford: Oxford University Press.

Schlick, M. (1936). Meaning and verification. *Philosophical Review, 45,* 339–368.

Schlick, M. (1948). *Law, causality and probability.* Vienna.

Schultz, A. (1967). *The phenomenology of the social world.* Evanston, IL: Northwestern University Press.

Schultz, D.P. (1969). The human subject in psychological research. *Psychological Bulletin, 72,* 214–228.

Schwayder, D.S. (1965). *The stratification of behaviour.* London: Routledge and Kegan Paul.

Scott, M.B. & Lyman, S. (1968). Accounts. *American Sociological Review, 33,* 46–62.

Scriven, M. (1958). Definitions, explanations and theories. In H. Feigl, M. Scriven, & G. Maxwell (Eds.), *Minnesota studies in the philosophy of science II.* Minneapolis: University of Minnesota Press.

Scriven, M. (1962). Explanations, predictions and laws. In H. Feigl & G. Maxwell (Eds.), *Minnesota studies in the philosophy of science III.* Minneapolis: University of Minnesota Press.

Scriven, M. (1974). Psychology caveat. *American Psychological Association Moniter,* December.

Searle, J. (1970). *Speech acts.* Cambridge: Cambridge University Press.

Secord, P.F. (1982). The behavior identity problem in generalizing from experiments. *American Psychologist, 37,* 1408.

Secord, P.F. (1987). Resolving the actor/subject dialectic in social psychological research. Paper presented at the *Conference on the Making of Social Psychology,* Barcelona, Spain.

Secord, P.F. & Backman, C.W. (1974). *Social psychology.* Tokyo: McGraw-Hill Kogakasha.

Sellars, W. (1963). *Science, perception and reality.* New York: Humanities Press.

Shapere, D. (1982). The concept of observation in science and philosophy. *Philosophy of Science, 49,* 485–525.

Shapiro, A.K., & Morris, L.A. (1978). Placebo effects in medical and psychological therapies. In S. Garfield & A. Bergen (Eds.), *Handbook of psychotherapy and behavior change* (2nd ed.). New York: Wiley.

Sheldon, B. (1982). *Behaviour modification.* London: Tavistock.

Shotter, J. (1981). Critical notice: Are Fincham's and Schultz's findings empirical findings? *British Journal of Social Psychology, 20,* 121–123.

Sigall, H., Aronson, E., & Hoose, T.V. (1970). The cooperative subject: Myth or reality? *Journal of Experimental Social Psychology*, *6*, 1–10.

Simons, C.W., & Pilliavin, J.A. (1972). Effect of deception on reactions to a victim. *Journal of Personality and Social Psychology*, *21*, 56–60.

Silverman, I. (1977). *The human subject in the psychological laboratory*. New York: Pergamon.

Simmel, G. (1908) *Sozilogie*.

Simons, C.W., & Pilliavin, J.A. (1972). Effect of deception on reactions to a victim. *Journal of Personality and Social Psychology*, *21*, 56–60.

Skinner, B.F. (1938). *The behavior of organisms*. New York: Appleton-Century-Crofts.

Skinner, B.F. (1953). *Science and human behavior*. New York: Macmillan.

Skinner, B.F. (1974). *About behaviorism*. New York: Knopf.

Sloane, R.B., Cristol, A.H., Pepernik, M.C., & Staples, F.R. (1970). Role preparation and expectation of improvement in therapy. *Journal of Mental and Nervous Disease*, *150*, 18–20.

Slobin, D.I. (1971). *Psycholinguistics*. Glenview, IL: Scott, Fcresman.

Smith, J.L. (1975). A games analysis for attitude change: Use of role enactment situations for model development. *Journal for the Theory of Social Behaviour*, *5*, 63–79.

Smith, J.S. (1976). Psychotherapeutic effects of transcendental meditation with control for expectancy of relief and daily sitting. *Journal of Consulting and Clinical Psychology*, *44*, 630–637.

Smith, M.L., & Glass, C.V. (1977). Meta-analysis of psychotherapy outcome studies. *American Psychologist*, *32*, 752–760.

Stace, W.T. (1952). *Religion and the modern mind*. New York: Harper & Row.

Steele, T. (1982). *Somatic selection and adaptive evolution*. London: Croom Helm.

Stoutland, F. (1970). The logical connection argument. *American Philosophical Quarterly Monographs*, No. 7.

Stricker, L.J., Messick, S., & Jackson, D.D. (1967). Suspicion of deception: Implications for conformity research. *Journal of Personality and Social Psychology*, *5*, 379–389.

Strong, S.R. (1978). Social psychological approach to psychotherapy research. In S. Garfield & A. Bergin (Eds.), *Handbook of psychotherapy and behavior change* (2nd ed.). New York: Wiley.

Strupp, H.H., & Hadley, S.W. (1979). Specific versus nonspecific factors in psychotherapy. *Archives of General Psychiatry*, *36*, 1125–1136.

Suls, J., & Gastorf, J. (1980). Has the social psychology of the experiment influenced how research is conducted? *European Journal of Social Psychology*, *10*, 291–294.

Suppe, F. (1977). *The structure of scientific theories*. Urbana: University of Illinois Press.

Tajfel, H. (1972). Experiments in a vacuum. In J. Israel & H. Tajfel (Eds.), *The context of social psychology: A critical assessment*. London: Academic Press.

Tajfel, H., & Fraser, C. (1978). Social psychology as social science. In H. Tajfel & C. Fraser (Eds.), *Introducing social psychology*. London: Penguin.

Taylor, C. (1964). *The explanation of behaviour*. New York: Humanities Press.

Taylor, C. (1971). Interpretation and the sciences of man. *Review of Metaphysics*, *25*, 3–51.

Taylor, C. (1977). What is human agency? In T. Mischel (Ed.), *The self: Psychological and philosophical issues*. Oxford: Basil Blackwell.

Taylor, R. (1974). *Metaphysics*. Englewood Cliffs, NJ: Prentice-Hall.

Tolman, E.C. (1948). Cognitive maps in rats and men. *Psychological Review, 55*, 189–209.

Toulmin, S. (1953). *The philosophy of science*. London: Hutchinson.

Turner, S.P. (1977). Complex organizations as savage tribes. *Journal for the Theory of Social Behaviour, 7*, 99–125.

van Fraassen, B.C. (1980). *The scientific image*. Oxford: Oxford University Press.

von Humbolt, W. (1936). *Uber die Verschiedenheit des Menschlichen Sprachbaues*. Berlin.

von Wright, G.H. (1971). *Explanation and understanding*. London: Routledge and Kegan Paul.

Waismann, F. (1945). Verifiability. *Proceedings of the Aristotelian Society*, Supp. Vol. 19, pp. 119–50.

Walkerdine, V. (1984). Developmental psychology and the child-centred pedogogy. In J. Henriques, W. Hollway, C. Urwin, V. Louze, & V. Walkerdine, *Changing the subject*. London: Methuen.

Wallace, W.A. (1984). *Galileo and his sources: The heritage of the Collegio, Romano in Galileo's science*. Princeton: Princeton University Press.

Watson, J.B. (1913). Psychology as the behaviorist views it. *Psychological Review, 20*, 158–177.

Watson, J.B. (1924). *Behaviorism*. Chicago: University of Chicago Press.

Watson, J.D. (1978). *The double helix: A personal account of the discovery of the structure of DNA*. London: Penguin.

Weber, M. (1949). *The methodology of the social sciences*. Chicago: Free Press.

Weber, S.J., & Cook, T.D. (1972). Subject effects in laboratory research: An examination of subject roles, demand characteristics, and valid inference. *Psychological Bulletin, 77*, 273–295.

Weimer, W.B. (1974). The history of psychology and its retrieval from historiography. I: The problematic nature of history. II: Some lessons for the methodology of scientific research. *Science Studies, 4*, 235–258, 367–396.

Weinberg, S. (1977). *The first three minutes: A modern view of the origin of the universe*. London: Andre Deutsch.

Westland, G. (1978). *Current crises of psychology*. London: Heinemann.

Whorf, B.L. (1956). Science and linguistics. In J.B. Carroll (Ed.), *Language, thought and reality: The selected writings of Benjamin Lee Whorf*. Cambridge, MA: MIT Press.

Wicklund, R.A., & Frey, D. (1981). Cognitive consistency: Motivational vs nonmotivation perspectives. In J.P. Forgas (Ed.), *Social cognition*. London: Academic Press.

Wilkes, K.V. (1984). Pragmatics in science and theory in common sense. *Inquiry, 27*, 229–361.

Wilkins, W. (1979). Getting specific about nonspecifics. *Cognitive Therapy and Research, 3*, 319–329.

Will, D. (1980). Psychoanalysis as a human science. *British Journal of Medical Psychology, 53*, 201–211.

Willis, N.H., & Willis, Y.A. (1970). Role-playing versus deception: An experimental comparison. *Journal of Personality and Social Psychology*, *16*, 472–477.

Wilson, G.T., & Rachman, S.J. (1983). Meta-analysis and the evaluation of psychotherapy outcomes: Limitations and liabilities. *Journal of Consulting and Clinical Psychology*, *51*, 54–64.

Winch, P. (1958). *The idea of a social science*. London: Routledge and Kegan Paul.

Winch, P. (1964). Understanding a primitive society. *American Philosophical Quarterly*, *I*, 307–324.

Winch, P. (1972). The universalizability of moral judgements. In *Ethics and action*. London: Routledge and Kegan Paul.

Wittgenstein, L. (1953). *Philosophical investigations*. Oxford: Basil Blackwell.

Yardley, K.M. (1982). On engaging actors in as-if experiments. *Journal for the Theory of Social Behaviour*, *12*, 291–304.

Zaffron, R. (1971). Identity, subsumption, and scientific explanation. *Journal of Philosophy*, *68*, 849–850.

Author Index